595.44

D1085849

spiders
learning to love them

Lynne Kelly is a science writer who is fascinated by all aspects of the natural world. With degrees in engineering, computing and education, Lynne spent many years teaching physics, mathematics, science and gifted education, and has written a number of educational textbooks. She has also written a novel for Lothian and two popular science books for Allen & Unwin: *Skeptic's Guide to the Paranormal* and *Crocodile*. She is currently working on her doctorate in the English Department at La Trobe University.

About twenty years ago, Lynne's arachnophobia started to get out of control and she decided to do something about it. She resolved to study spiders seriously in order to overcome her irrational fear, and through books, help from an arachnologist and many hours spent observing spiders, her fear slowly turned to fascination. In the course of her research for this book, Lynne has been privileged to talk to some of the most respected arachnologists in the world.

Lynne lives with her husband on a bush block outside Melbourne where they document the wildlife in words and photographs.

LYNNE KELLY

spiders
learning to love them

JACANA BOOKS

ALLEN&UNWIN

For Abigail and Leah Heitbaum

Jacana Books, an imprint of
Allen & Unwin
83 Alexander Street
Crows Nest NSW 2065 Australia
Phone: (61 2) 8425 0100
Fax: (61 2) 9906 2218
E-mail: info@allenandunwin.com
Web: www.allenandunwin.com

National Library of Australia
Cataloguing-in-Publication entry:

Kelly, Lynne, 1951–
    Spiders: learning to love them

    ISBN: 978 1 74175 179 6 (pbk.)

    Phobias. Spiders. Spiders—Psychological aspects.

616.85225

Set in 11/15pt Adobe Garamond by Midland Typesetters, Australia
Printed in Singapore by KHL Printing Co Pte Ltd

10 9 8 7 6 5 4 3 2 1

CONTENTS

ACKNOWLEDGEMENTS

My journey from arachnophobe to obsessive arachnophile was all about flying into the cloud and becoming swathed in its silver linings. Many people have helped extensively with that journey and the book.

Alan Henderson was instrumental by sharing his knowledge of spiders very patiently with me. More importantly, his enthusiasm defied me to do anything but share it. His wonderful photographs enhance this book, but there would be no book had he not spent so much time sharing his real spiders with me. I appreciate his help more than he can realise.

Many experts gave freely of their valuable time and expertise. I am enormously indebted to Barbara Baehr, Ian Cope, John Daez, Mark Elgar, Volker Framenau, Mary Ann Hamilton, Duane Harland, Mark Harvey, Patrick Honan, Bill Humphries, Geoffrey Isbister, Robert Jackson, Barbara York Main, Norman Platnick, Barry Richardson, Robert Raven and Rick Vetter among many others.

I also appreciate the friends, relatives and acquaintances who put up with my endless enthusing about creatures with eight legs, who gave freely of their own experiences and offered invaluable support in the writing of this book. They include Jennifer Burge, David Curzon, Lauren Demke, Jen and Sam Ginsberg, Debbie Gwyther-Jones, Kathleen Hawkins, Rebecca and Rudi Heitbaum, Ian Irvine, Val and John Jacobson, Lisa Jacobson, Lewis Jones, Edna King-Smith, Peter and

Della King-Smith, Tony and Lynn King-Smith, Sue King-Smith, Ian Rowland, Tony Russell and Win Smith, Jill Lawrence and the students of G.A.T.E.ways.

At Allen & Unwin, I would like to thank my publisher, Ian Bowring, for his ongoing support for my writing and Aziza Kuypers for her terrific work on the final production. I would particularly like to thank the wonderful Catherine Taylor for her superb editing skills and her ability to accept excited endless emails with close-up photos of spiders with enthusiasm.

Although my husband Damian sees our house as a bird hide for his photography, I see it as a framework for my spiders to weave upon. I thank Damian for his unwavering support, for his incredible tolerance of spiderwebs and their owners, inside and out, and for being the person he is. I also thank him for photographing the spiders and then for training me with the camera when he could no longer stand being called to a burrow or web every time he sat down for a quiet cuppa.

And finally, thanks to those to whom I have dedicated this book, Abigail and Leah Heitbaum. The first thing they do when they visit is to look for the spiders. 'Theresa', the name of one of my wolf spiders, was among Abigail's first words. It is their young lives which give so much value to mine. Their enthusiasm for life reinforces just how valuable the natural world is and how crucial it is that we ensure it is still there for them, and their children, to enjoy.

Lynne Kelly,
Cottles Bridge, 2009

INTRODUCTION

Yet again I was screaming in my sleep. Giant spiders were marching towards me as I lay petrified in my bed. Too often were these monstrous creatures intruding on my dreams, my frantic cries waking the whole family.

Reason told me that the cure for an irrational fear was knowledge, but I found it difficult even to touch photographs of these eight-legged monsters. Without any real understanding of the reasons for my phobia, but determined to overcome it, I forced myself to start on a process of understanding, observing and identifying the creatures of my nightmares. Within months they had become fascinating fauna and I was a confirmed arachnophile. When I found myself crying at the death of a wolf spider I had named Theresa, I knew my cure had been overdone and I was now obsessed.

I want to take you on my journey. You don't have to leave the comfort of home to start observing spiders. Within a few days you will be able to predict your spiders' behaviour as they become individuals. You'll know when the house spider will emerge from her tunnel and how quickly she will retreat when she detects your presence. Spend some summer evenings in the garden and you will soon learn when the orb weaver is about to start the nightly construction of her perfectly engineered web. You may even manage to find her camouflaged daytime resting place. Once you get to know your arachnid residents as individuals, your life will never be the same again.

I'll introduce you to some of the spiders who have taught me so much about their surprisingly dramatic lives—Legless, Theresa, Erio, Annie and Twiggy—all of whom let me photograph their highs and lows. Then there's sex. No-one does it like spiders do. Frank and Helen did it all in front of Alan Henderson's perfectly poised camera.

Our journey will take us across the world in search of the biggest and the weirdest. Which are the most venomous and how dangerous are they really? We'll dispel some myths and discover some enthralling behaviour. If you thought spiders were simple, instinct-driven invertebrates, wait until you meet *Portia*, a little spider with abilities beyond those you would ever credit a spider.

As you are introduced to the engaging arachnids, you will also meet some of the small band of dedicated arachnologists from all over the world who wrestle with the vast numbers of spider species still to be classified. At the time of writing some arachnologists estimate that less than an eighth of our global arachnid species has been classified. While there are few willing to spend their professional lives unravelling the complexities of the many and varied arachnid species to create a viable taxonomy, there is a rich tradition of the well-informed amateur adding to the collective understanding. Much of spider behaviour, ecology and biology is a blank page—one just waiting to be filled in by amateur and professional observers the world over. And to be involved, all you need to do is go outside and start watching these incredible animals. They are everywhere, hiding from you. They can be found, if you just learn the signs. I hope this book will help you to identify the spiders you find in your home and garden and to find as much joy in getting to know them as I have.

1

ARACHNOPHOBIA

Little Miss Muffet
Sat on a tuffet,
Eating her curds and whey.
Along came a spider,
Who sat down beside her,
And frightened Miss Muffet away.

The Reverend Dr Thomas Muffet or Mouffet (1553–1604) loved spiders. He wrote of the house spider that 'she doth beautifie with her tapestry and hangings'.

Although there is no proof, Miss Muffet was probably his daughter, Patience. The good doctor liked to treat many ailments with the application of spiders. For example, 'The running of eyes is stopped with the dung and urine of a House Spider dropt in with Oyl of Roses, or laid on alone with Wooll'. Is it any wonder that his daughter ran away?

My arachnophobia crept up on me. I had never liked the little critters, but this didn't become a huge problem until I was in my thirties. I can't recollect any specific incident which triggered it, but I certainly remember how it made me feel.

Night after night, legions of huge, black, menacing spiders would climb my bed and march towards my face. There was no escape. I would scream, waking everyone, leap from my bed and turn on the light. It would often be hours before I slept again.

A simple bushwalk left me a nervous wreck, as I spent most of the time brushing imagined spiders from my face, arms and legs. They were hiding everywhere with the sole intention of getting me. I could feel their crawling hairy legs tickling my skin all the time. My arachnophobia was getting out of hand.

My black house spider, Legless, doing her horror movie impression. Get the angle and the lighting right and you can create a horror from any spider.
(Photo D. and L. Kelly)

So I did the only rational thing I could think of. I started studying them. How successful I was in overcoming my arachnophobia you will be able to judge for yourself in this book. Trying to understand more about arachnophobia, I contacted other arachnophobes. Tony Russell was a factory manager and tertiary lecturer who is now a fanatic birder. He described himself as: '72 and petrified of sp . . . s, see, don't even like writing or saying the name—all my life. I don't mind the tiny ones too much but anything bigger than 5 mm gives me the horrors, and the bigger they are the more they scare me.' Understanding of his phobia, Russell's family and friends would remove spiders for him. He remembers fondly his large Doberman, who saved him many times by hunting them out and eating them.

Rationally, Russell knows that most spiders can do him little harm, except of course those such as red-backs or the Australian funnel-webs. It's the look and possible feel of spiders which horrify him. Resident in Adelaide, Russell says that he's not that worried by red-backs, but more the big, hairy-looking ones.

Russell has thought a great deal about his phobia and how to distinguish between fear and horror. The 'look' of spiders and the thought that one might land on him generate his feelings of horror and revulsion, but he questions whether or not what he feels is fear. He claims that he could 'whack' a spider if necessary but it would still look horrible and he could never touch even a dead spider. He regards crabs as ocean-going spiders, and wonders how people can eat them. The thought revolts him.

Russell checks for spiders every time he goes into a room or a shed or a tunnel or a cupboard or walks through a forest where there might be webs. He won't walk through bushes or trees after dark because the feeling of a web on him would put him 'in a frenzy'. When I asked Russell where he thought his arachnophobia might have come from he said that his mother and three older sisters were equally horrified by spiders so he probably learned it from them at an early age. Unfortunately his three grown-up sons have caught it from him! When I mentioned overcoming my own arachnophobia through learning about spiders, Russell responded:

> Your suggested cure of learning about them seems impossible to me since I can't even look at pictures of them—it just gives me the creeps and then I think about them when in bed in the dark. Ugh ugh ugh!
>
> Surely it's got to be a learned thing! I was an educator for 15 years and I know that what is learned can be unlearned. But sp . . . s? You've got to be dreaming!

I was intrigued to learn that most of the psychological research on arachnophobia comes out of England, a country where there is not a single dangerous spider, and certainly none large enough to instil panic. Those who choose to treat arachnophobics by exposure to their perceived fear import the necessary tarantulas.

One BBC3 programme, *Panic Room*, features Dr Lucy Atcheson, a counselling psychologist and psychotherapist. Atcheson explains that she treats phobias 'through cognitive behaviour therapy which is very successful, as it takes the person out of the sphere of irrationality back into the rational'.

The research material for *Panic Room* lists arachnophobia as the most common phobia of all, although Atcheson acknowledges the difficulties in making such a claim, one of which is distinguishing a phobia from an exaggerated fear. What is not under dispute, however, is that arachnophobia is very common and not linked in any way to stupidity or a generally fearful or timid personality.

The Panic Room itself is a wildly dramatic enclosed space in which the phobic is exposed to increasingly fearful situations, involving the object of their fear, over three intensive days. Arachnophobe Gemma

Rigg's ordeal began with constant repetition of the word 'spider' and ended with her being able to have a live tarantula walking on her hand for ten seconds. This experience left her elated.

Rigg described what it was about spiders which caused her such terror:

> I think that spiders come and find me because they know that I'm scared. I hate their colour, how they move. I hate that they get into little gaps and so you don't know where they are and you can see one one second and not know where it is the next . . . I was in the back seat of a car and one actually crawled onto my leg and I got out of the car—and it was moving . . .
>
> I once didn't go back into a room for a week or so after seeing one, and it was my bedroom . . . I don't like that it's something I can't control. I am quite a practical person. I like to be able to solve problems and this is one thing that on my own I can't solve.

So what's the best way to tackle an irrational fear? My method was gradual exposure to the real thing. As I compared different treatments for arachnophobia, the cures seemed to be fairly consistent in approach. Mine took me about six months of constant involvement and observation, but it seems others would prefer their recovery to be far quicker.

A real source of fear—a large spider appearing when you least expect it.
(Photo: Alan Henderson)

In the land of the least offensive spiders in the world, the London Zoo runs 'The Friendly Spider Programme', a course designed to ease or eliminate the fear of spiders. The course uses a combination of cognitive behavioural therapy and hypnotherapy—no live animals, photographs or illustrations. Costing over £100 sterling, this half-day course runs every month. A hypnotherapist's presentation on how phobias can become established is followed by questions to the participants clarifying just what it is about spiders they don't like. The zoo's spider expert, Dave Clarke, then presents spider facts to refute the fears expressed. This is followed by a group hypnosis session designed to remove any remaining negative subconscious feelings about spiders and support the newly acquired positive emotions. An optional visit to the invertebrate collection allowing participants to meet Frieda and Sharon, Mexican red-kneed tarantulas, and various British species is taken by about 90 per cent of the participants.

It's not cheap and appears almost ludicrously simple, but the zoo reports that since 1993 over 2000 children and adults have taken part in the course. Follow-up analysis shows that over 80 per cent of participants claimed to remain calm, confident and relaxed when they encounter a spider.

The National Geographic Channel's programme, *Phobia: Arachnophobia* emphasised the harmless nature of spiders, with an entomologist, Tom Prentice, handling a black widow freely on his bare hands, demonstrating that even 'deadly' spiders have to be severely provoked to bite humans. Even then, he says, only young children, the elderly or those with severe respiratory problems are at risk. The programme then introduced Alfred Kinsey, whose phobia was so extreme that when he found a spider in his bed, he grabbed a gun and was going to shoot it until his wife pointed out this was 'a pretty psycho thing to do'.

Kinsey is a young, healthy and confident man who has one extreme vulnerability which he acknowledges is not only totally irrational but also embarrassing. He seeks treatment, with Dr Michael Telch at the University of Texas, during which it is clear he is extremely fearful.

As the treatment's exposure to the spiders increases, Dr Telch refers to the tarantulas used in the therapy by name. When Kinsey uses their names, the tarantulas, Tammy-fay and Brad, become individuals and less horrifying. With Kinsey, Dr Telch points out the predictability of Brad's behaviour as Kinsey is on the floor with bare feet with a tarantula wandering around. Telch asks Kinsey if there is any evidence that Brad is sensing his fear and 'going after' him. Kinsey says 'No.' By the end of the treatment, Kinsey is happily handling two tarantulas at once in a pet shop with many other spiders around him.

I am convinced that my own fear reduced enormously as I named the individuals I was observing, and saw each as an individual spider living her own life on her web. Her behaviour became predictable. And it is that predictability which became hugely significant in my overcoming the fear. It took me quite a few photographic sessions to be confident enough to move to within centimetres of the wolf spiders you will meet in Chapter 6, despite my overwhelming arachnophobia being well behind me. I was reassured by the fact that they backed away down their burrows when my presence became uncomfortable for them—every time. Not once did they move towards me.

The many contradictory reasons given for the cause of arachnophobia would suggest that it is far from being well understood. Many psychologists suggest that phobias develop from an unpleasant experience in childhood which is recalled from the subconscious when a person is again faced with the object or situation of dread. Alfred Kinsey's father felt his son's phobia might have been the result of his brushing into a spider's web as a child and having it engulf his face. Kinsey described the experience: 'It was terrifying. It was just there.'

What Kinsey said, I think, holds the key, and is why I still have some residual fear. All of a sudden, a spider is 'just there' where before there was no spider. Moving silently, stealthily and unpredictably, the eight long legs move in that unsymmetrical way that they do—unlike those of any other creature.

The eight legs are often quoted as a source of disgust. I have to admit they played a large part in my own fears—their length and the way the spider moves, erratically and unpredictably. As my fear turned to admiration and, ultimately, infatuation, the legs still feature. I now find their elegance, and the extremely delicate way in which their owners place them, to be nothing short of beautiful.

The side view of a *Nephila* (golden orb weaver) hanging on her web depicted in Plate 1 of the colour picture section shows exactly what I mean.

Unlike the web weavers, burrowing spiders are cramped. The burrow is excavated to the exact size from which the cephalothorax or abdomen, whichever is the largest, can be extricated. The long legs are therefore pulled tightly into the body when the spider is in the burrow, but not when resting at its opening. While observing closely, I have only ever seen a burrow dweller backing away from me, back into the safety of its silk-lined retreat. I have never seen one emerge. Not once.

As she retreats, the spider moves her legs in the most delicate and graceful way—a sight I never tire of. The wolf spiders, in particular, manage their spectacularly long legs in the most exquisite fashion to press their bodies back to the safety of their chamber. As my more confident wolf spiders would perform this feat at quite a leisurely pace, I have been able to observe them many, many times. If you are lucky enough to come across a burrower, I promise you will be as intrigued as I am. There really is nothing frightening in the way a spider moves its legs. The wonder is in the efficiency and elegance with which they manoeuvre such long, delicate limbs.

The Brits aren't the only ones who are frightened by their common house or garden spiders. Patrick Honan is Invertebrate Specialist at the

Patrick Honan eases the fear of many people with his talks and displays of live spiders at Melbourne Zoo. He is accompanied by a golden orb weaver, Nephila sp. (Photo: D. and L. Kelly)

Melbourne Zoo. He receives phone calls on a daily basis from anxious residents about the spiders they have unearthed in their gardens or discovered lurking on their walls. He remembers one woman who had an orb weaver web strung between two trees in her garden. She killed the spider—then she cut down the two trees. Another caller rang to say that she had dug up a spider in the garden and had killed it with a shovel. As Honan said, wryly, 'She was so proud of the fact she went on and on about it. So I told her to go out and smash it a few more times just to be sure.'

Most of Honan's calls relate to the Melbourne trapdoor spider, (*Stanwellia sp.*). People are horrified to discover they have a trapdoor spider living in their backyards, but given their wide range and long lifespan, Honan points out that they have probably been cohabiting with their human neighbours for a long time. Most callers eventually accept that reality but some are at their wits' end and ask Honan if they can spray with insecticide, or pour boiling water down the burrows. As he says, 'They can try, but it won't do any good. They may kill a few but their neighbours' spiders will ensure they soon have a new lot.'

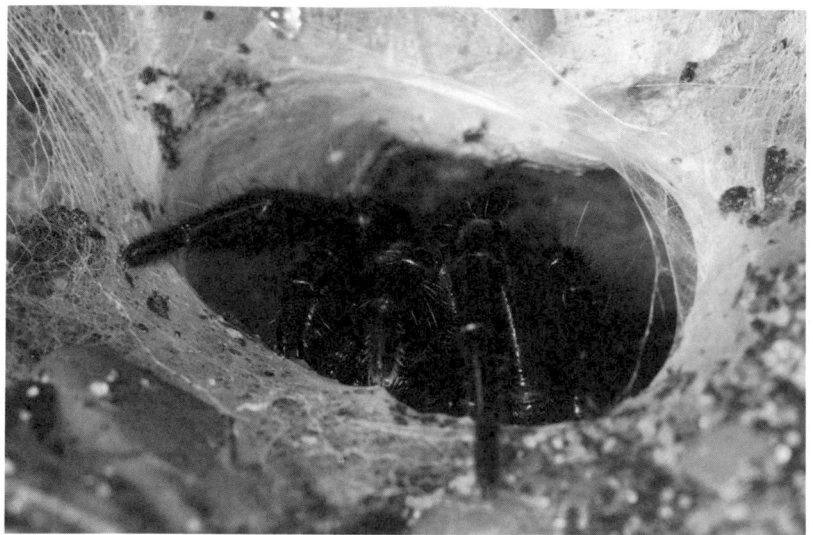

A Melbourne trapdoor, Stanwellia sp., *looking mighty scary. When I see them in the garden, as I do in their hundreds, they don't look scary at all. Out of context, anything can be made to look fearsome.* (Photo: Alan Henderson)

Although Honan can't really understand why people have an inherent fear of a creature that is pretty much harmless, he has his own theory on the cause of arachnophobia:

> It's often called genetic memory, a memory of when our ancestors lived with spiders and we carry on that fear. There's nothing wrong with the genetic memory theory or that a behavioural response can remain many generations later. Elephants can detect rumblings before a tsunami and run to higher ground even though it has been generations since there has been a rumbling then a tsunami.
>
> But if the fear of spiders is something to do with genetic memory, then we should be terrified of mosquitoes and have a much greater fear of rats. Yet the fear of spiders sits much higher than the fear of rats.

Honan's callers have given him many reasons for their fear of spiders—they're hairy, they have lots of legs, they move suddenly—all features that apply to other animals. Centipedes and millipedes leave spiders for dead on the number of legs. Tarantulas, the spider most featured in horror movies, are most of the time very slow-moving. As for hairy—well, pandas and koalas aren't exactly bald.

Any acceptable explanation for arachnophobia must take into account the fact that the less someone has to do with spiders, the more likely they are to be arachnophobic. Honan has found this to be so for people who come to Australia from Europe. With almost no large or threatening indigenous spiders, European visitors to the Melbourne Zoo are by far the most afraid of the exhibits. Honan has done his own research into this phenomenon:

> None of the theories that I have read makes any sense except one from a psychologist. In Europe in the Middle Ages, spiders were thought to spread disease. If a spider walked across your food, then you had to throw it out. If it fell in a well, then you couldn't drink the water. They thought it was spiders who spread bubonic plague.
>
> So arachnophobia applies to the European culture more than to any other and stems from the idea that spiders spread disease. From a psychological point of view, the response to spiders would be classified as disgust more than fear. The disgust reaction, according to psychologists, is the easiest to pass on from parent to child and within the culture.
>
> Arachnophobia appears to be a learned thing. Learned from parents. If you have to learn it, then it is not genetic or instinctive.

Honan places a lot of the blame on the media, which he believes are responsible for our paranoia regarding sharks and spiders. Newspapers beat up any shark attack or spider story because people read the stories to reinforce their own fear.

Honan remembers being contacted by a well-known Melbourne newspaper years ago to comment on a story about a man who had stumbled into a nest full of white-tailed spiders.

I explained that white-tailed spiders don't live in nests, so the story was not true. I explained that any reaction was not due to the venom, which is harmless, and that the necrotic blisters might be due to a micro-bacteria, which was the best we knew at the time. The reporter said that the possible effects sounds like leprosy. I disagreed. He asked if it could possibly be remotely like leprosy. I said I didn't think so, but there might be some superficial similarities. I was quoted with one line in the paper: 'The white-tailed spider gives leprosy-like symptoms.'

I like to think that Honan is right and that arachnophobia is a learned response passed on from generation to generation, but others have very different views. British science writer Lewis Jones was not convinced by my argument. He wrote:

As for learning to be phobic, I've never yet met any reasoned response to the fact that laboratory monkeys who have never seen a snake in their lives are terrified when presented for the first time with a toy snake (though not a toy rabbit). Nor does it follow that if something can be unlearned, it must have been learned. Bed-wetting can be unlearned, though it can hardly be said to have been learned.

I think that a lot of the problem is caused by the inappropriate use of the word 'fear'. Although people talk of being 'afraid' of spiders, in fact most so-called phobics are perfectly well aware that the creatures can't actually harm them, so fear is not involved. The sudden and unexpected sight of a nearby spider may produce a startle reflex, but this is by no means the same as fear.

Evolutionary psychologists have their own weird and wonderful speculations about how fear of certain things could have been useful in the distant past, and they're still producing groundless and untestable hypotheses about its survival value. Many of them don't seem to understand that evolutionary success only means that you have more offspring, not necessarily that the individual involved will survive better. I have no idea how they account for, say, the fear of flying—probably some scenario involving fear of heights in the treetops or at the top of some cliff.

Jones then pointed me to Steven Pinker's book, *How The Mind Works*, in which Pinker noted that chimpanzees born in captivity scream in terror when they first see a snake, while humans need not even see one to fear snakes:

We ought to be afraid of guns, driving fast, driving without a seatbelt, lighter fluid, and hair dryers near bathtubs, not of snakes and spiders . . . Parents scream and punish to deter their children from playing with matches or chasing a ball into the street, but when Chicago schoolchildren were asked what they were most afraid of, they cited lions, tigers, and snakes, unlikely hazards in the Windy City . . .

Few if any human phobias are about neutral objects that were once paired with some trauma. People dread snakes without ever having seen one. After a frightening or painful event, people are more prudent around the cause, but they do not fear it: there are no phobias for electrical outlets, hammers, cars, or air-raid shelters. Television clichés notwithstanding, most survivors of traumatic events do not get the screaming meemies every time they face reminders of it. Vietnam veterans resent the stereotype in which they hit the dirt whenever someone drops a glass.

I certainly can't trace my own arachnophobia to any particular event, nor was it even present when I was a child. I have never, to my knowledge, been bitten by a spider, nor had a sudden shock from one. Of course, that doesn't mean that some such scare is not a common trigger for others.

Over the course of six months, I questioned everyone I met who claimed to be *really* scared of spiders, about why that was so. A few mentioned a specific event, others the fear of being bitten, but most just shrugged, paused and then made some observation on the 'spideriness' of spiders.

Despite their lack of agreement on the cause, all the references agree on one thing—women are far more likely to be arachnophobic than men. The other point of almost total agreement is in the essence of the cure, if not the actual process. People must be willing to expose themselves to spiders and tolerate their anxiety until rational thinking overrules irrational fear. Some of us manage to overdo the cure.

In an interview, Dr Norman Platnick, one of the world's most respected arachnologists, was asked about being bitten by spiders. He replied that in 34 years as a professional arachnologist, much of that time spent in the field, he had never been bitten.

> And in general you have to work hard to be bitten by a spider—spiders eat insects. Anything big and noisy like a human is something they want to go away from. If it gets into your bedding and clothing, if it can't get away, it will bite you. But most don't have the strength to break your skin.

Platnick went on to point out that one of the most commonly cited movie images is that of a tarantula walking across Sean Connery's chest in the 1962 James Bond film, *Dr No*.

> The only thing [Bond] is in any peril of there is perhaps itching a bit! Tarantulas are not fatal. They're big, and they're also very good at faking.

If you do get a New World tarantula upset, they may actually rear up on their hind legs and spread their jaws and exude a drop of venom. This is all show. This is all to make you go away.

Not all silver-screen depictions of spiders are negative. The *Spiderman* movies may not have any real connection with spiders apart from the silk, but the spider's ability to create that silk is something fantastic. As we will see in Chapter 4, spider silk can expand enormously and retract again, and has a much greater tensile strength than steel at the same dimension. Spiderman uses those properties in the movies. As Platnick said, 'And any good spider press is great press. It's not like *Arachnophobia*.'

I had said I would not watch *Arachnophobia*, because I was scared of slipping back into my old ways, but I knew that for this book, I had no

An Arizona blond tarantula, Aphonopelma chalcodes, *showing the irritant hairs it can release. That is about the worst it will do to you!* (Photo: Alan Henderson)

choice. So I hired the movie and sat down to watch. I did jump at the spiders' unexpected appearance. So much of our fear of spiders arises from the fact that, unlike wasps and bees which signal their presence, spiders are silent and emerge from narrow and concealed spaces—spaces we do not even realise exist. Since watching my house spiders, I have discovered crevices in my walls, and entrances to them, which I had previously totally overlooked.

For most of the time spent watching *Arachnophobia*, however, I wanted to see them more completely—not just legs emerging and shadows stalking. My main reaction was one of disappointment that the creators had not taken a little more time to understand spiders.

The creature that dropped from the trees was clearly modelled on a tarantula or baboon spider. Although some of these species do live in arboreal retreats, they do not build orb webs. As soon as I saw the huge orb web in the opening sequences, I hoped they would not make its creator a primitive spider but, sure enough, the tarantula-like spider wove a distinctly non-tarantula-like web. This is fiction, I told myself. Literary licence. Then, transported to rural America, the creature built its web in a barn. In the dusty light, the huge web was clearly visible. The film-makers, in their wisdom, had given the usually sticky orb web the woolly, dust-gathering properties of a cobweb, and added some cobweb-like strands to enhance the effect. The spiders had crossbred, not only across species, but even across families and infraorders—tarantulas breeding with huntsmen. In fact, the producers used hundreds of huntsmen in the filming. The rearing tarantula-like beast in the final scene had the large eyes of a tiny jumping spider!

In the film *Harry Potter and the Prisoner of Azkaban*, the students of Hogwarts are asked to imagine their worst fears. Harry's best friend, Ron, immediately conjures up a huge spider. In the film *Harry Potter and the Chamber of Secrets*, spiders running up a wall or across a floor are a portent of evil. As the danger increases, so does the size of the spiders. Told by their giant friend Hagrid to follow the spiders, Ron mutters 'Why spiders? Why couldn't it be "follow the butterflies"?' Harry and Ron enter the unnerving Forbidden Forest, in which more and more spiders accompany their every step. Webs abound in the grey light while larger spiders descend on silk. As they bid farewell to the most horrific and gigantic of all, Aragog, they are descended upon by very realistic, if oversized, spiders. Aragog says:

> Go? I think not. My sons and daughters do not harm Hagrid on my command, but I cannot deny them fresh meat when it wanders so willingly into our midst. Good-bye friend of Hagrid.

At which point, the apprentice wizards are attacked by hundreds of huge spiders. The spiders were wonderfully well done.

Film director Wes Craven specialises in horror movies. He says:

> There's something about the configuration of a spider's body that looks like a hand but it doesn't have a mind attached to it that you can relate to. I mean, you can't look into its eyes, you can't quite guess its personality, and it has venom. I think most all animals which have venom are high on the list of human phobias.

In retrospect, I quite enjoyed *Arachnophobia*, because I compared it to *Eight Legged Freaks*. *Arachnophobia* was the hands-down winner in terms of plot, production and performance. The giant eight-legged freaks of their self-titled film were apparently male orb weavers, who wrapped their prey live to be offered to the females as a bribe, something I have never heard of orb weavers doing, although some nursery-web spiders have a similar mating strategy. The film gave spiders an ant-like social structure, in which they acted as a colony to attack. Effectively blind carnivores with an innate predisposition to eat the nearest moving object are not great social animals. In fact, out of over 40 000 species of spider now described, only about twenty are truly social. Some may live in conglomerate webs, but very few actually cooperate in prey capture, breeding and creating a social web.

The eight-legged freak version of orb weavers hunted prey, which rather defeated the purpose of weaving their orbs. The webs they did weave were cobwebs anyway. These cobweb-building, hunting orb weavers had tarantula-shaped bodies with fangs which were sometimes attached to their jaws, sometimes to their shortened front appendages known as the pedipalps. These spiders moved in a way no spider has ever moved, leaping and bounding on legs which varied between stout, hairy tarantula legs to long, thin limbs. Spiders have no hearing yet, attracted by noise, they made sounds reminiscent of bad digestion, while emerging into the light from trapdoors. Even allowing for literary licence, this film was ridiculous.

It is easy to create a horror movie out of nature. Spiders aren't the only animals to have been treated this way—dogs, sharks, birds and bees have all been cast as villains. Perhaps where spiders differ is that so little is known about their behaviour. The unknown is always more frightening than the known. If you get to know some of the individual spiders who share your house and garden, I guarantee that your arachnid neighbours will at least intrigue, and perhaps even enchant, you.

2

SPIDERS, SPIDERS EVERYWHERE

The fire-ravaged bush is dead, black and empty. It appears desolate, but experience tells us it will recover. The first animals to return don't need plants; some don't even need food for a while. There is no doubt the food will arrive and the familiar cycles begin again.

The first back will be the spiders. Some will emerge from their burrows, having survived the heat in their underground lairs. Others will arrive by air. Newly hatched spiderlings, miniature versions of their parents, will float in on tiny silken sails. Some will die in water, many will become instant meals, but others will land and commence their solitary lives.

The spiderlings alight onto blackened branches still smoking from the fire. The lack of food may force them to cannibalise each other, but the insects will not be long behind them. The spiders wait on their tiny webs, or in their newly staked hunting grounds. The first of the insects will fall prey to the waiting hunters. The spiders will grow. Other insects will come and breed, strengthening the food chain. The carnivores will feed on the spiders. Later, when the new green shoots appear, the herbivorous insects will add to the variety.

After the spiders and the insects come the birds. The rain brings them water and the new plants begin to provide cover. Small ground mammals also feed on the invertebrates. They start to reappear, first at the edges and slowly throughout the forest. The bush is being repopulated. It is different: young and raw, but it is alive again.

When Krakatoa exploded in its volcanic catastrophe in 1883, not a single animal was left on the island. The first living creature later found there was a spider: a linyphiid, the same family as Europe's money spiders. Within 50 years, 90 different species of spider had been identified on Krakatoa. Jumping spiders have been found on Mount Everest, at an elevation of 6700 metres, while ballooning spiderlings have been collected in planes at a height of 1500 metres. Charles Darwin noted large numbers of the gossamer spiders floating onto the HMS *Beagle*, when the ship was nearly a hundred kilometres from land.

Separate studies in both England and America estimated that over two million individual spiders reside in one acre of grassy field. Spiders are everywhere. No matter how clean, how stark, how sterile your home, the spiders will come. Spiderlings will balloon in and wait for the insects that will appear. Adult spiders will walk in. As you destroy one, another will take its place. Spiders are like that.

As you are reading, you are almost certainly in the company of spiders. In a dark recess, whether under your couch or behind the buffet, the cupboard spider sits on her tangled web patiently waiting for dinner. The funnel-weaver has just emerged from her funnelled web in the corner of the window to wait, just as patiently, for flying insects to flutter into her net. Under the eaves, a delicate, common house spider has her tiny brood around her on the web.

The hunters are more active. The wolf spider roams the floors while the huntsman roams the walls. The search for a mate eventually will be more important than the search for food. Many are on a death march, the act of mating being their only reason for living. Having sown their seed, they will die soon after. Others will become food for their cannibalistic mates.

Before you recoil in horror from the next spider who wanders into your house, take a deep breath and remind yourself that as you are neither a female spider nor a potential meal, you are of no real interest at all. You are simply a horrendously large predator and should be avoided at all costs.

The next step is to have a look—you won't need to be too close. As with my male wolf spider in Plate 2, you will see eight legs, each with seven segments, poised for flight. In front of them you will see two smaller appendages, like legs, but which don't quite make the grade. These are the pedipalps, more often referred to simply as palps. If the ends of the palps are enlarged, as if the spider is wearing miniature boxing gloves, then it is a mature male. The palps contain the spider's sperm, ready to be deposited should he find a mate who accepts his attentions.

Look at the spider's abdomen. You will see a soft fur, and perhaps a delicate pattern. The legs too are sometimes barred. The spider's head and thorax, referred to jointly as the cephalothorax, may also be patterned. What do you think about the spider now? You may be starting to see it as a small animal, beautiful in its own way. Or is that asking a bit too much?

Spiders basically divide into two distinct groups. The mygalomorphs are usually fairly bulky and, as spiders go, often on the large side. They are referred to as 'primitive' spiders because their ecology is similar to that of the arachnid ancestors. They are distinguished from the araneomorphs, or 'modern' spiders, by their fangs. In mygalomorphs, these point downwards, which is why the spider rears up before striking. If you hear the word 'arachnid' and think immediately of a large black spider with its cephalothorax raised threateningly above its hapless victim, then you are visualising a mygalomorph. Grasping its prey firmly in its front legs, the mygalomorph lifts its fangs above its quarry then strikes, fast and hard. The large fangs penetrate deep into the victim before delivering their venom.

The 'modern' spiders, or araneomorphs, have fangs which strike together horizontally. The vast majority of spider species you will meet are araneomorphs, from the elegant orb weavers to the deadly widows, athletic little jumping spiders to the patient house spiders. They vary in size from microscopic to over seven centimetres in body length. They vary in appearance, from dull brown or black to ornately jewelled and patterned. Some reflect light in gorgeous colours. They vary in their hunting methods, some actively pursuing their prey, others preferring to wait for the unwary to fall into their elaborate silken snares. And they vary in what they hunt. Some are so selective they will eat only a particular type of moth, and then only the male. Others will jump on anything that moves. The variety is extraordinary.

Most primitives live in burrows and females can live to twenty years of age or more, often in the same site. Males take over five years to reach maturity and then set out to find their females. If a male survives the mating game, he will die soon afterwards.

The moderns are more egalitarian. Both sexes usually die in their first or second year of life. The males mature and find their females. Some may become a post-coital snack for their recently impregnated mates or die soon afterwards, others cohabit with their mates and live to mate again. Some females die after producing their eggs, others soon after the young are hatched. Some will live to tend their young. Some will breed a second season.

With such extraordinary variation, the spider world offers real-life drama right outside your back door. Your spiders have been keeping as low a profile as possible because to them you are a threat. Large creatures eat spiders and you are a *very* large creature. Once you start recognising the signs, however, you will find spiders everywhere. They say we are always within a metre of a spider. I don't doubt it for a minute.

AROUND THE HOUSE

My first step towards overcoming my arachnophobia was to find a spider in a web—admittedly, on the outside of the window frame—and give it a name. Then talk to it each night. That's how the recovery started. Slowly, from the safety of the other side of the glass, I came to fear them less, then become mildly interested. By the time I could bear to be on the same side as them, I had started to rather like the little things. I didn't know then that I would grow to love them and eventually develop what can only be called an obsession. The whole process took about six months. My arachnophobia has gone. So have the nightmares and sleepless nights. The webs now stay—inside and out.

The first spiders I learned to tolerate made their funnelled webs on the other side of the kitchen window. As I watched Tiny, Cutesy and their fellows I found I could predict their behaviour. At the same time each night, they would emerge and rest at the entrance to their retreats. I began trying to estimate the time of their emergence to the minute. I was often very close. Sitting there, front legs resting on their web, they would wait for prey. Each morning, they were gone, tucked into the furthest corner of their retreat.

I later learned that these were young black house spiders (*Badumna insignis*, family Desidae). The older ones are much larger, but my housekeeping had kept them at bay. My windows grew messy, but these youngsters taught me a valuable lesson about just how shy they were. When I finally ventured out to get a closer look from *their* side of the window, they retreated instantly. I could not get near enough to see them closely.

A red wattle-bird, one of our common honeyeaters, chose to do my housekeeping for me. One morning, as we were eating breakfast and watching the birds, a large, feathered spider-eater worked her way right across the window, picking off Tiny, Cutesy and all the other young spiders I had been observing. I was horrified.

That was the day I knew my arachnophobia was well on the way to a cure, although I had no idea how much I would come to love these black house spiders.

The spider experience across different countries and vastly different environments has much in common. The average home in any temperate region is likely to host twenty if not more, species of spiders. Some of these may be in significantly large numbers. There will be different species, although some global travellers will be found almost everywhere. There will be different specialists, found only in a particular location, but all of us have similar spider niches. We all have hunters and web-builders, burrowers and jumpers.

The difficulty is that we all use different common names for spiders which are very similar. This is why arachnologists always refer to spiders by their families. Without family names, lists of commonly seen spiders from different parts of the world look very different. Add in the families, and we see a startling familiarity. (For a list of spider families see Appendix 1.)

Common spiders I see include the brown house and common house spiders (family Theridiidae), daddy long-legs (Pholcidae), humped spiders (Uloboridae), garden orb weavers and St Andrew's Cross spiders (Araneidae), jumping spiders (Salticidae), huntsmen (Sparassidae), flat rock spiders (Trochanteriidae), trapdoor spiders (Nemesiidae), flower spiders (Thomisidae) and wolf spiders (Lycosidae).

In their *Spiders of Southern Africa*, Astri and John Leroy list the spiders found in and around the home and garden as button spiders and comb-footed spiders (Theridiidae), daddy long-legs (Pholcidae), feather-legged spiders (Uloboridae), jumping spiders (Salticidae), rain spiders (Sparassidae), scorpion spiders (Trochanteriidae), crab spiders (Thomisidae), baboon spiders (Theraphosidae), trapdoor spiders (including Nemesiidae), and wolf spiders (Lycosidae). They list the garden orb weaver (Araneidae) as the genus *Argiope*. That genus I call the St Andrew's Cross spider. What they call simply orb weavers are very like those I call garden orb weavers.

In Europe, Asia and America, the common spiders in and around the home are from the same families again. In a fact sheet from the Ohio State University, Dr Susan Jones gives the common spiders found in and around the house in her state as cobweb spiders (Theridiidae), orb weaver spiders (Araneidae), funnel-web spiders (Agelenidae), cellar spiders (Pholcidae), wolf spiders (Lycosidae), jumping spiders (Salticidae) and crab spiders (Thomisidae).

What Jones calls a cellar spider, much of the world calls daddy longlegs (Pholcidae). Jones reserves that term for the harvestman, a close relative which is not a spider.

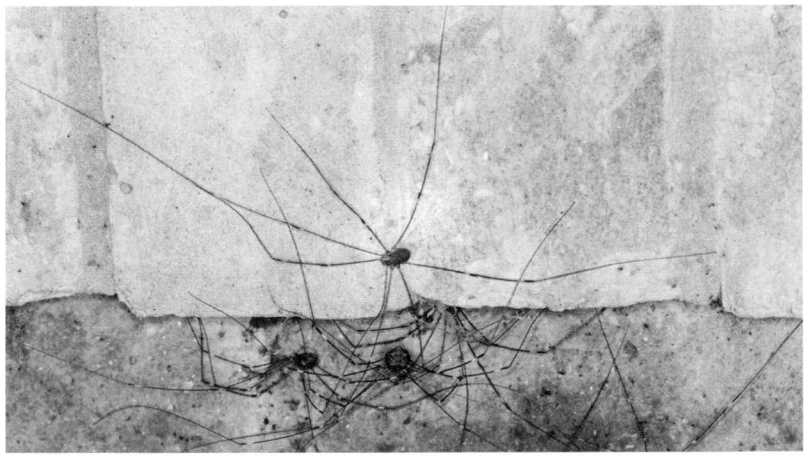

Harvestmen from Texas. (Photo: D. and L. Kelly)

The harvestman does have eight legs, but it is not a true spider, it is an opilionid. The harvestman is in the same class (Arachnida) and order (Araneae), as the spider, but in a different suborder, Opiliones. The opilionids have only a single body structure and do not build webs. They are omnivorous, eating fungi and plant material as well as dead and living arthropods, and rarely enter houses.

The true spider version of the daddy long-legs (Pholcidae) is in the genus *Pholcus*. Daddy long-legs, pholcids to arachnologists, can be easily identified—there are two parts to the body, separated by a narrow waist, the pedicel. Pholcids have eight eyes and eight very long, thin elegant legs. Pholcids often build their webs in corners. When disturbed, the spider will bounce rapidly on its web, causing it to vibrate. This is possibly a method to confuse potential predators.

Daddy long-legs are great spiders to observe—and you can do it without leaving your armchair. The corner of our kitchen was home to Mummy Long-legs, as I felt she was more appropriately named. A male stayed on her web for weeks, strumming out his courtship message. Mummy Long-legs responded, at which the male either beat a retreat or approached to strum yet again. Weeks later, Mummy Long-legs produced an egg sac, loosely bound with silk, which she held in her jaws. I could see each egg clearly.

Weeks passed as I constantly climbed the chair I had placed beneath her web to get a better view. I was amply rewarded for my persistence the day I was witness to the young emerging. Hundreds of spindly legs, freed from their trusses, slowly spread and the balls became miniature daddy long-legs. Over the following week, the young moved further apart on their mother's web as she ventured off to catch prey and feed again. When I climbed up on my chair, Mummy Long-legs would return to spread her long limbs protectively around her offspring. I was astounded how fast she would move if she was at the far end of her web and I accidentally knocked the wall.

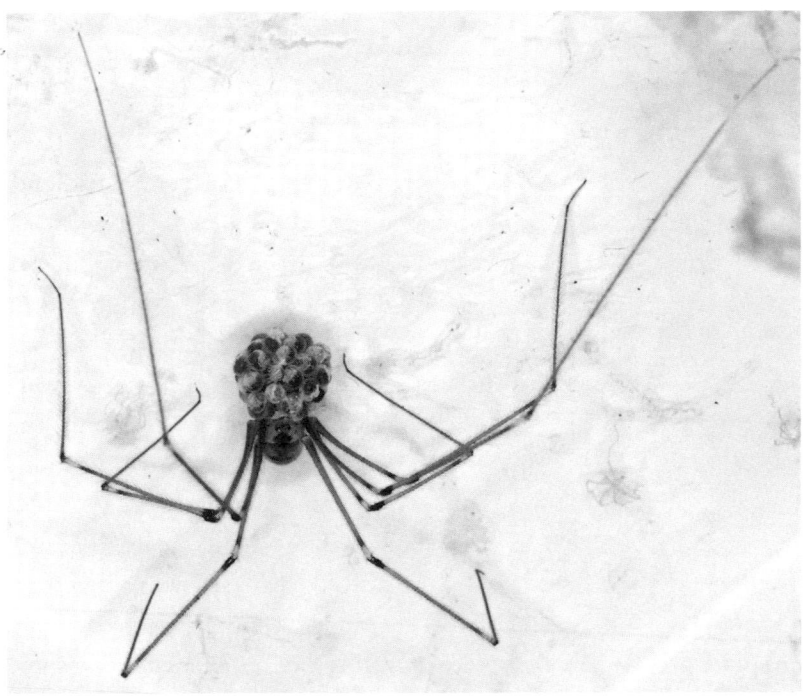

*The daddy long-legs (*Pholcus sp. *family Pholcidae) I named Mummy Long-legs with her egg sac held in her jaws.* (Photo: D. and L. Kelly)

Even before the young had all left their mother's protection to take up residence in every nook and cranny around the kitchen, two males danced attendance on Mummy Long-legs and the whole process started again.

There is a widely held belief that the daddy long-legs has the most deadly venom of any spider but its fangs can't penetrate the skin to deliver it. The truth is that the fangs can penetrate human skin, but delivers a bite which may cause only a mild local reaction, if any. So where did the myth come from?

The daddy long-legs has a favourite food—other spiders. As the daddy long-legs will prey upon and easily kill the red-back and other

Mummy Long-legs' young hatch.
(Photo: D. and L. Kelly)

widow spiders, human logic says: if it can kill the red-back and the red-back can kill me then the daddy long-legs can kill me even better! That was the Australian version—overseas versions require only the substitution of an indigenous venomous widow species.

The logic fails because biology doesn't work that way. Spider venom has evolved for use on spider prey. We are not spider prey. It is sheer coincidence that some spider venom affects primates and can kill us. It is nothing to do with evolution, just bad luck. But there is more to this bad science. In order to kill a red-back, the daddy long-legs wrap their prey in silk, using the length of their legs to avoid being bitten. So it isn't just the power of the venom, but the interaction between the spiders.

When I asked Dr Robert Raven, Senior Curator of Spiders at the Queensland Museum, why there have been no studies of daddy long-legs' venom, he said, 'It's just really boring venom. As there are no known cases of a pholcid spider ever causing the slightest problem having bitten a human, why waste valuable resources on testing it?'

In 2004, the television show *MythBusters* tested the daddy long-legs story. The spider's fangs measured about 0.25 mm, when the average thickness of human skin is only about 0.10 mm. After much time and effort, the show's host apparently managed to be bitten and the skin was penetrated. As there was little more than a brief, mild burning sensation, the venom appeared to be harmless to humans.

Once you know the difference between pholcids and opilionids, it's not too hard to distinguish a daddy long-legs from a harvestman. With spiders, however, establishing the exact species you are observing is often almost impossible. Classification to the species level involves peering at the genitalia of a dead spider through a microscope. A casual observer, able to identify the general group—the jumping spider from the huntsman, the wolf spider from the trapdoor—is doing very well.

I compared domestic arachnid scenes with Kathleen Hawkins, a friend and correspondent who writes of life in Flower Mound, Texas:

> These are the spiders I've identified here in Texas: wolf spiders, garden orbs, black fishing spiders (maybe), brown recluses, daddy long-legs (although I've heard they're not technically spiders), jumping spiders (maybe), golden-silk spider, cream house spiders (maybe), and crab spiders (maybe). Of course I've seen many more, but I'm beginning to think that identifying spiders is as hopeless for me as identifying birds. There are such subtleties sometimes between spider species that I doubt I could ever be accurate (except for identifying the very obvious ones). Actually, birds are easier for me to identify than spiders, although I still have trouble identifying the 13 kinds of woodpeckers. The best I can do is: small, medium, and large.
>
> We have a small black, furry spider. They're very alert spiders and make silken shelters. We've had them in the house and the mailbox (pity the mail carrier). I think they're quite common, but I've been to dozens of spider websites and haven't seen this exact spider.
>
> There are flat webs with funnels, and then one [spider] that spins random webs with balled up (what appears to be) egg sacs.
>
> Oh, yes, and we have tarantulas. I've seen the 'Texas Tan Tarantula' and black tarantulas. But I see them rarely, maybe once a year or less.

One day when I went outside to see if the mail had come, I reached back
to close the door behind me and saw a tarantula sitting on the doorknob.
It was startling. Once in a while I'll see one crossing our lane. They move
slowly, but steadily with purpose. I consider it a gift to see one.

The term 'house spider' is used all over the world, for spiders from
a great variety of families. Most often it is used to refer to the common
house spider, that messy cobweb-builder with all the egg sacs (*Achaearanea spp.*, family Theridiidae) as shown in Plate 3, which either occurs
naturally or has been introduced all over the world.

I met Kathleen's alert little nest-builders on a recent visit to Texas.
They are the bold jumping spider (*Phidippus audax.*, family Salticidae).
(See Plate 5.) Jumping spiders are common everywhere in the world and
I think they are drop-dead cute. As we will see in Chapter 6, they are
also incredibly smart arachnids.

I'm green with envy over the tarantulas (family Theraphosidae)
Kathleen sees wandering across the road—we have nothing even similar
in southern Australia, while further north we have the less spectacular
Australian tarantulas.

Kathleen mentions flat webs with funnels. In most countries, the
term 'funnel-web' is used to describe spiders in the family Agelenidae,
as shown in Plate 6. What we call funnel-web spiders would cause great
alarm if they were common around the house. Our funnel-webs are
primitives—bulky, large and aggressive black spiders of the family
Hexathelidae, and include the Sydney funnel-web (*Atrax robustus*), often
quoted as the most deadly spider on earth.

Other funnel-web spiders, or funnel weavers, of the family
Agelenidae are common all over the world. Their webs gather dust in
the corners of brickwork, windows, fences and other structures and are
typified by a funnel-like retreat in which the spider hides during the day.
Sheets of woolly, dust-gathering web stretch beyond the funnel to trap

insects and other invertebrates, including spiders. Sitting at the mouth of her retreat with her legs delicately touching the web, the waiting spider feels the vibrations when her web is disturbed and rushes out to claim her prey.

Many agelenids (as arachnologists call spiders of the family Agelenidae) are in the genus *Tegenaria* which includes the notorious hobo spider (*T. agrestis*), the domestic house spider (*T. domestica*), which is also known as the barn funnel weaver, and the giant house spider (*T. duellica*). *Tegenaria* runs on top of her dense, horizontal web when out hunting at night. The hobo spider (*T. agrestis*) is one of a small number of spiders in North America whose bites are feared, as is the brown recluse spider (*Loxosceles reclusa*, family Sicariidae) Kathleen casually mentions in passing. These will be explored more fully in Chapter 9.

The common house spider with her funnelled web in Australia is a completely different animal to her overseas equivalent, yet the ecological niche and behaviour are remarkably similar. The Australian black house spider (*Badumna insignis*) is in the family Desidae, and usually builds her web vertically against house walls or on fences.

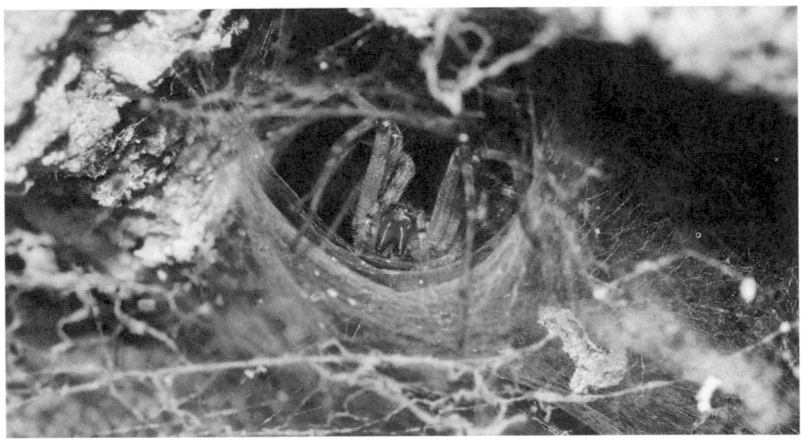

A Tegenaria at her funnel web entrance in Oxford, UK. (Photo: D. and L. Kelly)

Although thickset and reputed to have a painful bite, they do not deserve the fear they generate. In sudden extreme heat these spiders have been known to drop from their webs in hot tin roofs, but they will not, as some claim, deliberately jump on you.

There are a number of related species. The female of the larger, darker *Badumna insignis* can measure nearly two centimetres in body length while the male is only half that. Slightly smaller is the speckled grey house spider, *Badumna longinqua*, which has been introduced from Australia into New Zealand and California, where it has taken hold with ease.

Part of a group known as lace-web spiders, black house spiders are fanatical web-builders as becomes clear to anyone who tries to clear the web away. If the spider is safe in its retreat, the first signs of the web reappear the next day, and grow every night.

The web is made in sections of zig-zags criss-crossing almost parallel lines of silk, which gives a distorted ladder effect. The silk is described

*My favourite black house spider (*Badumna insignis*), Legless, in her nightly position, waiting for prey to arrive on her web.* (Photo: D. and L. Kelly)

*A black house spider having caught a European wasp (*Vespula germanica*). Without the spiders eating an insect or two a night, we would soon be overrun by insects.*
(Photo: Alan Henderson)

as 'cribellate', and is woolly rather than sticky (as we will explore more fully in Chapter 4). The insect who has the misfortune to fly or walk into the web gets entangled rather than stuck. As the victim struggles to free itself, vibrations travel along the web to alert the spider to its presence and the spider emerges to wrap up the next meal. Black house spider webs are often filled with discarded arthropod remains.

Spiders have no true jaws. They can only eat a liquid lunch, preferably pre-digested. To ensure their food is properly prepared, spiders inject the prey with digestive juices, creating insect-innards soup or consommé of centipede, ready to be sucked up.

The typical zig-zag pattern of a cribellate web, with the weaver in her daytime retreat below.
(Photo: D. and L. Kelly)

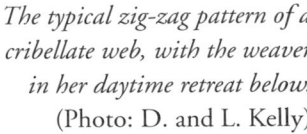

Web-building house spiders have regular habits. They emerge at almost the same time each evening to sit poised, ready for action. The long front legs rest delicately on the web, detecting the slightest of movements. These spiders have very little sight and no hearing. Their hairy legs tell them what is happening in the world around them. You are just a blur of light and dark. You are of no interest unless you become a threat. Then the spider will retreat.

The woolly lace-web collects fine dust and so soon loses its fresh look. Closer examination reveals last night's work. It is the shiny silken lines or the fresh, new ladder of web, still exhibiting neat zig-zags, undamaged by the deadly activities of spider and prey.

The first of my long-term black house spider companions was Noirville, as I named her (in strangled French). She lived on the window over my desk in the shed which I call the 'Garret'. It is where I write, my favourite place on earth. She made her lace-web on the top of the window until she experienced the blazing heat of her first Australian summer, whereby she moved to behind the rug beneath the window. She left her old web adorned with one hapless male wrapped in his shroud of silk, three spidery legs extended beyond the shroud bearing mute testimony to his failure. She stayed behind the rug for nearly two years.

Noirville emerged each evening, but her long dark legs on the web were the only indication she was there. Should any small insect be caught in her web, she would dash out and carry it back into her retreat. She never left the web. If I became over-familiar, she would disappear into her retreat, to stay there for at least an hour. Then the familiar feet would appear again.

One night, I watched a smaller spider approach the web and realised it was a male. He took his time, sitting motionless on her web for hours. As he moved nearer her retreat, he began tapping on her web. Then he entered the tunnel and emerged—alive. I have watched male black house spiders reside with females for a week or more.

One day, a host of miniature Noirvilles appeared on her web. Over the next few days they departed, most, I guess, out the window which I left open for them. A few months later, a small web appeared, across the other side of the rug from Noirville.

The intriguing part was the differences in behaviour. Noirville was out each night and stayed out while I worked. Noirville II was very shy. If I turned on the light, she would disappear. I could see her if I shone a torch behind the rug, but she would never emerge while I was there.

Since Noirvilles I and II, there have been many more *Badumna*. Over last summer, there were over twenty individuals I talked to every night. David Attenborough commented in an interview with Michael Parkinson:

I think spiders are absolutely extraordinary, I mean we brush away a cobweb and you think of the complexity it takes to build that and that tiny little creature with a minute, microscopic little brain knows how to do that and what's more they all have real characters, you can get half a dozen spiders of the same species . . . I was working with a camera-man, Kevin Flay, and Kevin had been looking at a whole row of them and he had them on sprays of leaves in milk bottles and he said, 'That one, hopeless, does nothing. This one, doesn't like light at all, that one very temperamental. But this one, she goes for anything, doesn't matter how frequently she's eaten.' That meant that these little spiders which we tend to dismiss as mechanical, tiny little, with no character—they each had a separate character.

And so it is with my black house spiders. Legless was very confident. Uppity tolerated my light and camera—most of the time. Topsy, the largest, was very shy. I had to do my best sneaking to see her. Named after her position on the top of the kitchen window on the back verandah, she would disappear on my approach unless I moved very slowly.

Spiders are not hairy in order to scare the hell out of us. The web-builders are almost blind, but through her hairs and the slight air vibrations I caused, Topsy knew exactly where I was and how I was moving. I used to demonstrate this to visitors. We would all approach Topsy's side of the window, very slowly, stand still and then I would blow very, very gently in her direction from about two metres away. On cue, every time, she would be gone. Blink and the dash would be missed. And she wouldn't come out again for hours.

Uppity was less shy. A few spiders down from Topsy, she always hung upside down at the entrance to her retreat, something none of the others did. I never saw her in any other position.

*Uppity, a black house spider (*Badumna insignis*) in her funnel entrance, upside down. She was the only one of the many black house spiders to rest this way.* (Photo: D. and L. Kelly)

As the summer progressed, Uppity became very large in her abdomen and much more difficult to photograph. Even at my sneakiest, she was usually gone before I had but the briefest glimpse of a spider in rapid retreat. Then her young appeared. Just like Noirville a few years before, Uppity's web was covered in miniature versions of herself. Another spider, not much larger than Uppity's young, was crossing the web preying on the young who had left the retreat, and Uppity's protection, only hours before. A baby spider's life expectancy isn't good.

But that summer, my favourite was Legless.

Legless was so named as she had one leg less than she should have. It's not uncommon for spiders to be a leg or two short. They have the ability voluntarily to amputate a leg if something grabs it. This is known as autotomy and is common in arthropods and familiar in lizards, who will drop their tail to escape a predator. An immature spider will regrow

Uppity's young emerge from her retreat. One had barely emerged before being taken by a spider. (Photo: D. and L. Kelly)

Legless was so named as she had one leg less than the full complement. The stump of her hind leg can be seen. Spiders drop a leg voluntarily when they are caught. (Photo: D. and L. Kelly)

the leg in its next moult. The new leg will grow within the exoskeleton, squashed in by the hard outer case. A seven-legged spider will moult, and emerge with eight full legs. The new leg may be thinner and shorter, but it will be a complete leg. Legless remained deficient. She was already mature. A leg autotomised after the final moult is gone forever.

Legless' name creates the awful image of a spider with only a body and none of its characteristic legs. I was distressed to read that researchers have created such a sad sight. In one French experiment, a spider was induced to autotomise all eight legs. The immobile spider was kept on a soft bed and fed artificially. All eight legs regenerated at the next moult. These new legs had all their segments. Regenerated legs which were autotomised were again regenerated at the next moult.

Experiments have shown that anaesthetised spiders cannot autotomise their legs, so it is a deliberate act. The leg is usually disconnected at the end of the first of the seven leg segments, the coxa (see the diagram of the ventral view of a garden orb weaver on p. 65). There does not need to be an external force to cause the limb to disconnect. The spider actually jerks the coxa upwards, leaving the rest of the leg in place. The single muscle which traverses this joint readily detaches itself from the top of the trochanter. This muscle withdraws into the cavity left in the coxa and, with surrounding muscles, serves to seal the wound. As a spider's body cavity is full of blood, any piercing or tear will cause a fatal blood loss.

Spiders usually autotomise legs which have been caught by a predator or another spider. An aggressive response from a female to a male can result in the rejected suitor autotomising the gripped limb and beating a hasty retreat. If a spider is stung in the leg by a bee or wasp caught in its web, it can automise the limb before the venom reaches the body.

When shedding their skins in a moult, spiders will sometimes autotomise a leg which won't come free easily. In such cases, spiders have been seen eating the severed limb, wasting nothing. It's such a common occurrence that up to a fifth of all spiders in the field has at least one leg less than their full complement. Spiders seem to function fine with a few missing limbs. Orb weavers with only three or four legs have been found to build perfectly functional webs.

I grew fonder of Legless each night as she would tolerate almost any number of photographs and allow me to creep very close before she would disappear into her retreat in the external brickwork near the laundry door.

Legless added to her messy web until it crossed over onto the laundry door. Once or twice a week we passed that way and disturbed the web. Legless industriously replaced it the following night. At one stage we had some renovations done. The builders went in and out the laundry door all day. Arriving one morning while it was still dark, the builders met Legless. By the end of the week, they could be heard mumbling 'Sorry, Legless' each time they slammed the door. After a week of determined replacement, Legless gave up. She extended her web around the brickwork in preference, only months later choosing to replace it over the door again.

One night, I saw a smaller spider on Legless' web with her. Enthusiastic about the chance of photographing her mating, I moved over to take the first photograph. In the instant I focused I registered the distinctive white tip on the abdomen of the newcomer. It was a white-tailed spider (*Lampona cylindrata*, family Lamponidae). Its leg was almost touching Legless, poised for the final, killing leap. The favourite food of white-tailed spiders is black house spiders like Legless.

A good scientist observes, records, photographs and lets nature take its course. I screamed, dropped my expensive camera, with its brand-new, thousand-dollar lens, and blew on Legless. I blew hard, between her and her attacker. Legless disappeared into her retreat in a flash. I grabbed a twig and brushed the white-tailed spider off the web.

I have to admit I panicked, checking regularly to see if the white-tailed spider had returned. It was a long wait until the following night when I was relieved to see Legless appear at the entrance to her retreat as usual. But for the next few weeks she would scurry away as soon as I approached her web. It was nearly a month before I could photograph her again.

A few weeks later I noticed a common house spider (*Achaearanea sp.*, family Theridiidae) I had named Lady Macbeth, due to her seemingly constant supply of victims, bailing up a prey. It was a white-tailed spider. I started photographing, feeling less upset than I would usually at the sight of a spider meeting such an end. This very victim, I told myself, was probably responsible for the demise of one, if not more, of my black house spiders, whose numbers had decreased by half over the summer. As Lady Macbeth sank in her fangs, I noticed a

*Legless is about to be jumped by a white-tailed spider (*Lampona sp.*). Black house spiders are their favourite food.* (Photo: D. and L. Kelly)

strange white ball on the tip of the struggling spider's abdomen. I had no idea what it could be so I showed the image in Plate 4 to Dr Robert Raven.

'It's probably shitting itself,' he said.

It's a spider-eat-spider world out there.

One morning, breakfasting early on the verandah, I noticed Legless appear even though it was light. I had never seen her in daylight before. She was soon gone, and a stroll to her corner revealed the remains of a beetle body beneath the web. Enjoying the company of the morning birds at the feeding table, I decided to finish my cup of tea and toast before photographing the remains of Legless' meal, only to find I was nearly too late. The ants were removing the last of the leftovers.

Another of my black house spiders was still feeding on a large beetle in the early morning sun. I watched in horror as the swarm of ants

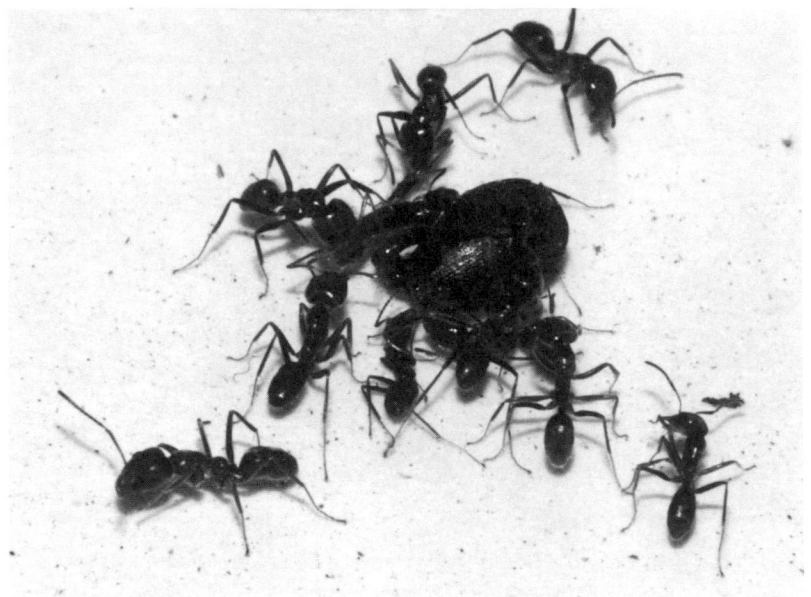

Legless' leftovers soon disappeared in the mandibles of the ants. (Photo: D. and L. Kelly)

climbed the door frame to finish off her meal, taking her as well.

Many of the beetles I observe are dung beetles, feeding on the droppings of our kangaroos, wombats, wallabies and possums, perhaps even those of birds and dogs. If it weren't for those beetles, we'd be knee-deep in dung. If it weren't for the spiders, we'd be knee-deep in beetles. If it weren't for the birds, we'd be knee-deep in spiders. If it weren't for the ants we'd be knee-deep in the remains of all of them.

Legless was in the middle of a food chain, her small world mimicking the giant interconnected ecosystem which is our planet. Unfortunately, birds are not the only creatures which feed on spiders. I was heartbroken the night I found a mite sucking Legless' lifeblood as she sat on the web.

Legless and the mite near her back leg, indented into her abdomen.
(Photo: D. and L. Kelly)

Legless built a woolly lace-web, Lady Macbeth a sticky tangle-web. Only metres from their webs was the huge orb of a garden orb weaver. When Legless' web was damaged, she would repair it overnight. The garden orb weaver, by contrast, builds a new web every night. It's time to meet one of the most accomplished arachnid engineers.

3

GARNISHING
THE GARDEN

The spider's touch, how exquisitely fine!
Feels at each thread, and lives along the line.

Alexander Pope, *Essay on Man*

Erio changed my life. In 45 minutes, one small spider turned me into a fully fledged arachnophile. How often have you come across a single thread of silk strung across your path? The next time, instead of brushing it aside, note the location and return just after dark, and you may be rewarded by seeing your own Erio building her web.

Erio was a garden orb weaver (*Eriophora biapicata*, family Araneidae) who lived on the maple in front of my home when I lived in suburban Melbourne. Spiders of her species, or their close relations, inhabit gardens the world over. Wandering outside one evening, I was stopped by a pale, moving object in front of my face. Closer inspection revealed Erio, rushing across a single thread spread between the tree and a neighbouring bush. Twice more she travelled its length, feeding

A huge garden orb web in the morning dew. (Photo: D. and L. Kelly)

out thread with her back legs. The last of her threads was left slack.

Travelling back on her slack thread, Erio suddenly stopped in the middle. Dropping towards the ground with her slack thread, she formed an inverted triangle. Stopping again, this time half-way to the ground, she appeared to survey the mid-air triangle now above her. She then dropped on a single thread. Her slack thread was now shaped as a capital Y. The bottom of her Y was attached to a rock, and she climbed up again.

With her triangle now strongly attached to the rock below, Erio set to work on the outer framework. Back up to the triangle she ran. She then dragged a slack thread up to the bridge line. She attached this thread to the end of the bridge line, and then tightened it to form part of the frame and another radius, as shown overleaf.

In and out she ran with slack threads. Out along a radius and down a frame, where she would attach her slack thread to create yet another radius. A few times she attached threads to the ground. The outer frame-work now measured about two metres from tree to bush, and just over two metres above the ground. Sometimes she would pause, and I wondered if it was to rest or because she had sensed my presence. But then on she would go, either refreshed or reassured by my stillness.

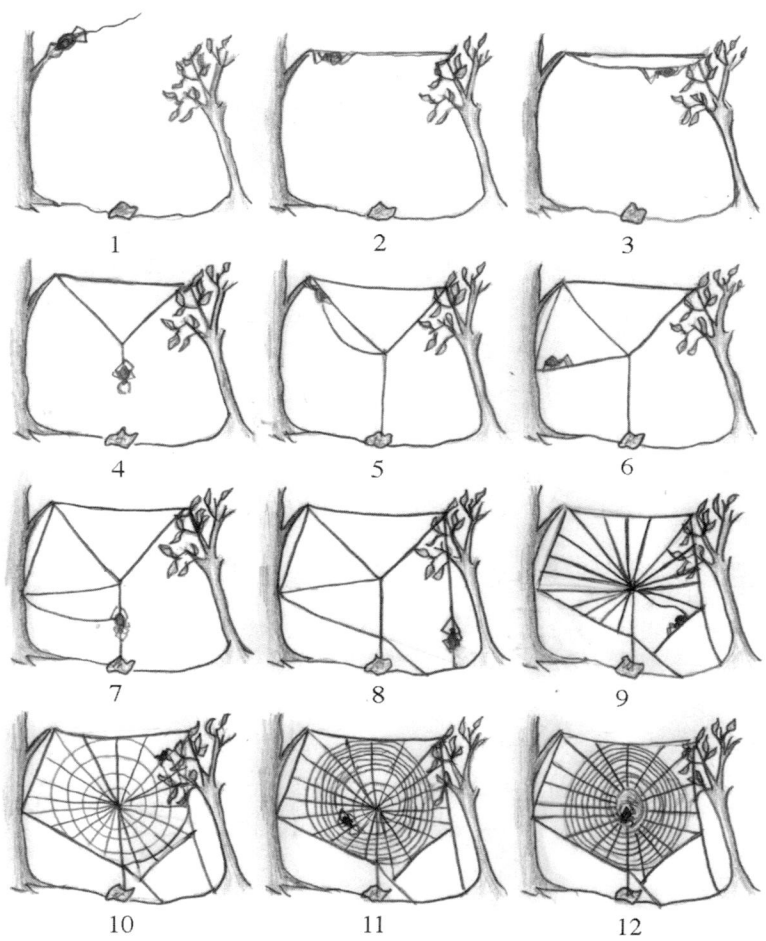

Stages of orb-web construction. (Diagram: L. Kelly)

As Erio added more and more radii to the framework, the mass of threads in the centre became thick enough to appear white. Erio would take what appeared to be rest breaks, always head down, on this central platform. The first lap of the spiral was spun. Erio would climb out on the radius as far as she could while still being able to reach back to her previous circuit. Her leg span became her measuring stick, as shown in Plate 9. Out and out from her hub the structural spiral emerged. Occasionally she would turn and add spiral in the reverse direction, but mostly it was a perfect formation.

Up until now, Erio had been using dry silk, but now that her spirals had reached the outer rim, it was time for her to lay down her sticky trap. This was much more closely spaced than her structural coils. Back she came from the outer rim, spinning her new threads and rolling up her first weaving. As she added each thread of her new spiral, from one radius to the next, Erio would pause momentarily and tug the thread with her abdomen, releasing tiny globules of glue. I was mesmerised by her little bottom, tensioning her structure with such precision. My engineering background told me how precisely she must be adjusting the tension for different parts of the web to bear her weight so evenly. My admiration soared with every tug. Almost back to the centre, she stopped spinning, collected a few more dry rounds, then returned to her resting place—head down.

Erio's web was complete. She consumed the collected thread, not wasting any precious protein, and I assumed she would now have a well-earned rest on her lovely soft white cushion, at which moment she snipped out the central pad and ate that as well. The centre of her web was now a vacant space. In 45 minutes of frantic movement, round and round, back and forward, with only a few rests in the middle, Erio had completed a shiny, perfect orb web. It was stunning, and so was she.

Over the following weeks, I was able to predict the exact time Erio would make her web. I made sure no-one walked through the single strand she left up each night, so she would revisit it. And every day I hunted for her resting place on the tree. Hunted and hunted and hunted.

At last I decided the time had come to insist she reveal her sanctuary. Armed with a chair and a drink, I took up position well before dusk and stared at that tree trunk. As the sun began to set, a small piece of dark bark stood up, stretched itself and walked out onto the thread. I had stared at that exact spot so many times yet had never seen her. From then on, of course, every time I looked at it I could see the eight elegant legs, tightly folded and the compact shape totally absorbed into the texture of the bark. A pale-coloured spider with red markings on her legs became a black patch of bark and I have no idea how.

One evening, Erio's single bridge strand between her tree and one of the nearby bushes was broken by a visitor. Erio emerged as always, climbed out to her branch and lifted her abdomen. Light reflected from the emerging strand of silk as her hind legs fed it into the air. Suddenly she turned, tugged at the thread and, reassured it was well attached, ran across to a bush close to her usual anchorage. Back and forth, up and down, in and out, then around and around and around. Forty-five minutes later and the perfect web was in place, its creator head-down in the centre.

Each time Erio's bridge strand was lost I watched her lay down a new one. Only twice was the air so very still that she was unable to catch a breeze and, after an hour or so, she gave up. No webs were spun those two nights.

Late in February, Erio's web was constructed with less care than usual. A few days later, she didn't take it down properly. There was a half-built orb, a sort of standing memorial to my spider. She hadn't returned to her resting place on the bark. I searched the ground but couldn't find her body. I searched the tree but couldn't find an egg sac. I missed the little entertainer who had given me so much pleasure over the summer.

Erio must have hidden her egg sac well. By next spring, nine tiny orb webs had appeared on the branch where Erio had once rested. I hoped they would reach maturity. Then there were eight. Then there were seven. One day I saw a gecko on the branch. Then there were none.

The joy of watching a garden orb weaver strut her stuff is on offer most summer nights in gardens the world over. With a variety of genera, they are all stocky spiders with hairy bodies, but vary enormously in colour and patterning. In Europe, garden orb weavers are often called by their genus, *Araneus*. In his delightful book, *Spiders of Britain and Northern Europe*, Michael J. Roberts writes:

> *Araneus diadematus* is without doubt the commonest and best known of this genus of orb weavers, and has a distinctive white cross on the abdomen. This species is sometimes known as the 'garden spider', although it is by no means the commonest spider in the garden and is generally commoner on gorse bushes away from human influence. The abdominal markings give rise to the names of 'diadem spider' and 'cross spider'; the latter seems to have unduly vexatious implications. In Denmark, the species is known as the 'korsedderkop' and in Germany the all-embracing name 'Gartenkreuzspinne' is used. Whatever you want to call it, it is a good species in which to observe web-building, prey capture and mating. The female places her spherical egg sac in a sheltered spot, remaining with it until she dies in late autumn. The spiderlings emerge the following May and, initially, cluster together in a fuzzy ball which 'explodes' at the slightest disturbance.

HOW DOES AN ORB WEAVER KNOW HOW TO SPIN HER WEB?

I have often heard it said that the construction of an orb web is just the application of a formula, unvarying instinctive behaviour followed like a computer programme. As evidence, we are reminded that orb weavers cannot learn their skills from a parent as the mother is usually dead before the young leave the egg sac, yet tiny spiders weave tiny, perfect orb webs. While instinct must have something to do with it, my observations of the garden orb weavers made me doubt that spider weaving can be put down to a simple algorithm, or even a complex one. Orb weavers respond to the different situations in which they find themselves—location and weather. If you observe the same orb weaver make her web night after night, you too will conclude that she is making reasoned decisions. The laboratory is in your own backyard. As Barbara York Main wrote in her classic *Spiders*:

> The actual sequence of placing frame-threads and radii varies from spider to spider and even in the webs made successively by an individual spider. The site of the web and the intensity of the wind both influence the details of the web.

Last summer, I watched three orb weavers, Erio-three, Erio-four and Damiana, weave their webs in their three locations, all within 30 metres of each other. Erio-three lived on a hakea bush, her resting place at head height among a group of hakea nuts. She was grey, like the nuts which camouflaged her so well. Erio-four lived on the brown eaves of the house and wove a web from the house to the nearby trellis fence. She was distinctly brown. Damiana was golden with the most stunning markings. She was still weaving late in summer, a month after the other two had left to produce their young. A male was a completely different colouring again. (See Plates 7 to 12.)

Erio-three was the one I observed most closely, as she wove her web at head height.

All day, wet or dry, Erio-three would imitate a hakea nut, in perfect stillness. Each night, she would emerge from her resting place and test the thread to see if it had stayed in place from the night before. If so, she would add a strengthening line and get to work. If the thread had been broken, Erio-three would raise her abdomen and release thread

A male garden orb weaver, almost certainly the same species as my females, had very different markings, almost black with a distinctive white stripe. (Photo: D. and L. Kelly)

until a breeze caught it. Only once it was firmly attached to shrubbery on the other side of the driveway would she start to create her strong baseline.

Late in the summer, Erio-three's web was being broken during the night by the kangaroos that drought had forced to venture near to the house in search of food. Erio-three moved her web higher in the small hakea bush, out of harm's way. She wove her web in this new location for the rest of the summer. From the same resting place, she

Erio-three on her completed web. (Photo: D. and L. Kelly)

now climbed and wove every night in a different position to that which she had used for months. I don't believe that kind of behaviour can be attributed solely to instinct. I witnessed another spider make a similar decision that summer.

Damiana was still weaving well after the others had gone. Her magnificent web was strung between two wattles, well above head height, leaving a clear gap over the pathway regularly used by the kangaroos.

Late in the summer, I still had not found Damiana's resting place. The frame of her orb web disappeared into the trees way above my head. One evening, I went out when it was still dusk, and watched for Damiana to emerge. I became aware of a descending object a few centimetres above my head. I stepped back and turned the torch to reveal Damiana, who immediately climbed to a small knob of silk at the height of her usual hub. She had been descending from her hub to place her ground anchor.

I watched her climb to a branch five metres above my head, taking her silk line and hub with her. Hours later I found her blowing around in the wind on a half-sized orb web near the branch on which I assume she rested during the day. The following night I resisted going out until late, hoping she would descend to her usual height, but she again had built high up near her branch. She never again descended to the level of the torch-bearing Godzilla.

Up until I'd inadvertently scared her off, Damiana had been using a totally different initial process to all the other orb weavers I had observed. Every night, she would drop from a great height down to the bushes below, attach her line to the ground and then climb to use the breeze to get her silk to the bushes. On the last night she came to ground, she met me. She decided not to build where danger threatened and, learning from that experience, never built there again.

In *Life's Other Secret: The new mathematics of the living world*, one of my favourite authors, Ian Stewart, argues that evolution favours the rules which govern behaviour, not the behaviour itself.

A few rules, with built-in contingency planning, can encapsulate a *huge* range of behavior, adaptable to a huge range of circumstances. Rules, quite simply, require less information . . .

The common garden cross spider *Araneus diadematus*, for instance, builds around 200 webs during its short lifetime. Each web differs subtly from the others, depending on the surroundings in which it is to be built. These variations demonstrate the enormous flexibility of the spider's web-building system: too flexible to be just a simple list of actions coded in the spider's genes. Rules, however, are another matter entirely. The shapes of webs are clues to the spider's rules.

As any computer programmer very well knows, rules take far less information storage space than final images. Fractals, for example, some of the most complex images ever produced, can be computer coded in a few lines. Professor Fritz Vollrath and his team at Denmark's Aarhus University created cyberspiders to weave cyberwebs, based on observations of real spiders. Orb-web construction varies between spider species in detail but not in the basic characteristics: evenly spaced radials overlaid by an evenly spaced spiral. Adding in genetic algorithms, Vollrath coded his cyberspiders with rules for making webs. Introducing crossbreeding and natural selection, he found it took no more than 50 generations to 'breed' cyberspiders who made highly efficient orb webs, matching those generated by their real models.

Stewart concludes:

> The message here is mathematically exciting but biologically sobering. It is that *apparently* complicated and flexible animal behaviour patterns can be generated by much simpler, and more rigid, rules. Evolutionary selection is based on the effectiveness of the webs—but selection works by eliminating the spiders whose web-building *rules* produce less effective webs.
>
> What drives spider evolution is the rules, not the webs—and the same probably goes for much animal behaviour, individual or collective.

All spiders evolved on earth in normal gravity, so what can spiders weave in microgravity? Three experiments have been attempted with spiders in space, on *Skylab* (1973), the ill-fated *Challenger* (1986) and then the equally unlucky *Columbia* (2003). The first spider was not fed, and hence starved. It had managed to build orb webs. The Australian garden orb weavers (*Eriophora sp.*) on *Columbia* soon managed to build very good orb webs, after some initial less-than-perfect ones. Once they were building their normal webs, they did so in much less time than the control spiders on earth. Unfortunately, most of the detailed data were lost with the *Columbia* and her crew.

I don't *know* how a spider knows how to build a web, although I suspect it is a combination of instinct—those genetically coded rules—and learning from experience. What I do know is that I have no better proof that nature is awesome.

SMALLER ORB WEAVERS ABOUND

The large orb weavers are not the only master weavers working their nightly wonders in the garden. Small, very small and absolutely tiny spiders are creating scaled-down versions of the large orb webs. Once I had found one little orb web, I saw another and another and then a few more. One branch of a pelargonium, not more than ten centimetres long, had at least ten permanent residents each with their own tiny orb.

I became particularly fond of the largest of my tiny residents. I called her Itsy. I called her even smaller neighbour Itsier. Each was clearly a different species. Each night I would photograph Itsy and Itsier at their work. During the day I could see Itsy fairly easily, but it was a real strain to find Itsier, her camouflage was so superb.

Itsy rested under the top leaves of the branch above her permanent orb web. One day she was busy weaving. The first egg sac was ready. Then a second. A few days later a third. I watched her wrap prey so I knew she was still hunting and eating. A fourth egg sac and she was done. Most of the next week she rested on her egg sacs, totally passive. I checked her morning and night, knowing that if she was missing I would never know if she had died or been eaten.

One morning Itsy was dead, her tiny body strung in her web.

I couldn't see any damage when I zoomed in close on the photographs. Itsy was woven into her web, outstretched, and didn't have the

Itsy on her web. (Photo: D. and L. Kelly)

Itsy resting with her four egg sacs and prey, so she was still eating. (Photo: D. and L. Kelly)

Itsy's little body, woven into her web. (Photo: D. and L. Kelly)

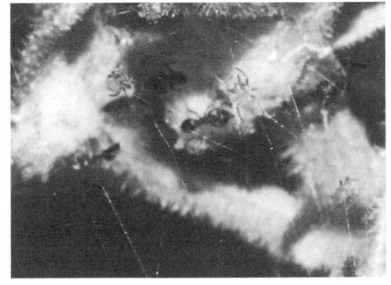

Itsy's babies hatched. Within a few hours, ants raided the egg sacs. (Photo: D. and L. Kelly)

usual shrivelled appearance of a dead spider. Could she possibly be presenting herself for food for her young? Or as a decoy for predators? The next day, her web was damaged and the tiny body gone.

I checked the unattended egg sacs constantly over the next few days. Suddenly there was a horde of tiny replicas of Itsy emerging over her web. The egg sacs were still there, torn open. As I watched the spider-lings a dozen ants appeared. Over the month I had been watching this small branch, I had never seen an ant on it. Now Itsy's egg sacs were covered in them, the babies all actively dashing about on the web below. Half-an-hour later, the ants, and the empty egg sacs, were gone.

An hour later the spiderlings were also disappearing, ballooning off to new pastures. I hope some of them are in my garden still.

While the orb weavers are the undisputed leaders in web-building, all spiders produce silk. But how? And what is this wonderful substance that has a higher tensile strength than anything we can produce, despite all our technological achievements?

4

LET'S GET PHYSICAL

Garden orb weavers are very good at resting, legs splayed, in the middle of their orb webs—an ideal position for you to identify their body parts.

The first photograph shows Erio-three on her web, followed by a representation of a spider's dorsal structure. The photo on the following page shows Erio-three's other side, followed by a diagram giving the ventral structure. The final figure is a diagrammatical representation of spider innards.

While insects have three body parts—head, thorax and abdomen—spiders have only two. The head and thorax are fused into a single part, known as the cephalothorax or prosoma. The cuticle is the hard outer skeleton which encloses the cephalothorax and legs. Despite being pliable, the cuticle cannot grow, and thus has to be shed regularly during a spider's life in a series of moults. Once modern spiders reach maturity they stop moulting. Primitive spiders, such as the trapdoors and tarantulas, will continue to moult throughout their long lives.

Garden orb weaver—dorsal view. (Photo: D. and L. Kelly)

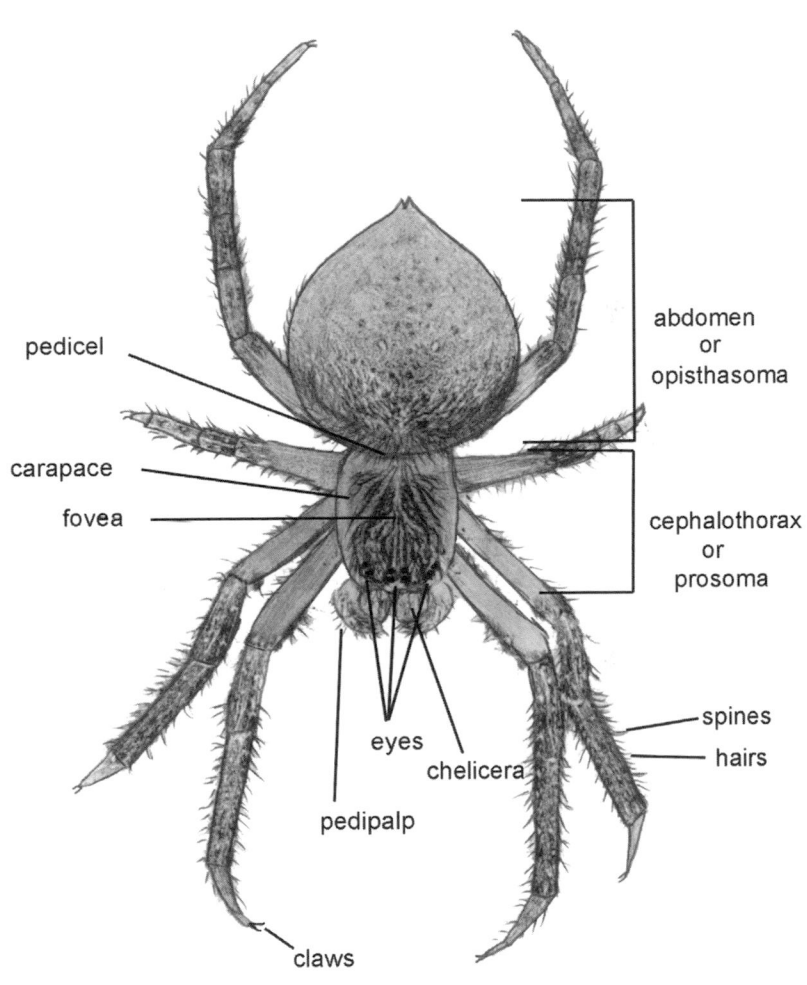

Garden orb weaver—dorsal physical structure. (Diagram: L. Kelly)

Garden orb weaver—ventral view. (Photo: D. and L. Kelly)

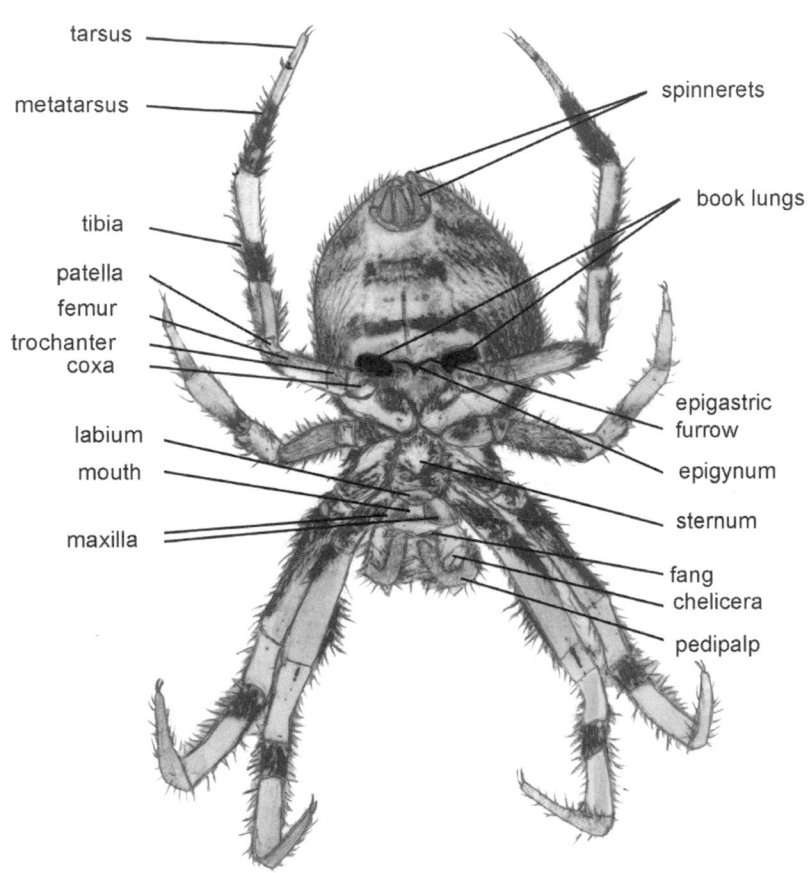

tarsus
metatarsus
spinnerets
book lungs
tibia
patella
femur
trochanter
coxa
epigastric
furrow
labium
epigynum
mouth
sternum
maxilla
fang
chelicera
pedipalp

Garden orb weaver—ventral physical structure. (Diagram: L. Kelly)

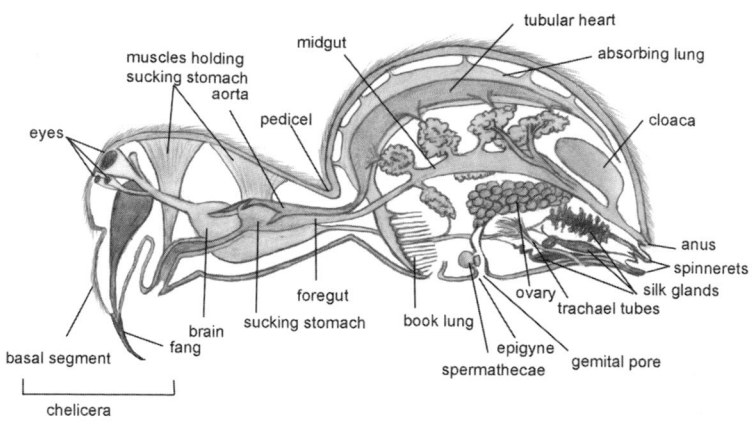

Spider internal physical structure. (Diagram: L. Kelly)

The soft abdomen of a spider can expand freely, and does so every time it feeds. The cephalothorax and legs are covered in a hard exoskeleton. New cuticle grows beneath this outer shell, wrinkled and soft. With each moult, the spider grows a little. The time between moults depends very much on the species, but also on the environmental conditions and on how much the spider has been able to feed. Small spiders may go through as few as five moults to maturity, while larger spiders may need about ten. Males, often being smaller than the females, may need a few less moults before they gain their sexually mature palps and can head off on their quest to find a mate.

When a spider is ready to moult, it withdraws into its retreat for a few days and ceases to eat. My wolf spiders cover their burrows with silk and leaf matter, to appear a week or so later with the entrance expanded. Many of my trapdoor spiders cover their doorless burrows with a thick covering of silk. There are many reasons they may do this, but moulting will certainly be one of them. There is no end of interest if you find individual spiders and watch them over time!

Some spiders construct silken retreats to prepare for the moulting process, while those who have permanent abodes stay inside. A definitive sign that the moulting is to begin is when a spider drops from a thread—the moulting thread—and then starts to split open. The freshly moulted spider is a glorious sight as it performs a gymnastic display, flexing and stretching the new body covering carefully as it sets. (See Plate 13.)

Smaller spiders can moult in as little as ten minutes, while the larger tarantulas can take hours. Not all spiders use moulting threads. Tarantulas, for example, lie on their backs while they moult. But all spiders do pass through the same three stages. With increased heart rate and thus increased pressure of their haemolymph, the cuticle of the cephalothorax begins to split along the side join. Lifting off the upper surface, the carapace, spiders split open the sides of the covering of the abdomen. They then free the abdomen and draw out the legs from their restrictive tubes. If the spider becomes stuck here, maybe because it's too dry, the result can be death. If it is just a leg which is caught, then the spider may choose to autotomise it, starting the next phase short a limb or two. At this stage, a spider is defenceless—the fangs are soft. The spider often lacks pigment as well as strength.

The image overleaf is the most defenceless you will ever see a live Sydney funnel-web, reputed to be the most deadly spider in the world.

The abdomen, or opisthosoma, is soft and usually covered with a velvety fur. A narrow waist, the pedicel, joins the cephalothorax to the abdomen. The cephalothorax has a hardened upper surface called the carapace. The carapace contains a slight hollow called the fovea. It is here that the internal muscles are attached.

On the carapace and on the front, are the eyes. Unlike insects' compound eyes, spider eyes have only a single lens in each and are known as simple eyes. There are never more than eight, which is now believed to be the primitive number. Usually in two or three rows, the front eyes are referred to as 'anterior', the rear ones as 'posterior'.

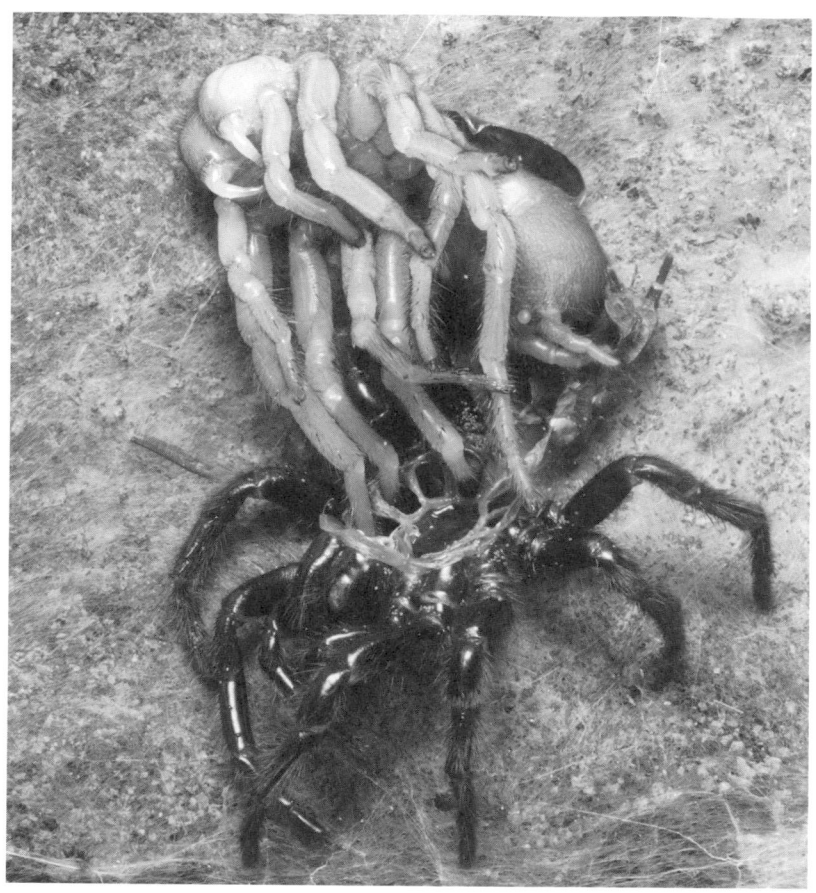

*A Sydney funnel-web (*Atrax robustus, *family Hexathelidae) moulting. Note the split carapace on its back, and the soft, white fangs. Without colour or a hardened exoskeleton, the spider is defenceless.* (Photo: Alan Henderson)

The wolf spiders (family Lycosidae) have two very large posterior median eyes. In front, is a row of four smaller eyes, referred to as the anterior row. In the posterior row, wolf spiders also have two posterior lateral eyes, giving them vision to the side.

Wolf spider eyes. A mother wolf spider (Lycosa godeffroyi) *peers from her burrow with one of her young.* (Photo: D. and L. Kelly)

Some spiders, the tarantulas for example, have their eyes raised above the surrounding cuticle. Some midget spiders even have them raised out on stalks. Not all spiders have eight eyes, some have only six. The median anterior pair appear to have disappeared in species such as some of the daddy long-legs and all of the spitting spiders. Some have only four eyes, some two. Some cave-dwelling spiders have lost their eyes completely. As we shall see in Chapter 5, the eye pattern is a key criterion for spider classification.

Erio, being a garden orb weaver, relied very little on sight and almost entirely on touch. She had small eyes, just visible in the middle of the front of her cephalothorax. The wolf spiders and jumping spiders, being hunters, rely much more on sight so their eyes are significantly larger. The wolf spiders seem to be able to detect movement visually, but only the jumping spiders appear to have eyesight good enough to enable them to identify other jumping spiders and their prey. Most other spiders only seem to be able to distinguish light from dark and hence day from night.

The chelicerae are the parts attached to the front of the cephalothorax, comprising a stout basal segment and the fangs. Some spiders have cheliceral teeth, projections from the chelicerae which are used in crushing and chewing prey.

The Melbourne trapdoor spider is a primitive spider more correctly known as a mygalomorph. The fangs are paraxial, that is, they work

*Paraxial fangs of a primitive spider (*Stanwellia sp.*), in this case a Melbourne trapdoor.* (Photo: Alan Henderson)

parallel to each other. The spider raises its cephalothorax above its prey before striking down with its fangs, pinning its victim to the ground. The spider then drags the prey back to its retreat. Most primitives have distinctly visible chelicerae.

The garden orb weaver and wolf spider, and most other spiders you will meet, are modern spiders, araneomorphs, so their fangs are directed inwards, or diaxial. The spider grasps the prey, much as you would do using kitchen tongs or pincers, to insert their venom. All spiders use digestive juices to reduce the soft parts of their prey to fluid. Some spiders use teeth on the inner rim of their chelicerae to chew the prey into a pulp to aid this process. Others simply suck out the now-liquid innards, leaving the empty shell for you to identify.

The spider's mouth is a simple opening covered by a plate called the labium. On either side of the mouth is a small flexible plate, the maxilla. The maxillae can move freely.

The opposing fangs of a modern spider, in this case, a wolf spider.
(Photo: Alan Henderson)

To ensure the spider takes in no solid particles, the maxillae have a thick border of hairs which acts as a filter. A smaller plate inside the mouth, the palate plate, acts as a finer secondary filter. Anything caught there is spat out by the spider and brushed away with the palps.

It's a very efficient filtering system. In experiments in which spiders were fed a suspension of black India ink in a neutral red solution, the gut content turned red but all the tiny ink particles were trapped and expelled.

The pre-digested food then passes from the mouth through the oesophagus, a tube which leads to the stomach. In spiders this is not a digestive organ, but acts as a sucking device, so it is called the sucking stomach. It is attached to the carapace by very strong muscles. When these contract, the stomach expands and 'sucks' up the liquids from the mouth. When the muscles expand, the juices are then forced from the sucking stomach to the foregut. The foregut is the section of the gut in the cephalothorax. Passing through the narrow waist, the pedicel, the gut then broadens into the midgut, from which the nutrients are absorbed into the body fluid. Nitrogenous wastes are removed by a kidney-like structure, the Malpighian tubules. The substances from these tubules, along with those from the waste from the gut, are stored in the cloaca to be released as blobs for you to find on windowsills beneath spiders' webs.

There are considerable differences in fang size between species. Orb weavers' fangs are quite small. Hunting spiders can have huge fangs. Wolf spiders and burrowing primitives also use their large, strong fangs to dig, often in very hard ground. They break down the soil piece by piece and carry it in their fangs to the surface.

The venom glands are usually located in the cephalothorax extending to the tip of the fang, although in some spiders, such as the tarantulas, they are contained entirely in the basal segment of the chelicerae. The cephalothorax also contains the brain, from which the main nerve cord passes through the narrow pedicel to the abdomen.

Most people know that spiders have eight legs. When I ask people to do a quick spider sketch, however, about 80 per cent will attach the legs to the abdomen. Yet in real spiders, all the legs are joined to the cephalothorax. The legs are usually drawn as short, fat, single curves whereas most spider legs are long, thin and elegant, their beauty in the combination of the seven straight segments. They also have a pair of reduced legs with only six segments attached to the maxillae—the pedipalps or, simply, palps.

The seven leg segments are the coxa, trochanter, femur, patella, tibia, metatarsus and tarsus. On the tip of the tarsus are two claws which extend the spider's foot and can be seen with the naked eye—if you look very closely. Some spiders have a third, middle claw. This claw is particularly important for web-builders who use the claw to grip the web as they move across it.

Beneath the tarsus, between the claws, are the all-important claw tufts, which can be best seen under a microscope. (See Plates 14 to 16.)

Most spiders use these tiny claws and tufts on their tarsi to crawl up walls and across ceilings. Rough surfaces don't present any problem but smooth or dirty surfaces are more hazardous. When spiders slip off a surface they will release a dropline of silk to break their fall. They can then climb up the line to their original location. Large heavy spiders, such as tarantulas, can die as the result of a fall.

Adam Summers and his colleagues from the University of

The three claws of a web-builder and the two claws with claw tufts of a free-ranging spider. (Diagram: L. Kelly)

California studied Costa Rican zebra tarantulas (*Aphonopelma seemanni*) as they climbed a glass wall. They were surprised to find that the tarantulas left a trail of fragments of very fine, sticky silk, each a few centimetres long. Summers and his team hypothesised that the spiders were laying down these short sticky strands to help climb the smooth wall.

Closer investigation revealed microscopic spigots, similar to those found in the spinnerets, in the tarantulas' feet. Although the tarantulas are mygalomorphs, or primitive spiders, Summers proposes that these foot spigots are a relatively recent adaptation, as they are not found on other primitive spiders.

Spiders have no ears, so they don't technically hear. The extremely sensitive hairs on their legs and bodies allow them to sense sound as vibrations of the air. Spiders have many different types of hair, which serve a wide range of purposes. Scaring humans is not one of them. The palps and front legs have olfactory hairs—their chemotactile receptors allow the spiders to 'smell' by touch. Jen Burge, a Texan tarantula owner, told me about the time she placed one of her tarantulas on the hands of a woman who had recently applied hand lotion. The spider squatted down on its abdomen and lifted all eight feet. It didn't like that lotion!

The spiders' legs are covered with two different types of sensory hairs. Sensilla are movable bristles which sense touch and vibrations. Trichobothria are upright hairs set in broad, deep sockets. Like a car's gearshift, the hair can move in every direction within that socket. These hairs detect the movement of prey, and the direction the movement is coming from. The membrane connecting the trichobothria to their socket is extremely flexible, which means that the slightest air vibration will start them moving and send the signals straight to the spider's brain. The strength and type of movement dictate the spider's response. A heavy human twang on a web will send the spider in the opposite direction, or on a dropline to the ground. Something of an edible size will be risking its life sending signals to the trichobothria.

The heart is a longitudinal tube running right along the upper surface of the abdominal cavity. The blood from the cavity passes back into the heart through a number of openings, to be pumped to the cephalothorax through the aorta to feed the head, legs, palps and other appendages. Flowing into the cavity of the cephalothorax, the blood then moves back onto the abdominal cavity to re-enter the heart. Spider blood is usually bluish, because of its copper-containing respiratory pigment rather than the iron-containing pigment in our haemoglobin. Unlike mammals, spiders don't really need a blood pigment which is highly efficient in storing and transporting oxygen as they are inactive a great deal of the time and consume very little oxygen when at rest.

Spiders can be very active, and a hunting or frightened spider can move extremely quickly. Two of the spider's leg joints (the femur–patella and the fibia–metatarsal joints) do not have muscles to extend the leg. Puzzled arachnologists eventually discovered that the extension is a hydraulic mechanism. The spider contracts its cephalothorax, increasing blood pressure to the legs. That is why dead spiders are curled up.

The spiders' open circulatory system is quite different to the mammalian system. They don't depend on an efficient oxygen feed through an endless mesh of vessels and veins—their blood fills the entire body cavity between the wall and the organs. The drawback of such a system is that any small puncture of the soft abdomen will cause a spider to bleed to death.

Spiders' lungs are also very different to those of warm-blooded creatures. To breathe in oxygen, they have book lungs, so-called because of their many fine leaves. However, book lungs have a large surface area through which water can evaporate, which means that spiders are very vulnerable to dehydration. All mygalomorphs, like the burrowing trapdoor spiders, have two pairs of book lungs, and stay well out of the sun.

The araneomorphs have only one pair of book lungs but have evolved tracheal tubes which take oxygen directly to the organs. The tubes lead to a spiracle, an opening in the underside of the abdomen just in front of the spinnerets. The system can be closed off, making the tracheal system far more effective when the weather is dry. Hence some araneomorphs can be far more active during the day.

Some extremely tiny spiders have done away with lungs altogether, relying entirely on the tracheal system to deliver oxygen to the blood. The dwarf orb weavers of the family Symphytognathidae are less than two millimetres in body size and are some of the smallest spiders known. Their body parts have evolved to the absolute minimum for survival but they still build perfect orb webs, with all the features of the glorious constructions of their (relatively) giant cousins. Able to fit on the head of a pin, they weave their tiny webs in the moist moss of the forest floor, creating a miniature version of the web-hung forest canopy.

Between the book lungs, on both male and female spiders, can be seen a fold. This is the epigastric furrow, which hides the sex organs. These organs, and the practices to which they are put, are so extraordinary that Chapter 8 has been devoted to that topic.

The spinnerets at the end of the abdomen are the external signs of the spider's unique silk-making machine.

SILK, ASTOUNDING SILK

Spiders aren't the only animals which produce silk. Caterpillars spin themselves cocoons, weaver ants stitch leaves together using silk from their larvae, held between their pincers as living shuttles and silkworms spin over a kilometre and a half of the stuff each. But spiders produce the strongest, most flexible and most variable forms of silk. Spider silk is the strongest, toughest fibre known.

A teaspoon of silk is enough to create a million webs. A strand of spider silk long enough to encircle the entire planet would weigh less than 500 grams. It is extremely flexible, capable of stretching to three times its length with ease. It is resistant to fungi and bacteria, so it doesn't rot.

All spiders produce silk from the group of modified limbs you can see at the base of their abdomens, called spinnerets. Watch a spider on a web and you will often be able to see the hind legs drawing out the amazing thread from the spinnerets. Many species, including the orb weavers, produce seven different kinds of silk.

Extremely strong is dragline silk—the life-saving thread which allows a spider to drop suddenly to the ground when danger threatens. Baby spiders, and some adults, balloon off into the atmosphere on threads of gossamer—the same silk as used for draglines. It is also used for the radial lines on an orb web which require the extra strength to support the entire structure and the battering it will take as insects fly into the web. Dragline silk has been measured at five times the breaking strength of steel of the same density. Tests are done on very sensitive machines which record just how much weight a given thickness of silk can take before breaking. Density is calculated as the mass in a given volume. Given the extreme lightness of silk, even extraordinarily thin thread can support a great deal of weight for its thickness.

The orb weaver uses dragline silk, which is known technically as major ampullate silk, for the radials of the web. Temporary scaffold silk forms the outward spiral (minor ampullate) and is replaced with extremely stretchy and sticky capture silk (flagelliform or coronate), which can be stretched to more than three times its length before snapping. As the capture silk is laid down, the orb weavers cover it with a gluey substance from the aggregate glands. You can watch an orb weaver twang each strand of her sticky web to produce globules of glue right along the thread, each filled with a coil of silk which can expand rapidly. This combination of strong, flexible and sticky silk is what makes the orb web such a formidable insect trap, able to absorb the momentum of a flying insect while retaining it in the web.

The rapidly produced shroud of silk with which the spider binds the struggling insect (aciniform) is now considered to be the strongest of all when considering both flexibility and breaking stress. Kevlar is the material currently used to make bullet-proof vests. Dragline and swathing silk are far tougher. Researchers are working hard to try to imitate the spiders.

The male spider uses aciniform silk to construct his all-important sperm web, as will be discussed in Chapter 8. The female uses aciniform silk for the outer wall of the egg sac, and will also produce a different kind of silk to construct her egg sac (tubuliform). Piriform silk comes from different silk glands again, and is used to attach webs and draglines to their anchor points.

Dragline silk is in the order of a micrometre in thickness, a millionth of a metre. The filaments used to create the catching silk of a hackle band web is a hundredth as thin as dragline silk. That is the woolly web which the many species of funnel weavers produce around your home. Cribellate silk is produced from an additional spinning organ, the cribellum, a small plate located in front of the spinnerets. The extremely fine thread is combed out of the cribellum by the rhythmic movement of a row of comb-shaped hairs on the metatarsi of the hindmost legs. This action can be easily seen when one of the hackle-web spiders is adding to its woolly web. Each thread of silk you see will be made up of many fine threads criss-crossed over a pair of straight axial lines.

Birds have long recognised that spiders not only taste great, but they produce a superb building material. Many bird nests are bound and lined with spider web, with some nests comprising up to 80 per cent of this flexible, soft, weatherproof wonder.

Most spiders don't build webs. They hunt from burrows or are wanderers. Yet they still use silk for their draglines and to capture prey, as well as to line their retreats and egg sacs. All spiders have silk glands, which take up a great deal of their abdomen. The silk emerges from thousands of tiny tubes in the spinnerets, known as spigots.

The silk glands produce a variety of proteins which form the layers of the silk. The highly viscous liquid silk flows through a long duct which gets progressively narrower as it approaches the spinnerets. The cells of this duct extract water through the lining. The resulting fluid is then subjected to a mild acidic bath in the duct before the stress being applied by the spider's pulling action converts the liquid protein into a solid silk fibre. Just before emerging from the duct, a thin, fatty coating is added to the silk thread. This solid silk fibre is dry.

Spiders produce a solid fibre from a liquid at body temperature without any of the noxious chemicals we use to make artificial fibres. If we could replicate spider silk, we could create light, flexible but very strong fibres for clothing. We could make ropes of incredible strength which are light to carry. At only a tenth the width of a human hair, this incredibly fine, strong thread was once used for firing sights on guns and telescopes. As the thread is chemically inert and does not dissolve in water, it would be perfect for artificial tendons and ligaments. The potential applications are endless, if only we could do what a millions of tiny creatures do all day, every day. We can't.

Scientists have been trying for years to replicate spider silk, but have not yet found a way to reproduce the very long protein chains produced naturally by the spiders. A Canadian company, Nexia Biotechnologies, is trying a new approach. By genetically engineering goats to produce spider silk protein in their milk, scientists hope to synthesise spider silk, an achievement Nexia president Jeffrey Turner claims is 'the Holy Grail of material science'.

Silk can be generated in the web-making which is so familiar, but it can also be sprayed in a rapid mesh, as I was to witness in awe. As I watched, a fly sprang into Erio-three's web. I say 'sprang' because nothing demonstrates the incredible flexibility of silk more than seeing an insect hurtle into it and then bounce back to the equilibrium position of the web. Erio-three moved very fast, but I was able to photograph the swathing band silk she spewed from her spinnerets as she rapidly, yet ever so elegantly, spun the poor creature with her legs and palps. (See Plate 8.)

When the insect was subdued by silk, Erio-three sunk her fangs into the now firmly bound body and retreated with it to the hub of her web, where she fed for hours.

Sometimes there is too much food. Erio-four's web was only twenty metres away. One morning there was a large bound prey still in her web, while Erio-four was back in her camouflaged rest position under the eaves of the house. It was nearing the end of the summer and her web had not been taken down as it usually was.

Suddenly, an insect leg emerged from the bindings. Then a second. This prey wasn't dead, just shrouded in strong silk. Soon a large, introduced European wasp landed on the bundle and started spinning it furiously. I assumed the European wasp was stealing from Erio-four's larder, but as the victim emerged, I could see that it, too, was a European

Erio-four's prey and rescuer in a wild swirl, just before they flew away together. (Photo: D. and L. Kelly)

wasp. Once free of its binding, the erstwhile meal flew away. Had I really witnessed a wasp rescuing one of its own species?

Not all orb weavers weave the circular webs which come to mind so easily. The Australian leaf-curling spider (*Phonognatha graeffei*, family Tetragnathidae) weaves a part-orb web and then draws up a leaf to create its retreat. Spiders have been seen dragging leaves up to four times their own weight from the ground to the centre of their web. The leaf is then stitched into place, the tension in the silk curling the leaf into a cylindrical retreat as it dries out. Research with leaf-curling spiders at the University of Melbourne by Professor Mark Elgar and his team, has shown they select their leaves very carefully. Drier leaves are harder to curl, breaking easily as the spider tries to bend them. The researchers commented that the decision-making process appears to be ongoing—some spiders decided to remove a dry leaf and replace it with a moister, greener leaf. When a tad on the lazy side, or fortunate enough to have the opportunity, a leaf-curling spider may choose to haul an empty snail shell into the web instead.

Argiope is a genus of spiders found all over the world, hanging elegantly in the centre of their huge permanent orb webs. Black, gold and white stripes often decorate their abdomens and in the United States they are known as black-and-gold garden spiders. In Europe they are wasp spiders, Japan *ogane-gumo*, while in Australia they are St Andrew's Cross spiders. In some parts of the United States they are known as writing spiders, because of the bands of white silk—stabilimenta—with which they embroider their webs. There has been much discussion about the purpose of these adornments—are they to strengthen the web, deter or confuse predators, deter birds who may otherwise damage a web by flying into it, or to provide a cooler shelter in high temperatures? They may serve all these purposes, but the most favoured explanation is that, as it is highlighted under ultraviolet light, the stabilimenta serves to attract insects. Many insects see ultraviolet

A *St Andrew's Cross* (Argiope sp.)
with stabilimenta. See also Plate 13.
(Photo: Alan Henderson)

reflections which we don't, and may see the web as either a flower which offers them pollen, or a gap in vegetation which elicits flight behaviour.

The golden orb weavers (*Nephila spp.*, family Nephilidae) also produce permanent webs which, as their name suggests, shimmer gold. *Nephila* adds to and repairs her web constantly, so it is always fresh and sticky. The circular orb section alone can be as large as a metre across, with the attachments reaching far further. Many of these webs contain smaller spiders which are often mistaken for the males or young of the huge, elegant female resting head-down in the middle. They are in fact kleptoparasites—who steal their giant hostess' food. These small, humped spiders of the genus *Argyrodes* belong to a completely different family, the Theridiidae, although most theridiids build their own webs. With over 2000 species, the Theridiidae can be found around houses everywhere in the world.

TANGLE-WEB, COBWEB, SPACE-WEB—THE VARIETY IS ENDLESS

With their long, spindly legs and pea-shaped abdomens dwarfing their tiny cephalothoraxes, the family Theridiidae can be found on their messy webs in almost every home.

*The common house spider
(*Achaearanea sp.*), like
most theridiids, will tackle
prey much bigger than itself.*
(Photo: D. and L. Kelly)

The common or American house spiders (*Achaearanea spp.*) have travelled around the world. I can count dozens on the house, inside and out, yet I have never seen one wandering. Countless egg sacs hang on countless webs, producing an abundance of young. The spiderlings hang around on their mother's web for weeks.

The vast majority of theridiids are harmless although a few are deadly. The widow spiders, including America's black widow and Australia's red-back, will be discussed in Chapter 9.

The theridiids build amazing webs. There is a variety of web types, but like the orb weavers, most involve some form of sticky thread. The upper part of the web is usually a non-sticky space-web, which is probably as random as it looks.

Many of the theridiids make tangle-webs with 'gum-footed' trip lines. These lines run from the web to the floor or wall below, while the spider waits, hanging upside-down, above. Very elastic, these threads contain globules of glue. Any insect which strolls into the thread is caught by the glue. Their struggles break the thread, which catapults the insect upwards and into more sticky threads. The spider races down, bites its prey and carries it back to the retreat. The gum-foot lines of some widow spiders are strong enough to trap small lizards and mice, the dried remains of which can be seen hanging beneath the web. Some arachnologists now think that the widow spiders feed on these small reptiles and mammals as well as their accustomed invertebral prey.

Some theridiids make more sheet-like webs without gum-foot lines, some do not use sticky silk at all, but most theridiids use their webs for extended periods, constantly expanding and repairing them.

It used to be thought that fang direction divided spider families neatly up into primitives and moderns, and moderns then divided neatly into cribellate and ecribellate (non-cribellate) spinners. It is now believed that all modern spiders were once cribellate, and many still are, but the cribellum has been lost in those such as the wolf spiders, huntsmen, jumping spiders and most of the orb weavers. However, cribellate species can be found in almost all spider families.

Trying to fully organise the spiders by their web construction seems to fail—they are just too varied and complex. The family Uloboridae, for example, is extremely common and builds small orb webs. These webs are usually either horizontal or at an angle, unlike the vertical webs of most orb weavers. Uloborids are the only spider family which produces no venom at all, and they build their orb webs with cribellate silk!

WEIRD AND WONDERFUL WEAVERS OF SILK

The sheet-web-builders of the family Linyphiidae have over 4000 species described. Some linyphiids are referred to as 'money spiders' in the belief that one of these tiny spiders landing on you will bring financial gain. The young of many spiders balloon, but tiny members of the family Linyphiidae continue to balloon as adults. When many millions of these tiny spiders release silk from their spinnerets to catch the wind and disperse, they can form a cloud of gossamer. The next morning, a field covered in dew-covered gossamer is one of the world's most spectacular natural wonders. They may be present in their millions one day and be gone the next, blown wherever the warm wind takes them. Linyphiids are found in nearly every environment in the world, including walking on, or under, snow at temperatures well below freezing.

While many spider species use their silk to balloon, only one uses it to create an underwater home. The water or diving-bell spider (*Argyroneta aquatica*, family Cybaeidae) is the only spider species to live totally under water for its entire life, even though they breathe air in the same way as other spiders and could survive on land. (See Plate 18.)

This extraordinary spider constructs a silken diving bell which it attaches to an underwater plant. It then uses the dense hairs on its body as an air trap and transports the air down to its diving bell. The spider will remain in its bell awaiting small aquatic invertebrates to eat while trying to avoid being eaten by frogs and fish.

The male water spider is unusual in being larger than the female. He builds his diving bell next to that of the female and then creates a tunnel between the two. Found in ponds in Europe, northern Asia and northern Africa, the spider usually appears silver due to the trapped air around its body.

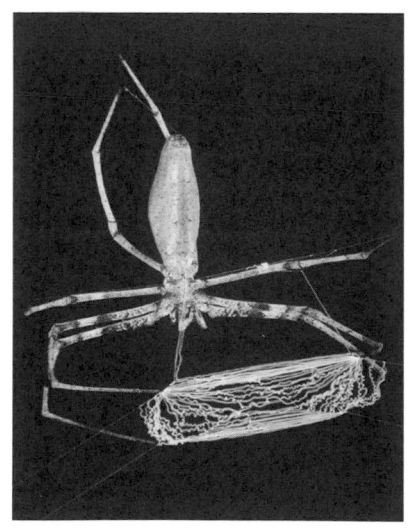

The incredible net-casting spiders (family Deinopidae) are found over much of the world, and often live close to human habitation. The genus *Deinopis* is also known as the ogre-faced

*The net-casting spider (*Deinopis subrufa*) waiting for passing prey.*
(Photo: Oceanwide Images)

spider because of its fantastic face, dominated by enormous posterior median eyes. These eyes are particularly adapted to the low lights in which *Deinopis* hunts.

Deinopis has an elongated body, about two centimetres long, with extremely long, slender front legs that manipulate a web in a way which can only be described as extraordinary. The spider first constructs a scaffold web which is attached to the vegetation over an area where prey will pass. It then positions itself on the web with its head up, combing out cribellate silk into a rectangular capture net. This woolly net can stretch to many times its basic size to entangle a prey.

With the net woven, the spider turns head down, holding the net by its four corners with its four front legs, and waits. Seeing a prey move past, or detecting the vibrations of a flying insect, *Deinopis* propels itself forward, stretches the net and ensnares the prey. The prey is then wrapped in the strong swathing silk and secured. Each evening a new capture net is created. Each morning it is rolled up and eaten.

The bolas spiders (family Araneidae) took the reduction of the orb one step further. They did away with it. They hunt by using a blob of glue silk on the end of a silk line, much like the rope-and-balls weapon used by the South American gauchos to capture animals by entangling their legs. Did the gauchos get the idea from watching spiders? With over 60 species in three different genera, bolas spiders are found in Africa, Asia, Australia and the Americas. In each case, the spiders lure their prey, adult male moths of a local species, by mimicking the female moth sex pheromones.

Hanging from a single silk line, the spider starts spinning the bolas as a moth approaches. When he is in range, she throws the line or swings it like a lasso. The hapless moth sticks to the bolas line and is hauled in to the waiting fangs.

But what do baby bolas spiders do? Big moths would knock the tiny spiders flying if they tried to lasso them, and baby moths are caterpillars.

They don't fly. Research on the bolas spider *Mastophora phrynosoma* showed that the tiny males and juvenile females attract flies in the genus *Psychoda* which look like moths and are known as moth flies, which they capture without using a bolas or a web. Instead, they balance on the edge of a leaf and use their front two pairs of legs to grab approaching prey. Like the adult spiders, they use the female pheromone, but of the fly, to attact their prey. The tiny males will hunt in this fashion all their lives. As the female bolas spiders become older and larger they graduate to hunting moths.

Then there's the spider who makes herself part of the web. *Hyptiotes* (family Uloboridae) builds a triangular web which is a triangular segment of an orb web. The best description of this extraordinary web-builder comes from W.S. Bristowe's inspirational *The World of Spiders*:

The spider sits inconspicuously, with her body touching a twig and with her front legs outstretched, holding a thread attached to the apex of the triangle. The first surprise is to discover that there is not a single thread stretching from the web to the twig. The spider herself forms a bridge between one thread, passing from the twig to her spinnerets, and another from the web which she is holding taut. This latter thread she has hauled so tight that there is usually a loop of slack which is held by the third pair of legs. In other words she is suspended in mid-air between two unconnected threads.

Complete stillness is maintained in this strained position until an insect touches the snare. The trap—for so it may be termed—is sprung once, twice and perhaps three times by the spider, whilst she simultaneously releases the coil of slack held by the third pair of legs, lets out more silk from her spinnerets and gathers up the trap line with her front legs. Each time the trap is sprung, she is projected forwards, closer to the snare and on reaching the insect, now firmly enswathed in the fold of the slacked spirals, she further envelops it in silk drawn from her spinnerets by her hind legs.

Cutting the bundle free and carrying it in her palps, she travels back towards the twig and pauses before reaching it to wrap the insect still more securely. With front legs stretched out at right angles along the single thread, and with abdomen hanging vertically downwards, she revolves the insect with her third pair of legs while the fourth pair draws silk from her spinnerets.

The watcher is amazed at the variety of different tasks allotted simultaneously to her different pairs of legs whilst she is poised precariously in the gap between the threads which link her base to the snare.

Hyptiotes is less than a centimetre long. Professional research has recorded very little spider behaviour. The arachnologists are too busy trying to classify the thousands of species. The sort of detailed observation necessary to discover an extraordinary animal such as little *Hyptiotes* is often left to the amateurs. If you take some time in your own backyard to get to know your own spiders there is every chance you will be the first in the world to witness something extraordinary such as *Hyptiotes* building herself into her own web.

While we are busy watching our spiders, the arachnologists are trying to untangle the taxonomy of what could be as many as a quarter of a million spider species around the world.

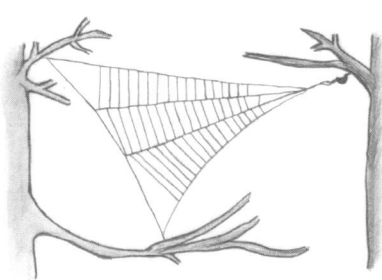

Hyptiotes *is a small spider who uses her own body as part of the web.* (Diagram: L. Kelly)

5

CLASSIFICATION CHALLENGES

What I do for a living is stare at genitalia.

Dr Mark Harvey

Dr Mark Harvey is a rare breed—an arachnid taxonomist. On row upon row of shelves, in row upon row of glass tombs, dead spiders wait for his microscope to be focused on their genitals. Their tiny reproductive organs are one of the key factors in determining their species.

The discovery of a new species of bird makes front-page news. A new species of spider is discovered every day. Phoebe Snetsinger's book, *Birding on Borrowed Time*, chronicles her lifelong quest to be the first person to twitch more than 8000 of the world's 9799 described birds. She had excellent field guides showing every bird from many angles to assist her.

No-one has ever attempted to twitch spiders in the wild. The number of described species has just passed 40 000 at the time of writing and Harvey says we may have classified between 10 and 20 per cent of them.

Dr Mark Harvey among his vials of dead spiders. (Photo: D. and L. Kelly)

At a rough guess, he estimates a world population of 250 000 species.

Dr Mark Harvey is Senior Curator in the Department of Terrestrial Invertebrates at the Museum of Western Australia. Buried in a world of spiders, water mites and pseudoscorpions, he works on the taxonomy and biogeography of eight-legged animals in this vast land. So well respected is he in the field that many creatures now have the species name *harveyi* in his honour, but not one has he named after himself.

Although trying to protect any threatened species is difficult, you will get some semblance of sympathy if you're talking about a bird or a mammal. It's much harder for spiders. Only twenty years ago, the first listing of an invertebrate was proposed in Western Australia. It was a cave cockroach.

'I'm not going to have any bloody cockroach on the Western Australian threatened species list!' was the response from the state's Minister for the Environment. Now there are well over 100 invertebrates on that list. As Harvey admits, 'None of them is charismatic. Most of these are cave spiders which are highly restricted in range, some to a single cave system.' He explained that cave spiders represent a bygone age, mostly relics from a much wetter time. Up until the Miocene, Australia had lots of temperate rainforest. Then it started drying out. Some spiders, instead of dying on the surface, found spaces in the soil and caves, surviving down there over millions of years. Some have no eyes left at all. They live in 100 per cent humidity and 100 per cent darkness.

This conversation was taking place in a staff room dominated by an enormous photograph of a cave spider (*Bengalla bertmaini*, family Ctenidae). With no pigment and no eyes, this surprisingly gorgeous spider could be seen through the window to the reception area. However, some reception staff had complained that the image was too disturbing so the window was kept covered.

Harvey told me about the warm summer evening when he could feel a small creature in his ear after brushing past a jasmine vine. When flushing the ear with water didn't stop the creature moving, he went to the local hospital to have it removed. He was delighted to be presented with the remains to identify. It was a *Euryopis* or close relative—small spiders which feed on ants and can often be seen hanging from a single thread with an ant in their clutches. Only a taxonomist would be so intrigued by such aural detritus.

The fear of spiders entering bodily orifices is high, but the danger of such a thing happening is very low. There is simply nothing to attract a spider into an ear, or even less so into the dampness of a mouth. It is often quoted that on average, people eat eight spiders a year. This myth originated in 1993 when journalist Lisa Holst created a list of 'ridiculous facts' for *PC Professional* in an article about the absurd things people will believe if they appear on a computer. Ironically, Holst's absurdity is now widely quoted as fact.

Taxonomists, such as Harvey, deal with the evidence they see beneath their microscopes. Taxonomists take the specific characteristics of a living thing and place it in ever more specialised groups. For spiders, the kingdom is Animalia, the animals. The phylum is Arthropoda, invertebrates with segmented bodies and exoskeletons. The class, Arachnida, are the arthropods with six pairs of appendages. Yes, six—four pairs of legs and one pair of reduced legs, the pedipalps. The arachnids are scorpions, whip scorpions, mites, ticks and harvestmen, as well as the spiders. After class comes the order, Araneae, which is just the spiders, which then divides up into suborder, family, genus and species, as shown in the classification tree overleaf.

The difficulty with spiders is that there are just so many of them. A birder might have a grasp of all the 9800 or so birds in the world, but to be able to recognise 40 000 different spiders, many of which are small, brown and free-ranging, is impossible. An amateur is doing well to get the spider into the right family. Hence it is almost impossible to know if the spider you have found is a new species because you first have to eliminate all the known species. Spider appearances can be deceptive. Most people struggle to tell a daddy long-legs spider from a harvestman and they aren't even in the same order! The fact that young spiders are numerous and much smaller, while the male may look nothing like the female, can lead to despair.

Spiders are in the order Araneae which, in turn, is divided into three suborders, Mesothelae, Myglomorphae and Araneomorphae.

The suborder Mesothelae includes 87 species which are today restricted to South-East Asia, Indonesia and Japan. These rare spiders are identified by their primitive characteristics, such as an externally segmented abdomen. They usually have eight spinnerets, although some have been found with seven. Unlike other spiders, these are located not at the end of the abdomen but near the middle of the ventral surface.

All other spiders have evolved to have no more than six, sometimes only two, spinnerets at the posterior end of the abdomen. These spiders are divided into the suborders Mygalomorphae and Araneomorphae.

The mygalomorphs—tarantulas, funnel-web tarantulas, mouse spiders and the many species of trapdoors—are often referred to as the primitives. They are stocky, burrowing spiders that live a more primitive lifestyle than the web-builders and hunters of the modern araneomorphs. With two pairs of book lungs and fangs which strike

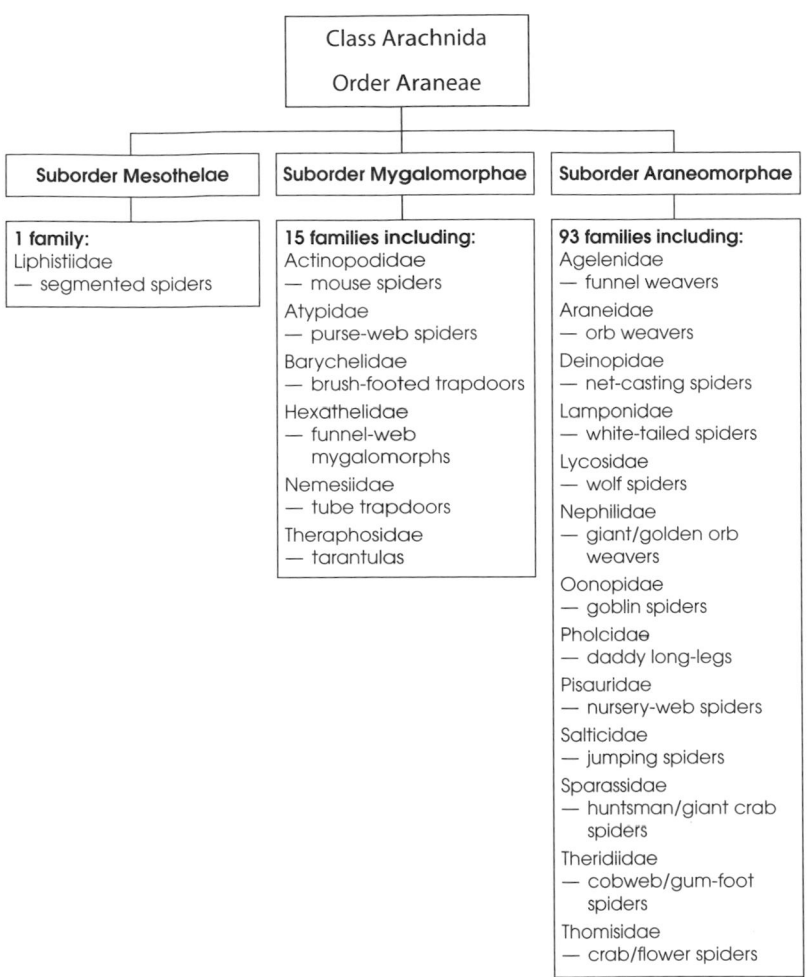

A simplified classification tree for spiders. (Diagram: L. Kelly)

downward, the mygalomorphs' resemblance to the truly primitive segmented spiders of the family Liphistiidae originally led arachnologists to believe they were the ancestors of the araneomorphs. It is now known that the segmented Liphistiidae are the ancestors of both groups.

The vertical (paraxial) fangs of a rearing mygalomorph or 'primitive' spider. (Photo: Alan Henderson)

For simplicity I will use the common terms 'primitive' and 'modern'. As we saw in Chapter 4, the moderns have evolved tracheal tubes, which means they are less vulnerable to dehydration than the primitives and therefore more active. Unlike the primitives, the moderns' fangs

The horizontal (diaxial) fangs of an araneomorph or 'modern' spider. (Photo: Alan Henderson)

Typical eye patterns for some spider families. (Diagram: L. Kelly)

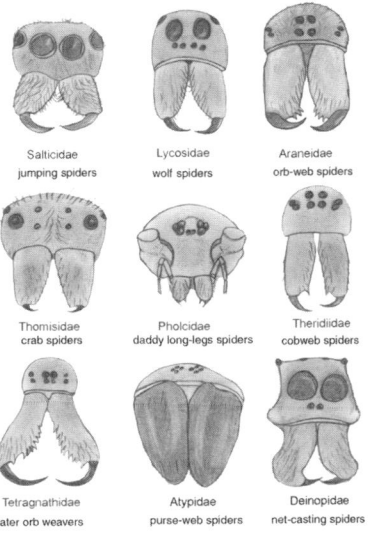

Salticidae
jumping spiders

Lycosidae
wolf spiders

Araneidae
orb-web spiders

Thomisidae
crab spiders

Pholcidae
daddy long-legs spiders

Theridiidae
cobweb spiders

Tetragnathidae
water orb weavers

Atypidae
purse-web spiders

Deinopidae
net-casting spiders

are horizontally aligned, or diaxial, and act in much the same way as pincers or tongs.

The next level of classification is that of 'family', and a spider's eye pattern is a useful indication of its family. To be sure of the genus and species, you need to look at the genitals!

Spiders do not have a strong fossil record. Their soft and fragile bodies are much more vulnerable to scavengers and weather conditions than the bones of the vertebrates. The spiders fossils that do exist are mostly in amber.

The world's biggest spider may be a trapdoor spider called *Megarachne servinei*, which dates from the Upper Carboniferous period, or 320 million years ago. Found in Argentina, *Megarachne* had a leg span of about 50 centimetres. That's half a metre. That's huge.

Some researchers now claim that *Megarachne* is a bizarre eurypterid, that is, a 'sea-scorpion', but whatever the outcome of the debate it is an enormous arachnid.

Spiders are the only arachnids to produce silk from abdominal glands that open through modified bristle-like hairs called spigots, located on the spinnerets. In fact, that is the identifying characteristic of a spider. Fossil evidence of spinnerets from the Devonian period (415 to 360 million years ago) has been found, which means that spiders were some of the first species to walk the earth.

What these Devonian spiders did with their silk is unclear. Aerial webs, made to trap flying insects, do not appear in the fossil record until the Carboniferous period, but they may have existed earlier. The Devonian spider was possibly like the living primitives, using its silk to line a burrow, weave egg sacs or make trip lines. Perhaps like the primitives it waited at the end of a burrow or tube for prey to wander past.

The primitives evolved from their Devonian ancestors with a gradual reduction in the number of body structures. Among other body structures lost, is at least one pair of spinnerets. These, in turn, have lost most of their segmentation. The fact that the remaining jointed spinneret segments have been shown to move in synch with spiders' legs leads some researchers to believe that the abdominal spinnerets may once have functioned like legs.

The primitives retained two pairs of book lungs, unlike the moderns. In most moderns, the second pair of book lungs became breathing tubes called tracheae. The moderns also took to the trees and made webs.

Dr David Penney of the University of Manchester has described a spider that was trapped and preserved in amber twenty million years ago. The four-centimetre long fossil was discovered during a visit to a museum in the Dominican Republic and is a new species of crevice weaver, family Filistatidae, commonly found in South America and the Caribbean.

A single piece of amber with a single spider in it has allowed Dr Penney to postulate a specific event which happened twenty million years ago. It appears that the spider was climbing up a tree when it was hit by fast-flowing resin. Droplets of the spider's blood reveal which direction it was travelling in, that it was hit on the head, and which of its legs broke first.

At the time of writing, just over 40 000 living spider species have been described, and the number is growing steadily. The authoritative (and regularly updated) list of spider species is given in *The World Spider Catalog* at <http://research.amnh.org/entomology/spiders/catalog/>. Version 9.0 was released on 23 June 2008. In the six months since the previous version, every one of the 108 families had some taxonomic adjustment, and a new family was added. That indicates the state of flux which enmeshes the taxonomy of spiders. Appendix 1 lists spider families, genera and species along with common names.

The spider world's cataloguer is Dr Norman Platnick, Peter J. Solomon Family Curator of the Division of Invertebrate Zoology at the American Museum of Natural History. A fierce exponent of modern cladistics, the sorting of organisms according to the evolutionary features they share from the common ancestors, Platnick is one of the world's most respected taxonomists. His primary methodology is to identify spider characteristics that will always lead to the same exact group of organisms. Platnick explains this in an interview he gave to the *New York Daily News*:

There are about 1.75 million species on this planet. Select from these all the organisms with abdominal spinnerets to produce silk—about 38 000 species. Repeat this process and select all organisms with modified male pedipalps for copulation. You end up with

Dr Norman Platnick
(Photo: D. and L. Kelly)

the same 38 000. This congruence of characteristics unites spiders uniquely from all others,' he said. Apply the concept with higher degrees of specificity, and species' characteristics emerge.

'You start with the null hypothesis that they are all the same. It doesn't take long to see that they are not,' he said. 'Then you divide them into groups of specimens more closely related to each other.'

As he explained the process, Dr Platnick dug out a paper describing a new species he had identified in Australia. 'The differences here are the male sex organs, or their pedipalps,' he explained. Carefully drawn in profile, one pedipalp had subtly different arrangements of sub-millimeter-sized bulbous growths.

These miniscule differences have put Dr Platnick and his museum at the centre of research on spiders, termed arachnology. With the museum already housing tens of thousands of arachnids in by far the largest collection of spiders in the world, Dr Platnick seeks to add to the number by cataloguing the world's biodiversity of spiders, one at a time . . .

Platnick has spent 40 years staring down microscopes at spiders, but has not lost his enthusiasm for classifying spiders:

What keeps it interesting is that so little is known. The last big project I did took several years. I was looking at a group of ground spiders in Australia, and by the end of the project it turned out that 90% of the spiders we were working with were new. I'm part of a project now with 32 people in 10 countries. It's an attempt to do a global inventory of a very poorly known family: goblin spiders. We expect that at least 80% of the species has not been described yet. Every morning I come in, and I'm looking at something that no one has ever seen before.

I met one of those 32 goblin spider professionals at the Queensland Museum.

Dr Barbara Baehr started the new millennium by moving halfway around the world—for spiders. As there are only about 800 spider species in Middle Europe, Baehr knew she would be unlikely to describe a single new species studying European arachnids. Australian arachnologists had already described over 2000 species, a number which was expected to grow tenfold. Accordingly, Baehr made the incredibly difficult decision to leave her son with her husband in Germany, and bring her daughters to Australia.

In the last few years Baehr has named and described nearly 400 Australian spiders and no doubt will name many more.

Many spiders from the southern continents do not fit readily into the families established to suit the better known European species. It is estimated that 99 per cent of European species have been classified but the rest of the world is still struggling to classify all their species. Working from their old type specimens, early arachnologists tried desperately to fit new spider species into the known families but as they found out more about the spiders of Australia, New Zealand and the Asia–Pacific region, they realised there was a need to add a significant percentage of new families. As more evidence of the evolutionary relationships between families comes to light, mass revisions are undertaken.

Arachnologists describe the current state of spider taxonomy in Australia as 'a mess' and yet it is far better than it was just a decade ago. European arachnologists have snap-frozen pholcids

Dr Barbara Baehr in her office at the Queensland Museum. (Photo: D. and L. Kelly)

(daddy long-legs) in every stage of copulation in order to study them in detail. The range of Australian spiders is so vast that almost no behavioural work has been done—yet.

'What arachnologist wouldn't want to be here?' Baehr asked me.

It wasn't only the thousands of unidentified species that appealed to Baehr, but the range of genera and families which provided an untapped evolutionary record unparalleled in the Northern Hemisphere where regular ice ages and ecological events rendered the population into a more fractured representation of the entire range.

When I arrived for my interview with Baehr, she was absorbed in the images at the base of her microscope. She leant back and let me see what she was looking at. Through the eyepiece, I saw a sight which was both repelling and intriguing. A male goblin spider in parts. Each body section was carefully laid out in its own amber box, horribly inert, yet revealing the detail of a single spider's anatomy. (See Plate 17.)

This is how spiders are described—every physical detail is photographed under the microscope and then minutely documented. It's a fiddly, time-consuming process, but one Baehr has already completed more than 400 times.

Baehr also draws these gorgeous creatures.

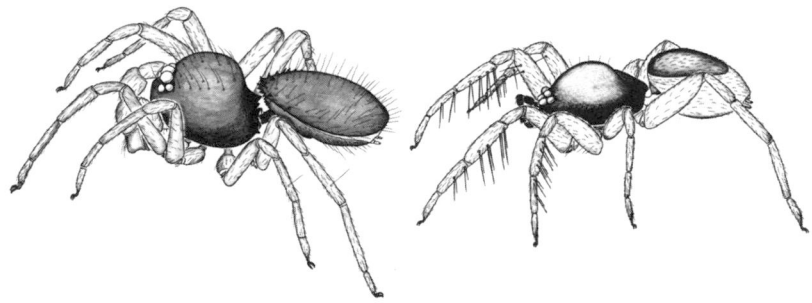

A goblin spider drawing by Dr Barbara Baehr.

Only a handful of professional arachnologists are based in Australia, so visits by overseas experts are welcomed. Baehr talked with great pleasure of the visit by a team led by Dr Platnick. While he was here, he completely rebuilt the taxonomy for the white-tailed spiders, family Lamponidae, from a family with 24 species to one with 186. There are now 191. Platnick also examined and reorganised the family Gnaphosidae, the ground spiders. It's a large family—over two thousand species, each with millions upon millions of individuals—one of which had been confusing me for quite a while. I called her Twiggy.

TWIGGY

Meeting Twiggy was no accident but the result of two fascinating years of learning about spiders. She taught me just how exciting observing can get when you begin to know what you are looking for. Twiggy's story isn't so much about a spider you might see, but the fact that you may well be watching behaviour no-one has ever recorded before. For much of the world, spider behaviour is still a fairly blank canvas—what is known has often been the original research of enthusiastic amateurs. Thanks to Twiggy, I have joined their ranks. I hope that by now, you are beginning to feel that you might too.

We have large huntsmen spiders a-plenty. Also known as giant crab spiders and rain spiders, members of the family Sparassidae come into homes around the world. Every now and then, however, I would see one which just didn't look quite right. The 'weird' huntsmen were extraordinarily flat, as if they had been squashed by the item I had just lifted to reveal their presence. After permitting me but a moment to look at it, the compressed creature would be gone. A flash of dark spider was all I saw as it disappeared into a sliver of space. For two years they played this game.

One day, I saw one dash under the toaster in the kitchen. I barri-caded the area. Armed with a camera-bearing husband, I very gently lifted the toaster. There was no escape. He was in the frame at last. Staring at the photograph I could finally see what my brain had been registering as 'not quite right' when I thought they were huntsmen. The third pair of legs on huntsmen are much shorter than the two front pairs. This was not the case with Flat Guy.

I sent the photograph in an email to Alan Henderson at the Melbourne Museum, who I had been pestering about my weirdo huntsmen. I checked my email hourly in anticipation of his response. He replied to gloat that his guess about my previously vague descrip-tions had been correct. Engorged palps confirmed that Flat Guy was indeed a male, of a *Hemicloea* species, probably *Hemicloea major*.

I read all I could find about *Hemicloea*, which was very little, but I did find out that females weave round, flat white egg sacs about two

Flat Guy after the toaster was lifted. (Photo: D. and L. Kelly)

centimetres across, often two or three at a time. I recognised these immediately as the dry white discs I had noticed on a piece of wood I'd turned over. I started searching, torch in hand, to be rewarded with a glimpse of the edge of just such an egg sac in a sawn-off trunk near the Garret, the shed where I write. Peering between the bark and trunk into the narrow black gap, I was greeted by a large, dark spider who moved rapidly over her egg sac and raised her thin cephalothorax aggressively, looking as threatening as she could. She was gorgeous. I had met Twiggy.

Most of the time Twiggy would be way down in her crevice, behind her egg sac. How long would she sit with her egg sac? It was a drought year and I had read that spiders need to balance their moisture intake. Was she sitting on dried-out egg sacs? Would she sit there until she starved? It was time to hit the spider books, the internet and the academic journals.

I found a few articles on classification and one small article on releasing some laboratory-bred young into the wild and noting their choice

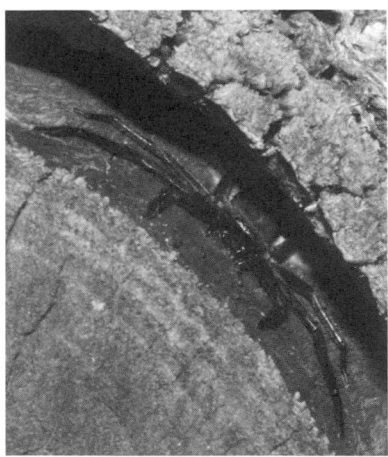

Twiggy being aggressive.
(Photo: D. and L. Kelly)

Twiggy on her egg sacs.
(Photo: D. and L. Kelly)

of home. Calling Twiggy a 'flat rock spider', only one book referred briefly to Twiggy's species while a few websites had photographs showing the extraordinary flatness. These are large, distinctive spiders, yet I could glean only fragments of information about them. Was I perhaps observing something which had not been recorded before?

Professor Mark Elgar at the University of Melbourne is one of the few zoologists in Australia working on arachnid behaviour. He confirmed the lack of research on this large, common spider. I also discovered the website of Dr Ron Atkinson, who mentioned *Hemicloea's* aggressive behaviour when defending her egg sacs. I wrote to him, asking for any information on the behaviour of Twiggy and her like. He replied:

> My experience with adult female *Hemicloea* spiders is that they tend to defend their egg sacs and newly-hatched spiderlings quite aggressively although they show minimal aggression towards humans at any other time. It would not surprise me to find them still occupying the same retreat even after the eggs have hatched and the spiderlings have dispersed but they should now prefer to run away rather than try to defend themselves. Most of their foraging for insects will be done at night for safety reasons so by day they will usually remain in their retreats. Being under bark they are better protected from the adverse effects of a cold winter and so can survive without feeding for months until the next spring brings a new batch of insects to feed on.

Hemicloea were quoted as being in the family Gnaphosidae, but Atkinson listed them as Trochanteriidae. My confusion arose from the fact that the guy at the very top had just revised Twiggy's taxonomy. Radically. Twiggy moved species, genus and even family. In 2002, Norman Platnick named her *Morebilus plagusius* and put her into the family Trochanteriidae, along with the world's scorpion spiders who have the same distorted sideways legs.

I confirmed this with Dr Mark Harvey of the Museum of Western Australia, who was listed as one of those responsible for this reclassification. He replied:

> Many thanks for your email regarding *Morebilus*. Yes, what used to be called *Hemicloea major* is now called *Morebilus plagusius*. Norm Platnick examined the original specimens of both species, and concluded that they represented the same species. Whilst species of *Morebilus* are often found under rocks, some specimens have been found under the bark of trees. I presume that there have been no studies examining the biology of rebiline spiders, so any observations would be useful.

Twiggy started greeting me with a leap to the top of her crevice, holding a threatening stance before retreating to defend her egg sacs from my attack. I hoped this indicated the imminent arrival of the young and checked many times a day.

One day I was sure the young had come. But no. A termite nest in the base of her log grew. Was this her private restaurant? No-one could tell me what *Morebilus* ate. Or what ate her! I never saw her prey but my view was very restricted as she would often retreat far down her crevice. There was a third actor on the small stage of the sawn-off log outside the Garret. Often I would see a skink, and sometimes two. One

Twiggy and her egg sacs attracted continuous interest from skinks.
(Photo: D. and L. Kelly)

day the two skinks were standing guard close to Twiggy and her egg sac. Did they know the young were to emerge? Twiggy was in her defensive stance—upper body raised and fangs expanded. But the young never did emerge. At the time of writing, the egg sacs are still intact, and Twiggy has abandoned them. She now lives on the far side of her log. She still leaps at me occasionally, but mostly just sits there.

I have located two more female *Morebilus*, and many males have passed my way. Now that I can recognise them instantly, I realise I see them far more often than the common huntsmen with whom I used to confuse them. So they must be breeding successfully, but I don't know how or where. I do know that I'll be observing *Morebilus* for many years to come.

AN ARACHNOLOGICAL TREASURE TROVE

After months of nightly excursions to Twiggy's log, observing and photographing, I glanced at the soil nearby. There was a small burrow and a small spider resting at its entrance. When, with help from Dr Robert Raven, she was identified as a young trapdoor spider, I started to look more thoroughly in Twiggy's alcove. My lack of observation skills horrified me.

I soon found many more Melbourne trapdoor spiders (*Stanwellia sp.*, family Nemesiidae). In the Garret's bolt handle was a tiny tube-web spider (family Segestriidae) with three of its pairs of legs just peeping from the front of the tube in the way that only segestrids do. I watched it grow, and discovered three more in crevices above the door. A young black house spider (*Badumna sp.*, family Desidae) had a web almost touching the bolt handle. Over the months I watched it grow its tiny snare into a glorious tangle of woolly web. Just inside the same door was a daddy long-legs, who had taken control of the entire region behind a cupboard. Under the eaves was an introduced common house spider (*Achaearanea sp.*, family Theridiidae).

It was another month before I thought to look up. In the branches directly above Twiggy's log were two orb webs. Each morning the little webs were gone. Each night they returned. I delighted in the knowledge that by summer the creators will probably be huge garden orb weavers (*Eriophora sp.*, family Araneidae). I checked the other side of Twiggy's log, only to discover a web I haven't been able to identify, constantly being enlarged by a spider I have yet to sight. Each night I hope she will reveal herself. And then there was the briefest glimpse of a spotted ground spider (family Gnaphosidae) dashing about its business, soon lost in camouflage. If all that wasn't enough, there are the lines of silk that decorate the alcove, almost certainly the draglines of jumping spiders. I now go down during the day to search for these diurnal hunters.

I want to know how this mini-community all fits together. I have photographed the skinks and birds who hang around Twiggy's log, defying them to touch her. There are wood lice, beetles, flies, ants, termites, moths, centipedes, millipedes, worms and the strange thing my tiny tube-web spider was eating, about which I have no idea at all. I need to learn about them all to understand what is really going on down there.

I have an entire world to explore in an area not more that two metres across and ten metres deep. What other group of animals could offer so much in your own backyard? And what other group of animals can tell you so much about the biodioversity and ecological health of your own little bit of the planet?

The ecosystem of Twiggy's log is reproduced in some form or another in every garden in the world—including yours.

The vast array of spider species offers an invaluable tool to the ecologist. Spiders are probably the best guide we have to a habitat's ecological health and to biodiversity in general.

In their 2006 taxonomical guide, *Spider Families of the World*, R. Jocqué and A.S. Dippenaar-Schoeman explain that spiders belong to a large taxonomic group that has adapted to its environment, some as generalists and some as inhabitants of only a very narrow ecological niche.

In contrast to other mega-diverse terrestrial groups with large numbers of species such as the Acari, Nematoda and Collembola [ticks and mites, roundworms and springtails], spiders are relatively large animals. Because their external copulatory organs are species specific, it is fairly simple to identify them . . . Surveys of spiders are, therefore, the most simple to conduct, and spiders appear to be the ideal animals to use for rapid biodiversity assessments. Simple identification, ease of collection and fine-tuned distributions make these animals study objects *par excellence* for decision-makers who require information about the intrinsic biological value of any particular habitat. Spiders provide such information about the value of any particular habitat better than higher plants or vertebrates, and thus offer the small-scale data for the selection of biodiversity 'hot spots' that is required for triage purposes.

And there is more! Jocqué and Volraith showed that size in spiders is dependent on the quality of the habitat. Monitoring their size can, therefore, be considered an 'early-warning-system', revealing changes in habitat quality. In assessing the quality of rainforest patches, the preferred indicator taxon is Ctenidae. The density of occurrence of these spiders can be reliably estimated by night collecting using the light from a headlamp that reflects off the tapetum in the back of their eyes.

Spiders are important in another way. They are a vital component of most terrestrial ecosystems, not least of agricultural systems. They strongly affect the density of insect populations and have been shown to limit insect pests in the agricultural environment.

Apart from the sheer pleasure my observations bring me each night, there is the satisfaction of knowing that I can make my own, very small contribution to a much bigger picture. Every record I keep is contributing to the knowledge of this intriguing group of animals. I never know who might be eating what, or who might be being attacked. Someone might be spinning, or there may be the joy of new young. Then again, there may be the grief of finding a mite on your very favourite.

Every night might be the night I discover something new. It is only in retrospect that I can identify the patterns of behaviour, after many hours of observing and photographing then zooming in on the photographs. Thanks to digital cameras, I can discover the secrets which were hitherto hidden. Twiggy, Erio and Legless will all die within a year or two, as the moderns do. But new individuals soon take their places. I am getting to know my trapdoors, all waiting at the entrances of their burrows each night. They can live over twenty years!

And I never have to leave my own backyard.

6

THE HUNTERS AND
THE HUNTED

Have you lost your belief in fairies? Never mind, I can tell you now that fairy stories pale into insignificance compared with what goes on in the bushes at the bottom of my garden, and yours. Even around the edges of the lawn, if you go down on your knees you might be able to see a harrowing life and death drama, or a delightful comedy, being played out before your eyes all in a matter of seconds. 'All the world's a stage . . .', and even a blade of grass, and the dramas played out beyond our back doors lose none of their impact through being scaled down in size and speeded up in time. The players are the insects and spiders, slugs, snails, centipedes and their kind.

So wrote the inspirational Densey Clyne in *The Garden Jungle*, a book and subsequent film extolling the excitement of the back garden. I had enjoyed the company of individual spiders before, even grown attached to them, but this was nothing compared to what I would feel for a spider I can only describe as 'beautiful'.

Glancing at the perfectly round spider burrow I'd been checking almost daily for months, I noticed a blobby thing. It had eyes. As I crept towards the blob, I allowed myself to hope that it might be what I'd been longing to see. The thing was covered in tiny bumps some of which were moving. A throng of tiny spiderlings, many deep, was clinging to the back of a wolf spider. I named their mother Theresa. (See Plates 20–28.)

I had seen photos of wolf spiders with clusters of young on their abdomens, but Theresa had so many babies that all I could see of her were her legs and face. The babies' tiny legs even covered six of her eyes, so many were battling for arachnid real estate. Any who ventured on to her large front eyes were dislodged with a swish of her palps, much as we'd use windscreen wipers to remove something blocking our vision.

All my wolf spiders are sun lovers, emerging to bake as soon as the temperature rises. Theresa sunned her babies each day at the edge of her burrow. I could not see how she would get herself, plus her young, down the narrow entrance to her burrow. She demonstrated. As spiders do, she suddenly took flight at my movement and disappeared into her burrow while I kept clicking. Examining the photographs closely I could see baby wolf spiders being knocked off by the top of the burrow entrance. In front of the burrow were those that had not been holding on tightly enough when Theresa turned to flee. A dozen or so tiny wolf spiders were running down the burrow chasing their mother.

A few days later and there were babies milling around the burrow entrance but no Theresa. The next day the babies were wandering further afield. If my reading on the mortality of spiders was right, most would not survive the week. Spiders are predators but they are also prey.

I thought Theresa's story was now complete, but that was only Act One.

Wolf spiders are found all over the world. With well over 2000 species, there is a great deal of variation in the lycosids. Some live in burrows, others as free-range hunters. I am very fortunate to have a large burrowing species in my garden, and consider my wolf spiders to be the most beautiful of all arachnids. Their two large posterior eyes have four smaller ones lined up neatly below. Another eye on each side of the carapace gives the wolf spider a distinctive face. The females carry the egg sacs on their spinnerets and they are the only family to carry their young on their backs, which are covered in special knobbly hairs for the young to cling on to. Having seen smaller wolf spiders roaming in the garden with egg sacs, I know I have at least two species, probably more. Most keen observers in gardens anywhere in the world will be able to find a wolf spider.

A few days after I had watched Theresa's babies leave the burrow, I was thrilled to see a familiar face appear. Theresa was still carrying a few babies on her back and she was looking a bit bedraggled.

A different species of wolf spider wandering on our back porch with an egg sac on her spinnerets. (Photo: D. and L. Kelly)

Theresa's young had shed their first skin and undergone their first moult before they had left the egg sac. While on her back they had shed again, leaving their rubbish behind them. It was hard not to empathise with her. When Professor Mark Elgar looked at the photograph, he suggested they may have been nibbling at her. As we will see in Chapter 7, some young spiders are known to eat their mothers alive.

A week or so later I was doing my nightly rounds when I noticed the most stunning visitor at Theresa's burrow. Slimmer and more distinctly marked, I first thought it was Theresa, resplendent in fresh colours and remarkably slimmed-down after her mothering role was complete. A close examination of the photographs showed no sign of engorged palps, but a check of the references told me this splendid visitor was a male. He had mated and was leaving. Alive. The following night, the more familiar brown Theresa emerged.

Theresa had already bred that summer so I assumed his visit was wasted and her life would now be a matter of enjoying her declining months in peace. Wrong again.

A few days later, Theresa's burrow was covered in twigs and bark. I assumed they had blown there and would prevent her from hunting. She would die! Despite my vow not to interfere with the spiders I was

Theresa receives a visit from an extremely good-looking male.
(Photo: D. and L. Kelly)

Theresa is herself again, out hunting at night and wonderfully camouflaged.
(Photo: D. and L. Kelly)

observing, I had become too emotionally involved with Theresa and so tried to remove the debris. It was woven firmly in place. A wolf spider knows far more about being a wolf spider than I do.

Approaching in the warmth of the afternoon sun the next day, I noticed something pale in a gap in the woven twigs. As I approached, there was a swift movement leaving a gap where the pale item had been. I approached the burrow an hour later and the same thing happened again. Theresa was being unusually sensitive to my approach. Reading up on wolf spiders, I came across a description of this very behaviour in Keith C. McKeown's *Australian Spiders*:

> For several days the burrow occupied by 'Sibyl' remained closed. Then the rain cleared away, and suddenly the sun made the wet grass a carpet of spangled glory. 'Sibyl' had opened her hole and made a steep little conical turret of sticks with a narrow hole, round in contour, at the apex. Just inside this hole, a pale object glimmered in the sun—we crept closer for a better view. There, held between the spider's hind legs, was a greyish-white translucent egg sac about the size and shape of a small marble. For three days the *Lycosa* held up her globe to the sun.
>
> In spite of being upside down in the hole, and therefore unable to see us, she nevertheless seemed extremely sensitive to our presence, and would slip below at our approach, so that it was only by exercising the greatest stealth we were able to view her precious egg sac.
>
> At the end of three days she closed in the top of the turret, so that it looked for all the world, like a tiny basket upside down.

I exercised the greatest stealth and was rewarded by the sight of wolf spider legs holding aloft a blueish-grey ball, just beneath the woven barricade Theresa had built to protect herself and her young.

I had assumed that the spider turning the egg sac was Theresa, but was it? I knew from my reading that wolf spiders looking for a new

Theresa holding her blue papery egg sac in the sun with her hind legs.
(Photo: D. and L. Kelly)

burrow can take over the home of another, the previous owner providing the first meal for the new resident.

I also knew that there were other wolf spider burrows in the vicinity of the house. One was in the zucchini patch, only metres from Theresa's and, like Theresa's, had been kept immaculate for a year. I had occasionally met the owner, who I named Chini for her nearby vegetables.

Now, however, Chini's burrow appeared derelict, covered with debris. As it was in the most frequented part of the vegetable plot, I presumed she had grown tired of the vibrations caused by spade, hoe and gardener.

Chini was gone and Theresa had only just bred. Was I watching Theresa's new egg sac or that of her killer? Had Chini escaped the perils of the vegetable patch for the relative safety of the pelargonium bed? I sought the help of Bill Humphries, Senior Curator of the Western

Australian Museum's Collections and Research Centre, and an acknowl-edged expert on wolf spiders. He wrote:

> Unless the spider was marked we will probably never know for sure. However, I have recorded a female *G. godeffroyi* producing another, very small, egg sac within 2 weeks of losing the first. So what you have observed is possible without having to postulate that the burrow was taken over by another female (also a real possibility). Females quite often produce two egg sacs, often in successive years. Covering the burrow mouth with a web has also commonly been observed when spiders are laying eggs or moulting (it serves to keep out ants), which suggest that the female produced the egg sac in the burrow and did not carry it from somewhere else.

I was confused. Should I love this spider as Theresa or hate her as Theresa's assassin? It was at that moment that I remembered that not so long ago I had been an arachnophobe. The cure of getting to know individual spiders had been too successful.

The next night a familiar-looking face appeared beneath the webbing, but I still didn't know whether it was Theresa. It was another week before a check of the vegetable garden revealed Chini's renovated burrow. There in the entrance was a now familiar sight—a wolf spider mother with young.

Back at Theresa's burrow, the egg sac was spun daily in the sun. As our hot, dry summer wore on, I started worrying. The spider's tough exoskeleton usually protects it from drying out completely, but in extremely dry conditions, such as during our drought that summer, it will seek water to drink. That is why house spiders are often found in bathrooms, caught in the sinks and baths whose smooth sides are so hard to climb.

It got hotter and hotter, drier and drier, until I was so worried about Theresa I started watering my spiders. Theresa, Chini, Twiggy and the smallest orb weavers, Itsy and Itsier, were all in exposed places so I watered them lightly. A few minutes later I saw one of Theresa's legs and a fang come up to the water. Itsy was clearly drinking as well, Twiggy's log was damp, and Itsier could be doing anything. At that size, I had no idea.

If you ever want to discourage a new acquaintance, even the most persistent will move rapidly to the other side of the room when you mention that you have been watering your spiders.

Theresa had stopped holding her egg sac up to the sun, but there was no sign of her, nor her babies. Nothing for days. Then one young appeared. Then another, but still no Theresa. I assumed the worst, that she had been worn out and was probably providing food for her young. Wrong, yet again.

Two days later I shed my first tears over a spider. Checking Theresa's burrow in the early afternoon, I saw it had been dug out to a depth of a few centimetres. The surrounding area was also scratched up. I was sure that a bird had spotted her and done all the damage, but had it caught her? I had once been irrationally afraid of creatures such as Theresa. Now I was irrationally upset at the possibility of her death.

I checked every half hour until late that night I saw a familiar blob standing next to her burrow surveying the mess. She let me watch for over ten minutes. Her back was covered with a mixture of babies, earth and detritus. Even her head was covered with debris. She looked terrible. Eventually she went over to the largest log (Theresa scale), grabbed it between her fangs and moved it back to its original place near the burrow. After a few more housekeeping chores, she descended slowly into the burrow, with her load of spiderlings and debris, and disappeared.

Over the next few days she began to look a bit more like a wolf spider should, appearing each day with a few less young and an improved burrow. Three nights later I could see the first hint of a silk binding at the top of an increasingly round burrow entrance. A week later, and there was no sign that the attack had ever happened. Theresa sunned her babies during the day and, as night fell, the mother and her load of young appeared poised at the burrow entrance, ready to hunt.

One sunny afternoon provided me with a spectacle the memory of which still thrills me. A light breeze was blowing when my regular check of Theresa's burrow revealed a tiny spider crossing a silk bridge between the bush above the burrow and the nearby pelargonium. The shrubs were spindly at best, it being a drought year and the garden bed quarantined to ensure its role as an arachnid reserve.

Theresa was at the burrow entrance, a few young still on her back and many more milling around her feet. The camera lens revealed the adventurer to be a tiny wolf spider. At each level of the nearby bush, he would release more silk. It would catch on the bush and he would climb. Up and up he went, covering the bush in trails of the finest of silk. Below, his siblings started to follow.

He climbed to the highest tip of the bush, at which point he raised his abdomen into the breeze and was gone. I had just witnessed my first ballooning. Many spiders species balloon to pastures new. Romantics can imbue the young spiders with a desire to establish their own territories, to strike out on their own, but the more pragmatic reason for their ballooning is to avoid being eaten by their siblings or their mothers!

Over the next quarter of an hour, at least 50 tiny wolf spiders climbed the pelargonium, crossed their sibling's bridge and followed him to the take-off point. (See Plate 28.) There, in groups of two or three, they raised their abdomens to the wind and flew off, some travelling only a few metres; others disappearing from view.

Over the following week, all the young disappeared, and Theresa spent her days sunning herself at her burrow entrance. As evening approached she would descend, and night time would bring her once again to the surface to hunt.

The day was sunny. The bees buzzed and the birds sang. Lazily, I watched a rather large family of the singers, in this case white-winged choughs, rummaging in the garden. I was slow to remember that one thing they rummage for is spiders. Too late, I arrived at Theresa's burrow. It had been dug out completely and she was gone. I was now so far from being an arachnophobe that I was crying over the death of a spider.

A week later, still unable to pass Theresa's pelargonium bed without casting a hopeful glance in the direction of the excavated burrow, I noticed another, smaller burrow wedged in safely against the wooden garden edging, not a metre from where Theresa had made her home. I peered down to see a miniature version of that familiar face. Was it one of Theresa's young? I can never know for sure but I choose to believe it was. And so the cycle started again.

Theresa wasn't my only wolf spider; Chini's burrow was also attacked that dreadful day, but as she had tunnelled beneath the brick path, I hoped she might still be down there somewhere. It was another anxious wait until night and a relief to see her emerge unscathed. She was much more skittish than previously, but she was still alive.

Over the following weeks, I learned that the choughs were not scratching around randomly in the garden. Each time they visited, some of my spiders would be dug up. The choughs' depredations revealed burrows I hadn't known about—sometimes those of wolf spiders but mostly those of the trapdoors you will meet in Chapter 7.

Chini was attacked again, this time much more substantially than before. I decided that night that if she survived the attack, I'd renege on my vow to let nature be. I was overjoyed

The last thing Theresa ever saw.
(Photo: D. and L. Kelly)

*Plate 1: A golden orb weaver (*Nephila sp.*) showing off the elegance of her legs.* (Photo: Alan Henderson)

*Plate 2: A male wolf spider (*Lycosa sp.*) on my front verandah in search of a mate.* (Photo: D. and L. Kelly)

Plate 3: The American or common house spider (Achaearanea sp., *family Theridiidae) with her egg sac. This genus is found all over the world.* (Photo: D. and L. Kelly)

*Plate 4: A common house spider, Lady Macbeth, (*Achaearanea sp.*) bailing up a white-tailed spider. Her egg sac is behind her.* (Photo: D. and L. Kelly)

*Plate 5: Kathleen's 'black, furry spider', the **bold** jumping spider,* Phidippus audax. (Photo: D. and L. Kelly)

*Plate 6: Funnel spider, the grass weaver spider (*Agelenopsis sp.*), actively hunting on a dewy morning in Texas.* (Photo: D. and L. Kelly)

*Plate 7: My garden orb weaver, Damiana (*Eriophora biapicata*) on her web.*
(Photo: D. and L. Kelly)

Plate 8: Erio-three, shrouding a captured insect with swathing silk.
(Photo: D. and L. Kelly)

Plate 9: Erio using her leg span as the measurement for the spacing of her spiral. (Photo: D. and L. Kelly)

Plate 10: My third Eriophora, *camouflaged Erio-three, in her diurnal retreat among the hakea nuts of a hakea tree. She is holding her legs in the typical resting position of garden orb weavers.* (Photo: D. and L. Kelly)

Plate 11: Erio-three testing her thread to start her new web. (Photo: D. and L. Kelly)

Plate 12: Erio-three releasing a new thread from her spinnerets as her bridge thread had been broken. (Photo: D. and L. Kelly)

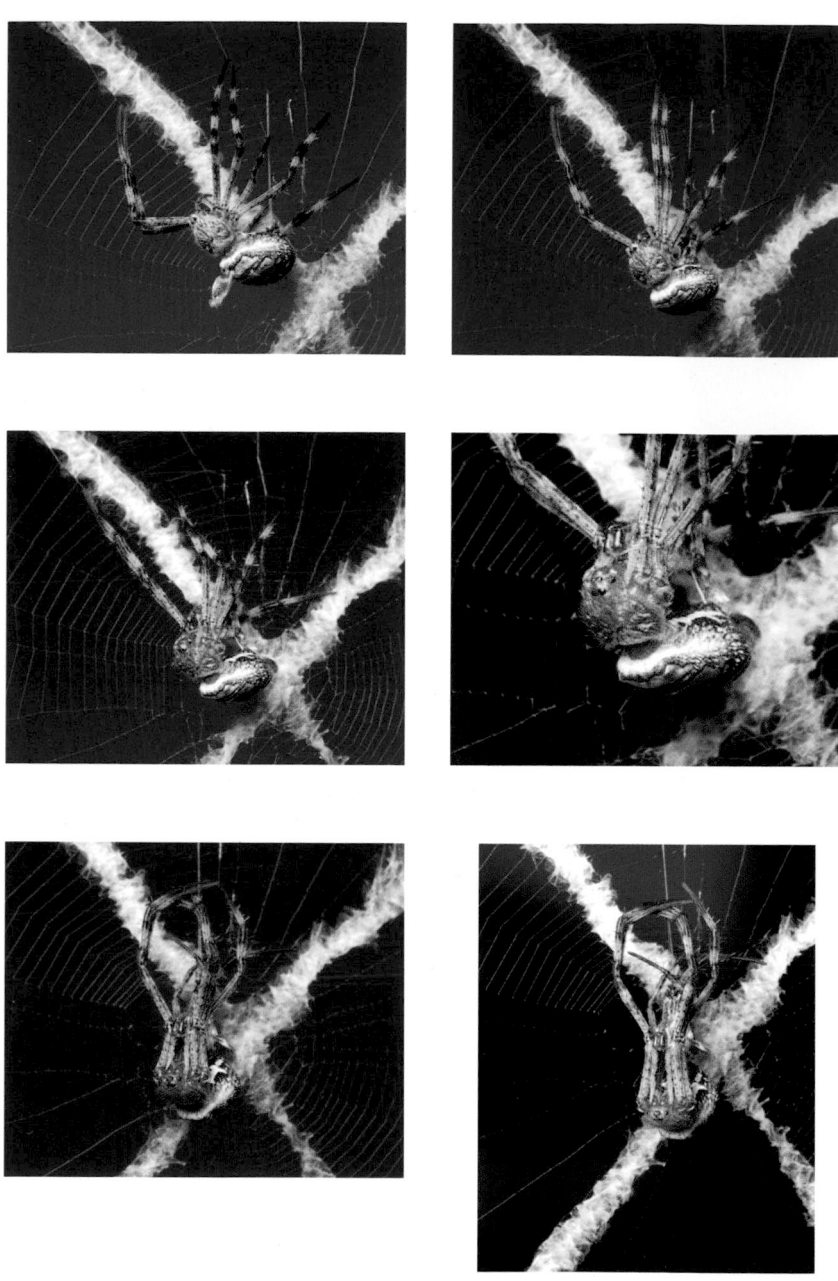

*Plate 13, this page and opposite: A St Andrew's Cross spider (*Argiope keyserlingi, *family* Araneidae) *moulting.* (Photos: Alan Henderson)

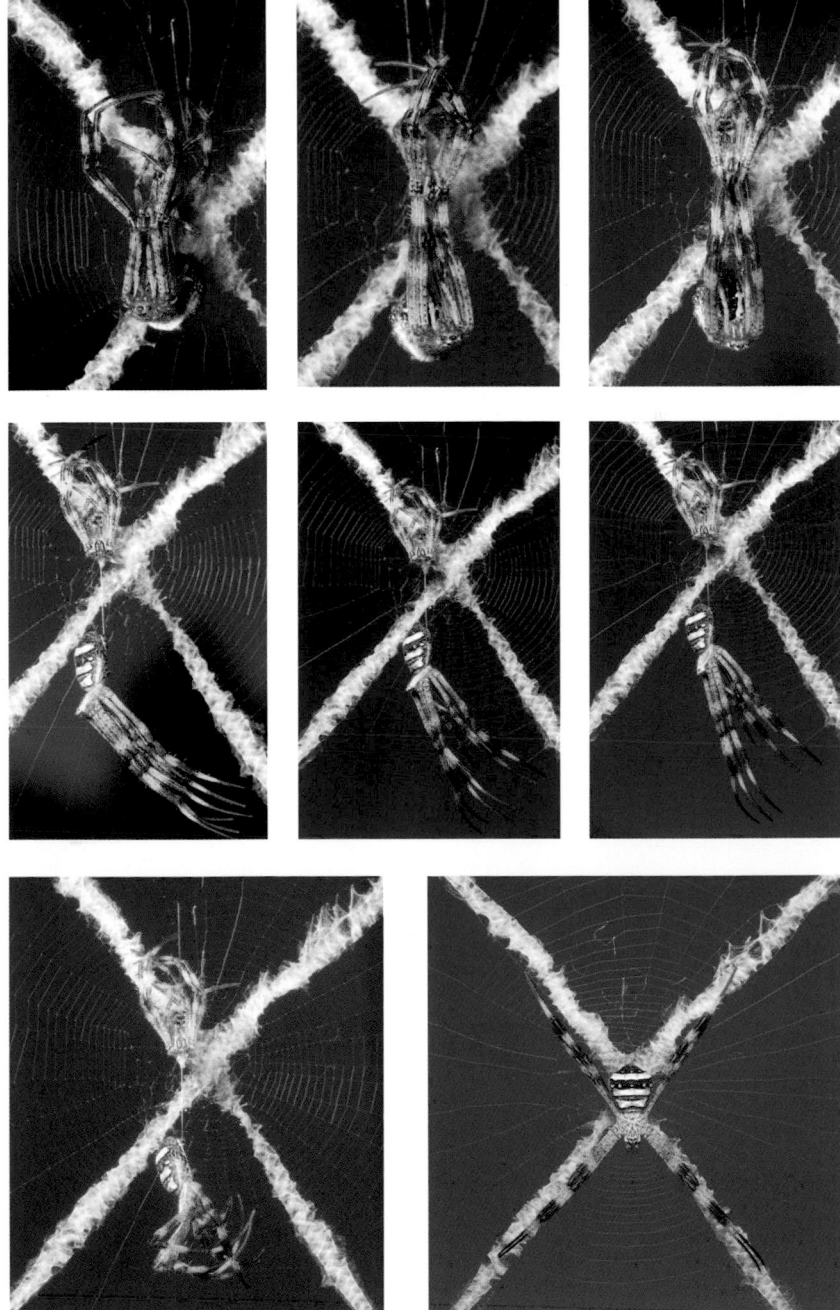

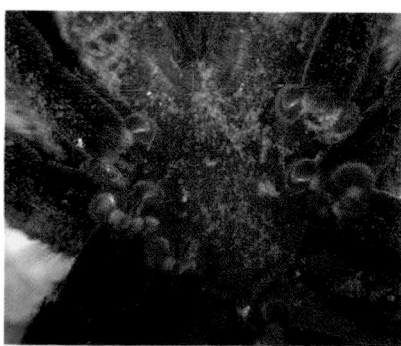

*Plate 14: A brushfooted trapdoor spider (*Idiommata sp., *family Barychelidae), showing the feet with claw tufts, which enable it to climb smooth surfaces. Note also the four book lungs typical of primitive spiders.* (Photo: Robert Raven)

Plate 15: The feet of a brushfooted trapdoor spider under a microscope, showing the claw tufts.
(Photo: Robert Raven)

Plate 16: A single foot of a brushfooted trapdoor spider showing the claws and tuft. (Photo: Robert Raven)

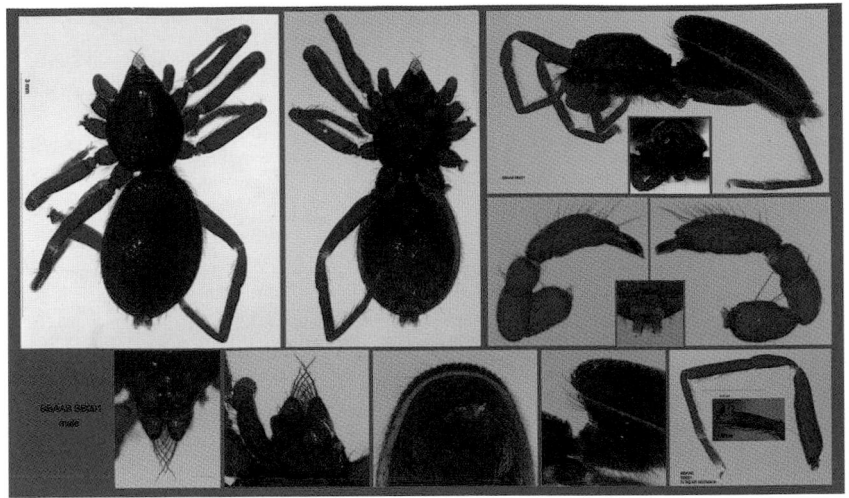

Plate 17: A male goblin spider (family Oonopidae) laid out for classification by Dr Baehr. (Photo: Barbara Baehr)

Plate 18: The diving spider (Argyroneta aquatica) with its silken, air-filled home. (Photo: Josef Hlasek)

Plate 19: A female Morebilus sp. *on a flower pot. She had been living in the narrow space between two empty terracotta pots stacked together.* (Photo: D. and L. Kelly)

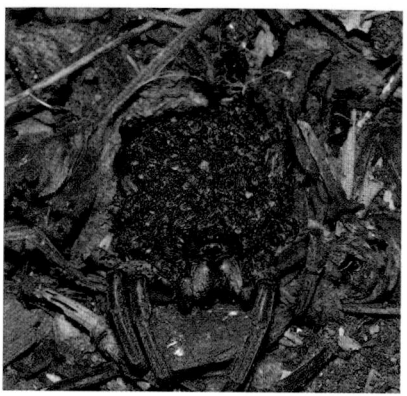

Plate 21: Theresa with her babies. Two at the top appear to be sparring. Children are the same everywhere! (Photo: D. and L. Kelly)

Plate 20: Theresa with her multitude of babies on her back. She's a wolf spider, Lycosa godeffroyi, *family Lycosidae. Note the dead pelargonium leaf on the left, which stayed by the burrow for most of the summer.* (Photo: D. and L. Kelly)

Plate 23: Some of Theresa's young were just not fast enough. They can be seen running after her. Others were knocked off on the top of the burrow as their mother dashed below. (Photo: D. and L. Kelly)

Plate 22: Theresa suddenly decided to retreat from the huge predator with a camera. She moved extremely fast. (Photo: D. and L. Kelly)

Plate 24: The first of Theresa's young leave home. The expression on this tiny face is daunting. (Photo: D. and L. Kelly)

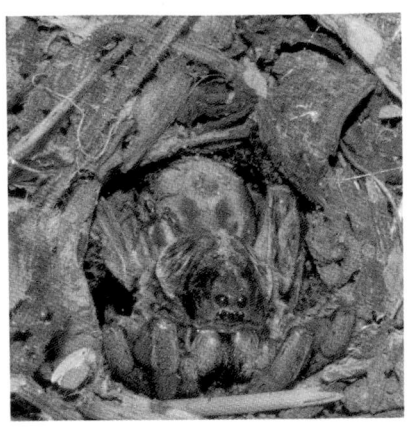

Plate 25: Theresa is looking haggard, probably having been nibbled on by her offspring. Bits of leftovers from the spiderlings' moulting are on her back. (Photo: D. and L. Kelly)

Plate 26: Theresa emerges from her burrow after her first bird attack. Covered in babies and debris, she just stood there while I watched her. The pelargonium leaf which has been in all her photographs is now gone. (Photo: D. and L. Kelly)

Plate 27: Theresa's 'log' had been moved away by the birds. She dragged it back into position before retreating into her burrow. She must have really liked that log. (Photo: D. and L. Kelly)

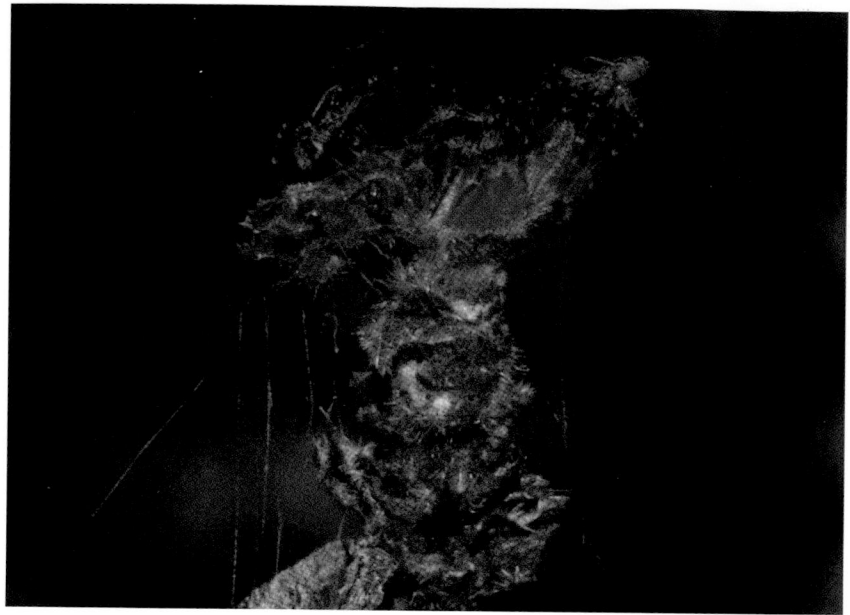

Plate 28: Theresa's young have climbed to the twig on the small pelargonium above her burrow to balloon off in the slim hope of surviving long enough to make their own burrows. (Photo: D. and L. Kelly)

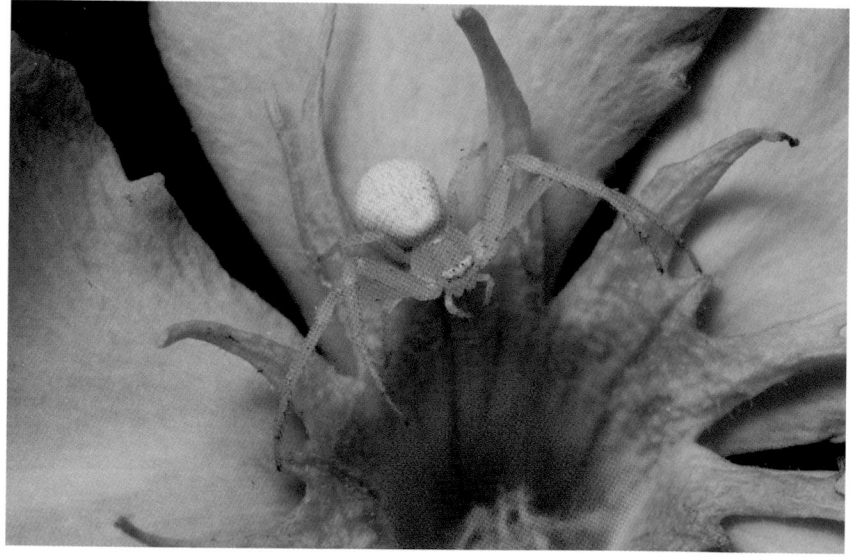

Plate 29: A crab spider, family Thomisidae. (Photo: Alan Henderson)

Plate 30: When it comes to cuteness, nothing beats the jumping spiders. No-one could be arachnophobic with a jumping spider around! This is the green jumping spider, Mopsus mormon. (Photo: Alan Henderson)

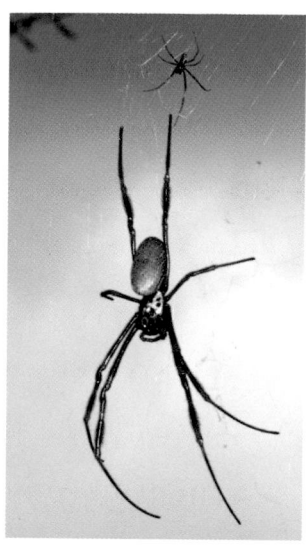

*Plate 32: A female mouse spider (*Missulena sp.,
family Actinopodidae*) rearing to show fangs.*
(Photo: Robert Raven)

*Plate 31: A huge female
golden orb weaver, (*Nephila
sp.*) with a tiny male
approaching to give his life
for the chance of offspring.*
(Photo: D. and L. Kelly)

*Plate 33: The distinctive red hourglass on the underside of the
abdomen in many widow spiders. (Photo: Alan Henderson)*

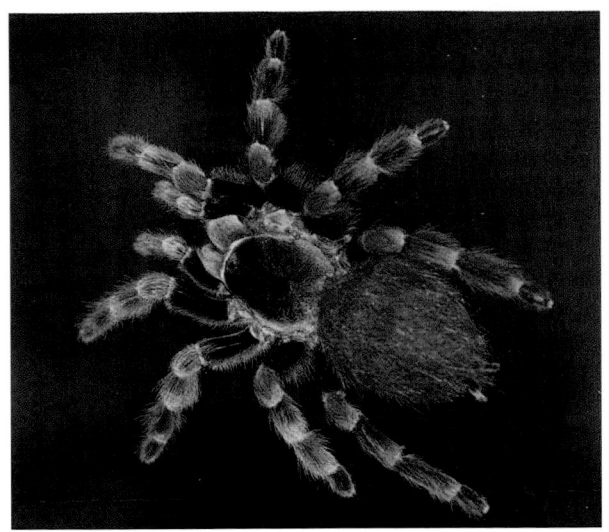

Plate 34: A Mexican red-kneed tarantula, Brachypelma smithi, *as displayed in* Bugs Alive! (Photo: D. and L. Kelly)

Plate 35: The Melbourne Museum's tiger huntsman.
(Photo: Alan Henderson)

Plate 36: Spinnelein pulling in her web systematically when she takes fright at my presence. It took her less than fifteen seconds to collect her web into a ball and escape to the cover of a leaf. (Photo: D. and L. Kelly)

Plate 37: Spinnelein has collected all of the web other than the main bridge line connecting the two bushes which supported her web. (Photo: D. and L. Kelly)

Plate 38: Spinnelein holds her ball of web in her fangs, ready to reabsorb the protein for future use. (Photo: D. and L. Kelly)

Chini peering out from her damaged burrow. She had survived the Attack of the Choughs. (Photo: D. and L. Kelly)

to catch a fleeting glimpse of my wolf spider. Chini got a fence.

There are many who have enjoyed the delights of lycosid company. My intention was to observe my spiders in the wild doing whatever is natural for them. I had read of many experiments with wolf spiders, in captivity and in the garden, being given a variety of materials with which to do the building for which they are famous.

Jean-Henri Fabre was a diligent observer of the wildlife of his native France. He described what happened when he gave his captive wolf spiders (*Lycosa narbonensis*) an endless range of building materials in his delightfully idiosyncratic book, *The Life of a Spider*, published in 1912.

Two months pass; and the result of my liberality surpasses my expectations. Possessing more windfalls than they know what to do with, all picked up in their immediate neighbourhood, my Lycosae have built themselves donjon-keeps the like of which their race has not yet known. Around the orifice, on a slightly sloping bank, small, flat, smooth stones have been laid to form a broken, flagged pavement. The larger stones, which are Cyclopean blocks compared with the size of the animal that has shifted them, are employed as abundantly as the others.

On this rockwork stands the donjon. It is an interlacing of raffia and bits of wool, picked up at random, without distinction of shade. Red and white, green and yellow are mixed without any attempt at order. The Lycosa is indifferent to the joys of colour.

The ultimate result is a sort of muff, a couple of inches high. Bands of silk supplied by the spinnerets, unite the pieces, so that the whole resembles a coarse fabric.

Fabre describes in exquisite detail the weaving of a mat on which the *Lycosa* lays her eggs. He marvels at her precision and elegant weaving, before shattering my illusions about the lycosid's maternal instinct.

Worn out with fatigue, the mother embraces her dear pill and remains motionless. I shall see no more to-day. Next morning, I find the Spider carrying the bag of eggs slung from her stern.

Henceforth, until the hatching, she does not leave go of the precious burden, which, fastened to the spinnerets by a short ligament, drags and bumps along the ground . . .

It is a sight worth seeing, that of the Lycosa dragging her treasure after her, never leaving it, day or night, sleeping or waking, and defending it with a courage that strikes the beholder with awe. If I try to take the bag from her, she presses it to her breast in despair, hangs on to my pincers, bites them with her poison-fangs. I can hear the daggers grating on the steel. No, she would not allow herself to be robbed of the wallet with impunity, if my fingers were not supplied with an implement.

By dint of pulling and shaking the pill with the forceps, I take it from the Lycosa, who protests furiously. I fling her in exchange a pill taken from another Lycosa. It is at once seized in the fangs, embraced by the legs and hung on to the spinneret. Her own or another's: it is all one to the Spider, who walks away proudly with the alien wallet. This was to be expected, in view of the similarity of the pills exchanged.

A test of another kind, with a second subject, renders the mistake more striking. I substitute, in the place of the lawful bag which I have removed, the work of the Silky Epeira [garden orb weaver]. The colour and softness of the material are the same in both cases; but the shape is quite different. The stolen object is a globe; the object presented in exchange is an elliptical conoid studded with angular projections along the edge of the base. The Spider takes no account of this dissimilarity. She promptly glues the queer bag to her spinnerets and is as pleased as though she were in possession of her real pill. My experimental villainies have no other consequences beyond an ephemeral carting. When hatching-time arrives, early in the case of the Lycosa, late in that of the Epeira, the gulled Spider abandons the strange bag and pays it no further attention.

Let us penetrate yet deeper into the wallet-bearer's stupidity. After depriving the Lycosa of her eggs, I throw her a ball of cork, roughly polished with a file and of the same size as the stolen pill. She accepts the corky substance, so different from the silk purse, without the least demur. One would have thought that she would recognize her mistake with those eight eyes of hers, which gleam like precious stones. The silly creature pays no attention. Lovingly she embraces the cork ball, fondles it with her palpi, fastens it to her spinnerets and thenceforth drags it after her as though she were dragging her own bag.

Let us give another the choice between the imitation and the real. The rightful pill and the cork ball are placed together on the floor of the jar. Will the Spider be able to know the one that belongs to her? The fool is incapable of doing so. She makes a wild rush and seizes haphazardly at one time her property, at another my sham product. Whatever is first touched becomes a good capture and is forthwith hung up.

If I increase the number of cork balls, if I put in four or five of them, with the real pill among them, it is seldom that the Lycosa recovers her own property. Attempts at enquiry, attempts at selection there are none. Whatever she snaps up at random she sticks to, be it good or bad. As there are more of the sham pills of cork, these are the most often seized by the Spider.

This obtuseness baffles me. Can the animal be deceived by the soft contact of the cork? I replace the cork balls by pellets of cotton or paper, kept in their round shape with a few bands of thread. Both are very readily accepted instead of the real bag that has been removed.

Can the illusion be due to the colouring, which is light in the cork and not unlike the tint of the silk globe when soiled with a little earth, while it is white in the paper and the cotton, when it is identical with that of the original pill? I give the Lycosa, in exchange for her work, a pellet of silk thread, chosen of a fine red, the brightest of all colours. The uncommon pill is as readily accepted and as jealously guarded as the others.

Having experimented with the egg sac, Fabre waits for the hatching and then experiments with the young, so unique in clinging to their mother's back in what I so much wanted to believe was evidence of Theresa's care.

The youngsters may be brushed off by a blade of grass. What becomes of them when they have a fall? Does the mother give them a thought? Does she come to their assistance and help them to regain their place on her back? Not at all. The affection of a Spider's heart, divided among some hundreds, can spare but a very feeble portion to each. The Lycosa hardly troubles, whether one youngster fall from his place, or six, or all of them. She waits impassively for the victims of the mishap to get out of their own difficulty, which they do, for that matter, and very nimbly.

I sweep the whole family from the back of one of my boarders with a hair-pencil. Not a sign of emotion, not an attempt at search on the part of the denuded one. After trotting about a little on the sand, the dislodged youngsters find, these here, those there, one or other of the mother's legs, spread wide in a circle. By means of these climbing-poles, they swarm to the top and soon the dorsal group resumes its original form. Not one of the lot is missing. The Lycosa's sons know their trade as acrobats to perfection: the mother need not trouble her head about their fall.

With a sweep of the pencil, I make the family of one Spider fall around another laden with her own family. The dislodged ones nimbly scramble up the legs and climb on the back of their new mother, who kindly allows them to behave as though they belonged to her. There is no room on the abdomen, the regulation resting-place, which is already occupied by the real sons. The invaders thereupon encamp on the front part, beset the thorax and change the carrier into a horrible pin-cushion that no longer bears the least resemblance to a Spider form. Meanwhile, the sufferer raises no sort of protest against this access of family. She placidly accepts them all and walks them all about.

The youngsters, on their side, are unable to distinguish between what is permitted and forbidden. Remarkable acrobats that they are, they climb on the first Spider that comes along, even when of a different species, provided that she be of a fair size. I place them in the presence of a big Epeira marked with a white cross on a pale-orange ground (*Epeira pallida*, OLIV.). The little ones, as soon as they are dislodged from the back of the Lycosa their mother, clamber up the stranger without hesitation.

Intolerant of these familiarities, the Spider shakes the leg encroached upon and flings the intruders to a distance. The assault is doggedly resumed, to such good purpose that a dozen succeed in hoisting themselves to the top. The Epeira, who is not accustomed to the tickling of such a load, turns over on her back and rolls on the ground in the manner of a donkey when his hide is itching. Some are lamed, some are even crushed. This does not deter the others, who repeat the escalade as soon as the Epeira is on her legs again. Then come more somersaults, more rollings on the back, until the giddy swarm are all discomfited and leave the Spider in peace.

JUMPING SPIDERS—THE SALTICIDAE

Fabre is not the only observer to be thoroughly umimpressed by the wolf spider's lack of mental actuity.

'Wolf spiders are intellectually destitute when compared to the salticids.'

These were almost the first words uttered to me by Dr Barry Richardson, when I contacted him to talk about jumping spiders. He dismissed my claim that the only spider who can challenge the wolf spiders in the arachnid photogenic stakes are the salticids. He denied that there could be any comparison at all.

'At least,' he went on, 'you're not into the macho mygalomorphs.' I shamefacedly confessed to having over 300 trapdoor spider burrows marked out in the area surrounding my home, with more being added daily.

Dr Barry Richardson is a researcher in the Australian National Insect Collection in CSIRO (Commonwealth Scientific and Industrial Research Organisation). He is interested in the process of evolution and how it actually occurs in the field. He is currently working on the taxonomy and biodiversity of Australian salticids. He likes to change the group of animal he studies every five years. Having produced award-winning work on mammals, he has diversified greatly: 'Tuna allowed me to work on the dynamics of large populations. Rabbits allowed me to study the effects of social structure on the genetics of populations and the salticids are just cute.'

As Richardson explained, even extreme arachnophobes do not seem to be frightened by jumping spiders: 'They move differently. They act differently. They just feel different. They're not spiders,' he concluded, 'they're salticids.'

With 5188 species in 560 genera—at the time of writing—the jumping spider family, Salticidae, is the largest of all spider families. Salticids are found in every country on the globe.

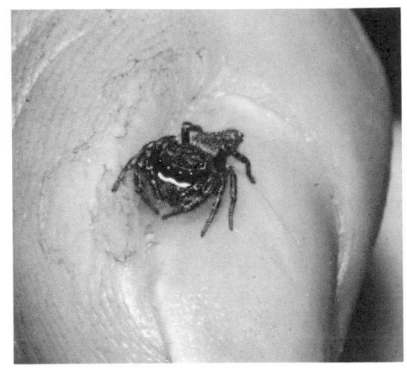

A jumping spider on the author's (not very clean) finger. Jumping spiders are curious, alert little spiders, well worth meeting up close. (Photo: D. and L. Kelly)

Richardson is particularly attracted by the salticids' visual acuity and chemical mimicry, their capacity to take on prey much bigger than themselves, and the complexity and sophistication of their hunting techniques. He is fascinated by their ability to adapt those techniques to a huge variety of prey, including those they can never have encountered before.

The diminutive salticids are the intellectual giants of the arachnid world. A surprisingly drab little creature, dull indeed when compared to her many coloured cousins, is the brightest of them all—*Portia*.

The seventeen species in this African, Asian and Australian genus have especially complex predatory strategies. Obviously there are both males and females of the genus, but the name *Portia* seems to lead many to use the feminine when waxing lyrical about this astounding spider who is less than a centimetre long. Richardson described what happens when *Portia* sights a prey:

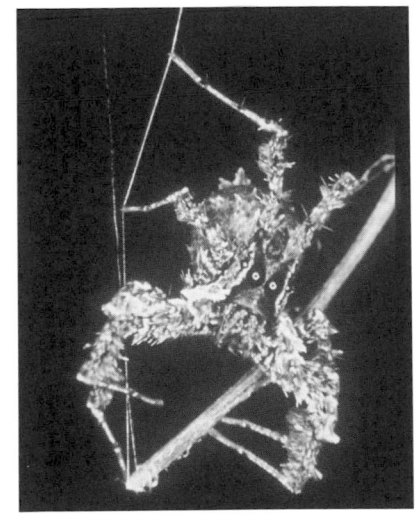

Portia—the tiny creature which is the intellectual giant of the arachnid world. (Photo: Robert Jackson)

She can visually identify complete and incomplete routes from here to there, select the best route and will follow that route even if it takes her out of sight of the prey. She can remember that she is hunting without the visual stimulus of the prey even with her tiny brain. Not many spiders can do that.

Like mammals with much larger brains, *Portia* will even move away from her prey initially, if need be. In laboratory experiments, *Portia* has been offered two alternative routes, only one of which leads to the prey. Having visually assessed the location of the prey in the environment, she almost invariably chooses the right route. A species of spitting spider (family Scytodidae) in the Philippines preys on salticids. Spitting spiders subdue their prey by ejecting a rapid zig-zag fire of sticky silk and venom from their fangs. The local species of *Portia* detours from a direct route to approach the spitting spider from the rear. Mind you, if the spitting spider is carrying her egg sac in her palps, *Portia* will attack from the front.

Preying mostly on other spiders, *Portia* employs behavioural sequences based on problem-solving and planning. Recent research has used *Portia* to study cognitive attributes that relate more to large predatory mammals, such as lions, than to very small spiders. Robert Jackson and Duane Harland, of the University of Canterbury in New Zealand, wrote:

What makes salticids special is their unique, complex eyes and acute eyesight, not leaping prowess. Salticids have large anterior medial eyes that give them an almost catlike appearance. No other spider has eyes like these and no other spider has such intricate vision-guided behaviour. The feline analogy is more than superficial, and a better common name for salticids would probably be 'eight-legged cats'.

As with a cat, a salticid uses more than its eyesight during prey-capture sequences. Chemoreception and other modalities also play a role. Like a cat, and unlike any other spider, however, a salticid locates, tracks, stalks, chases down and leaps on active prey, with all phases of these predatory sequences being under optical control. Using optical cues, salticids discriminate between mates and rivals, predators and prey, different types of prey, and features of non-living environment. No other spider is known to see this well.

The salticids' great claim to fame is their visual acuity. A dragonfly (*Sympetrum striolatus*), has the highest acuity known for insects. Its compound eyes are as big as *Portia*'s entire cephalothorax, yet the acuity of *Portia*'s sight exceeds it ten-fold. The other salticids are not far behind.

Salticids have eight eyes, six of which are along the side of the carapace. This means the salticid can detect movement through a 360-degree range. The two large front principle eyes are what make salticids unique. Wolf spiders have the same large eyes, but nowhere near the same acuity.

Spiders have 'simple' eyes, as do we, but the human retina contains more than 150 million photocells, *Portia*'s only a few thousand. Compound eyes with acuities approaching those of *Portia*'s principal eyes would not be physically possible on a body of *Portia*'s size. Humanlike spherical camera eyes require space and there just isn't enough inside *Portia*'s tiny cephalothorax. How, then does *Portia* manage to see so well?

The solution is amazing. The large corneal lens on the front of the eye has a long focal length, and can magnify distant objects. With binocular overlap, these two lenses cover about a 90-degree field of vision. The salticid is just too small to have a retina big enough to sample this field with the degree of acuity indicated by behaviour. A much smaller retina, which can only sample two to five degrees, fits inside the tube behind the eye. A second lens further magnifies the image, and sends the signal to four layers of receptors, each optimised for different wavelengths in the colour spectrum. The first three layers enable the salticid to discern green, blue and ultraviolet. The final layer of receptors enables high acuity in seeing shape and movement by bringing images near and far into focus at the same time, eliminating the need for a variable lens such as we have.

The final part to the solution is achieved by the eye tube swinging side to side while the corneal lens remains still. Sweeping the telephoto lens system in a complex pattern over the scene, the salticid achieves a 90-degree field of acute vision. Awesome as this is, Harland and Jackson conclude:

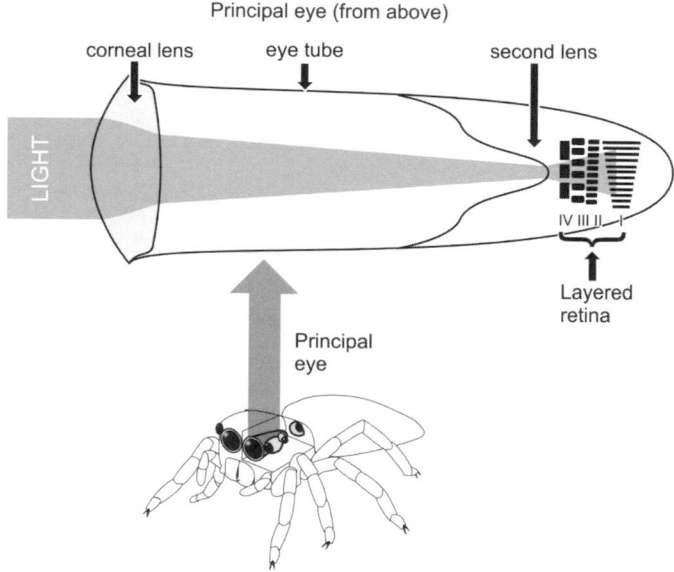

Internal structure of the salticid principal eye. Bottom: *Position of eye in cephalothorax.* Top: *Light passes through a corneal lens and down an eye tube where it is magnified by a second lens before falling onto a four-layered retina. Layers II-IV function in colour vision. Layer I functions in high-acuity perception of shape and form.* (Diagram: Duane P. Harland and Robert R. Jackson)

From many years of studying *Portia* our impression is that, although these spiders' feats of discrimination are impressive, they are often strikingly slow on the uptake. It may be that *Portia* can see more or less what we can see, but achieves this by means of a slow scanning process. Part of what it means to say an animal 'sees well' should perhaps be that it perceives what is out there quickly. On this criterion, *Portia* may see only poorly.

She may not be super-quick on the uptake, but *Portia* challenges anyone to deny her cognitive capacity is way beyond simple instinct. Most salticids hunt insects, but *Portia*'s preference is other spiders, especially those who build webs.

Jumping spiders build silken nests for resting at night, moulting, and egg-laying, but do not usually build webs to trap prey. *Portia* does. She builds a small web on the side of a larger web but she doesn't always eat her web catch. She uses the struggling insect to attract her host spider into her web. She also invades other spiders' webs and eats their eggs, steals their prey or attacks the inhabitants themselves.

Portia induces her prey to come to her by vibrating the web. She has pre-programmed signals for familiar prey, but tackles an unfamiliar species with a kaleidoscope of signals until she finds the one which works. She uses all eight legs, two palps and a flicking abdomen, in a huge variety of combinations to make an almost limitless array of signals. She may generate a signal which her prey interprets as a small insect caught in the web, drawing her prey right out to her waiting fangs. Once she gets the response, then she will focus on just that vibratory signal.

Portia fimbriata has been observed to perform this vibratory behaviour for three whole days before the victim decided to investigate. In laboratory experiments, *Portia* even responded appropriately to spiders that she would never encounter in the wild because their ranges do not overlap.

If the spider is a large one who would easily devour the smaller aggressor, then *Portia* either uses vibrations which draw it in slowly, or pacifies it with repetitive vibrations, while moving in for the kill. Should she tackle a daddy long-legs, a spider adept at overpowering other spiders the moment they touch its long, spindly legs, *Portia* has been seen to vibrate in a way which manoeuvres the victim into a position from which she can leap onto its body while avoiding its legs.

MASTERS OF DISGUISE

While *Portia* looks like a scrap of detritus on a web or leaf and uses her intellect to survive, some of her fellow arachnids mimic the insects with whom they share their space. Some spiders mimic their company to exploit their defences, such as the several hundred ant-mimicking species. Most don't look like ants in order to fool the ants themselves— poor-sighted creatures who rely on chemical and movement cues to detect prey and other members of their colony. Ant-mimicking spiders look like ants to make themselves unattractive to predators, such as birds, who feed on spiders but find ants unpalatable. Hidden among so many ants, the solitary spider is very hard for a predator to detect.

Appearance, movement, now scent. Ants don't have very good eyesight. They rely far more on chemical cues. A jumping spider, *Cosmophasis bitaeniata*, lives in the leafy nests of the green tree ant (*Oecophylla smaragdina*), where it preys on the ant larvae while avoiding direct contact with the workers. The workers aggressively defend their colony against various arthropod intruders or green tree ants from neighbouring colonies, yet chemical mimicry allows the little jumping spiders to enter the nests apparently undetected. Their cuticular hydro-carbon profile mimics that of the ants of a particular colony, and is acquired from that colony, not from the spider's genetic heritage. If changing colonies, the spider alters its cuticular profile to mimic the slightly different chemical cues of the new hosts.

Ants aren't the only insects to be mimicked by spiders. Another jumping spider, *Coccorchestes*, found in New Guinea and Australia, mimics beetles, while yet another jumping spider, the Australian genus *Abracadabrella*, mimics a fly. Among plenty more arachnid-mimics the world over, members of the genus *Graptartia* (family Corinnidae), mimic wingless wasps from the family Mutillidae. Southern Africa boasts small orb weavers (family Araneidae) who look like beetles and ladybirds, thought to be unpalatable to birds. Australia is host to another araneid, the bird-dropping spider (*Celaenia excavata*), whose disguise would be particularly effective on birds!

In *Biology of Spiders*, Rainer F. Foelix describes the unique strategy of *Callilepis nocturna*, a ground spider partial to ants.

Callilepis runs in short bursts; the motion resembles that of certain ants (for example *Formica*), but the body does not have an antlike appearance at all. Thus *Callilepis* cannot be considered as an ant mimic. The ant is always attacked head-on. The tarsi of the spider's front legs contact the ant's head and probe for the base of the

*The bird-repellent disguise of the bird-dropping spider on her egg sac. (*Celaenia excavata*). (Photo: Alan Henderson)*

antennae. Then follows a quick bite (0.2 seconds) at the base of one antennae, and the spider withdraws completely. A minute later *Callilepis* searches for the victim again and applies a longer bite. Initially the bitten ant is quite aggressive, but within a few seconds its injured antenna becomes limp and the ant starts walking in circles (right-hand circles if the left antenna was bitten and vice versa). Thus the ant hardly moves away from the spot where it was first attacked, and therefore can be easily relocated afterwards. *Callilepis* tucks the paralysed ant underneath herself and runs quickly for a hiding place. During the maneuver she is often attacked by other ants, but somehow she manages to dodge them. Once she has reached a safer place, she closes it off with a silken cover and starts feeding. The prey is never chewed, but is sucked from the 'neck' and abdomen. After one or two hours the undamaged cuticular shell is all that remains of the ant.

The very rapid and precise capture method of *Callilepis* represents an adaptation to cope with strong and potentially dangerous prey. The bite is placed only at the vulnerable base of an antenna, and the legs are immediately removed from the reach of the ant's formidable mandibles. The predation strategy of *Callilepis* is rather rigidly 'programmed': if both antennae of the ant are cut off, the spider still attacks but never bites it. Apparently the bite is 'blocked' when *Callilepis* cannot locate the antennal bases. On the other

hand, if one glues two antennae to the ant's abdomen, the spider will bite there. The antennae must therefore be considered the key stimulus for the spider's bite.

An ant-mimicking spider using its front legs to mimic the antennae of an ant. (Photo: Alan Henderson)

PARLOUR ETIQUETTE

'Will you walk into my parlour?' said the Spider to the Fly,
''Tis the prettiest little parlour that ever you did spy;
The way into my parlour is up a winding stair,
And I've a many curious things to shew when you are there.'
'Oh no, no,' said the little Fly, 'to ask me is in vain,
For who goes up your winding stair can ne'er come down again.'

Mary Howitt

Crab spiders are so fond of floral decor that the family Thomisidae are sometimes known as flower spiders. The beautifully camouflaged little killer overpowers unsuspecting insects much larger than itself when they alight on flowers.

The water spiders, *Dolomedes sp.* belong to the family Pisauridae, the nursery-web spiders. They prefer a parlour with water views. They effectively use the water surface as a web, the slightest movement alerting them to the presence of prey. Eating mostly small water creatures, *Dolomedes* can move very fast, galloping across the surface of their liquid hunting fields. They can even leap a few centimetres from the surface of the water when startled. It's an impressive feat. Can you imagine jumping more than your own height from the surface of water?

Sac spiders prefer to keep their parlours free of messy victims. Living in a thick silk tube found around homes and gardens all over the world, the spiders of the family Clubionidae rest, mate and produce their eggs in their silken sacs, but hunt free-range in the surrounding area.

Spitting spiders make their parlour anywhere there is food. The family Scytodidae spit down their prey. Ejecting a venomous sticky fluid from their fangs, it's all over in a flash. Zig-zagging from side to side, the prey is pinned to the leaf as if stitched by a sewing machine. The venomous thread binds then kills them.

As the behaviour of most spiders has not yet been studied, we are only just beginning to appreciate the extraordinary variety of their parlours.

THE HUNTSMEN—GIANT CRAB SPIDERS OR RAIN SPIDERS

Parlour-free, and named for their hunting prowess, there are over 1000 species of huntsmen spiders (family Sparassidae) across the world. Also known as giant crab spiders or rain spiders, none is dangerous, although all can deliver a bite which may cause mild pain and nausea. It is amazing the way they can enter a room which to all appearances was sealed. Much flatter than most other spiders, they can pass through very narrow gaps. Most spiders bend their legs vertically, but huntsmen move with their legs splayed in the horizontal plane with their knees to the rear. This gives them that flat, mobile huntsman gait perfectly designed for sneaking into your house through the smallest of cracks.

In the wild, huntsmen live under the bark of trees or in crevices in rocks and walls. The dark, tight spaces suit them beautifully. Their front two pairs of legs are significantly longer than the back pair, which gives them a very elegant and distinctive appearance. Huntsmen spiders have a wonderful courtship and breeding sequence, as we will discover in Chapter 8.

Huntsmen are a shy lot and rarely bite unless provoked or protecting an egg sac. Yet these are the spiders that are commonly held to cause an arachnophobic reaction on sight. I will still jump at the sudden appearance of a large huntsman—a common occurrence at home. It is their ability to materialise where moments before there was no spider, along with their ability to move fast and sideways, which leads to this reaction. My arachnophobic response is to the speed and unpredictability of their movements rather than the fear of a bite.

*A lichen huntsman (*Pandercetes gracilis*) with her egg sac, to which she has added lichen for camouflage.* (Photo: Alan Henderson)

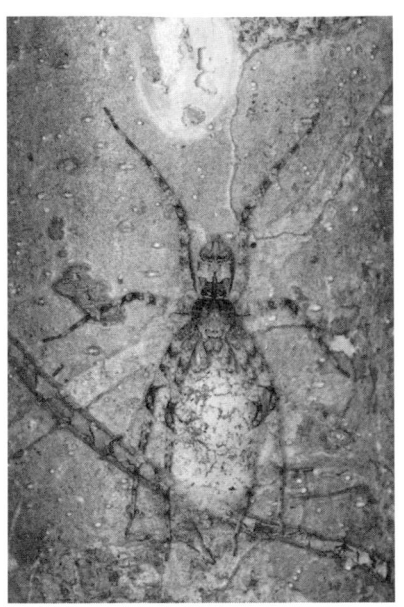

They are masters of camouflage, as the photograph of the lichen huntsman shows. There's a good reason for this, as free-range hunters are prey as much as predators. For some, death will come slowly as they are literally eaten alive by the larvae of wasps.

THE HUNTERS ARE ALSO THE HUNTED

Birds aren't the only winged predators to prey on spiders. There are also the wasps. We have potter wasps buzzing around the verandah, creating their nests in crevices in the brickwork and any other corner they find. I bought a new, elegant, thin-spouted watering can. When I tried to water from it, the spout was blocked with mud. I washed the blockage back down the spout only to find it blocked again the next day. Buzzing at the spout told me what was happening.

A persistent wasp was trying yet again to fill her chosen nest site. Twenty-four hours later the spout was plugged with mud. After an hour of gently forcing water down the spout, a glug and a gurgle told me the blockage had been dislodged into the can. I tipped twenty-five small spiders onto a towel.

A mud-dauber wasp (family Sphecidae) making a nest in the brickwork on the back porch to fill with live spiders. (Photo: D. and L. Kelly)

There appeared to be at least ten different species, yet there was not one I was familiar with. The little wasp had found each one in the vicinity of our back verandah and carried them to the spout, paralysed them, laid her larvae and stuffed them into the spout. I knew from my reading that the spiders were still alive. I felt it was a kindness to drown them.

Closer inspection revealed larvae attached to some of them, ready to feed on the still-living spiders.

One of the spiders with a wasp larva attached to her abdomen. (Photo: D. and L. Kelly)

Potter wasps, mason wasps or mud-daubers belong to the families Sphecidae and Vespidae commonly found around houses. Most are black or brown although many have striking markings in red, yellow, white or orange. Some have nests with multiple cells, each filled with spiders and larvae, while others have a single cell with a single larva. Some build exquisite little nests which look just like pots. It has been hypothesised that indigenous peoples based their designs on those of the wasps.

These macabre wasps have been found to be quite specific in the provisioning of their larval larder. The mud-dauber wasp, *Sceliphron laetum*, will provide a specific weight of spiders for her young, not a number. Bigger spiders, fewer spiders. *S. laetum* even adapts the total spider mass according to the sex of her larva. She places the spiders in order, lining up arachnid courses for the larva as it grows towards adulthood, when it finally emerges from the mud. The first spiders will be smaller, soft-bodied species, easy for the new larva to digest.

Spider wasps (family Pompilidae) are long-legged, solitary wasps. They place a single, paralysed spider in their nest or burrow, lay a single egg on the spider's abdomen and seal the nest or burrow.

I am not the first to be revolted by the parasitic behaviour of wasps. Charles Darwin found the gruesome behaviour of Ichneumon wasps, which infest many prey including spider egg sacs, incompatible with a Christian belief in the benevolence of nature. He wrote: 'I cannot persuade myself that a beneficent and omnipotent God would have designedly created the Ichneumonidae with the express intention of their feeding within the living bodies of Caterpillars, or that a cat should play with mice.'

All spiders suffer from parasitic mites, ticks, flies and wasps, even the tarantulas. Female tarantula hawk-wasps lure the large spiders from their burrows. Having stung the arachnid and laid its single egg the wasp entombs the paralysed spider, either in its own burrow or in a grave dug by the wasp beforehand.

Huntsman feeding on prey while a pompilid wasp larva feeds on it.
(Photo: Alan Henderson)

Another predator is the Gordian worm, that defies the concept of volume as it emerges from a spider's innards.

The aquatic adult worm, in the small phylum Nematomorpha, lays hundreds of eggs to be eaten by water-dwelling snails, insects and their larvae. The Gordian larvae turn into cysts. Should the worm get lucky, its aquatic host will leave the water and be gobbled up by a suitable terrestrial host, such as a spider. The worm larvae now becomes parasitic, feeding on the body tissue of the spider. After anything from four to twenty weeks, the adult worm leaves the dead or dying spider to find water and start again.

If birds, wasps, centipedes, worms, reptiles and mammals weren't enough, there's always other spiders. *Portia* is not the only spider to prey

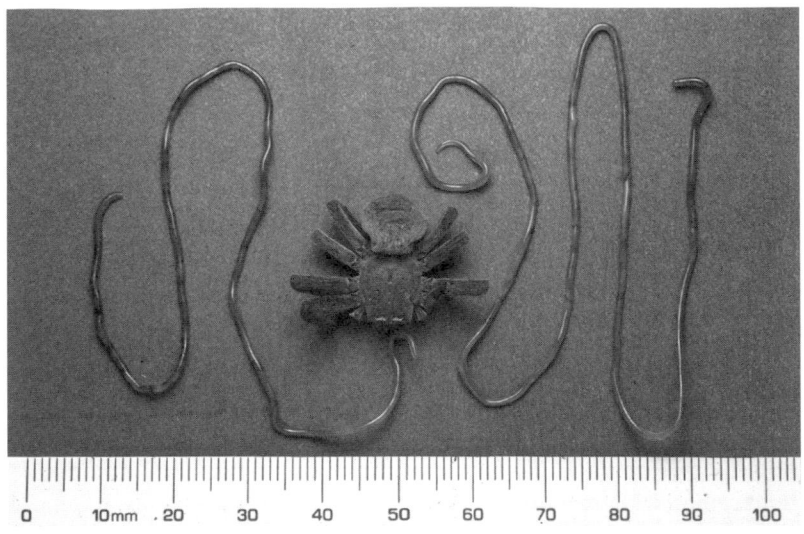

Two Gordian worms which have emerged from a single huntsman spider. It is hard to believe that they could fit inside! (Photo: Alan Henderson)

on her cousins. The family Mimetidae, known as pirate spiders, prey on web-building spiders. Like *Portia*, they attract their prey through vibrating the web, pretending to be a caught insect or a male seeking a mate. This is known as aggressive mimicry. Mimetids will also steal insects from another spider's web, or eat her eggs.

As we saw in Chapter 2, that familiar, placid daddy long-legs is not so harmless if you happen to be a spider. *Pholcus phalangioides* (family Pholcidae) will also wander over to other spiders' webs and use aggressive mimicry to lure their inhabitants to its gangly legs. Wrapping its prey at the tips of those long legs protects it from being bitten.

Pholcids are known to eat red-back and huntsmen spiders. They are also partial to the funnel-weaving *Tegenaria* species, including the hobo spider (*T. agrestis*), the domestic house spider (*T. domestica*) and the giant house spider (*T. duellica*). *Tegenaria* are found the world over, introduced into countries such as Australia, where they were not indigenous. It is the common daddy long-legs that helps keep *Tegenaria* populations in check.

Walking on the sticky and cribellate webs of other spiders can be difficult for daddy long-legs, which is why they are often seen cleaning their feet. Sometimes the pholcid will spin some of its own non-sticky web as it crosses the prey web, laying down an easier path for itself.

Like most theridiids, *Argyrodes* builds very sticky webs. Smaller than its better known cousins the widow spiders, *Argyrodes* hangs around on the webs of much larger spiders such as the golden orb weavers (Nephilidae) and garden orb weavers (Araneidae). *Argyrodes* steals the prey already caught by its host. By sneaking on the web while the host is wrapping the prey, the tiny thief will even feed on the same prey at the same time as the much larger host.

Taieria erebus (family Gnaphosidae) hunts in the open, as do most ground spiders, although some individuals have been observed making sticky webs, indicating that web-building is not uniform even within a species. But they can be even more variable than that. *T. erebus* has been observed to enter the tube web of *Segestria sp.* (Segestriidae), eat the inhabitant then remain in the web, catching prey in the same way as its previous owner.

Is it any wonder spiders hide from us whenever they can? Everything eats spiders, and we look just like huge predators. And sometimes we are. Chris Guest had read that tarantulas—the large primitive spiders—appear on menus in Cambodia and was curious to give it a try.

I'd been at the Central Market (Psar Thmey) in Phnom Penh earlier that day but they'd finished frying for the day, so I was quite excited to see a hawker selling fried tarantulas at Sisowath Quay opposite the Royal Palace. I chased after him and bought two for a dollar each.

Chris Guest eating tarantula in Cambodia. (Photo: Wilma Guest)

I'd seen them fried in peanut oil in a large pan outdoors in the central market. They were sold at highly inflated prices to tourists, but locals would eat them too. I believe crickets may have been more popular. The spiders tasted quite savoury, with crispy legs and a body that resembled egg yolk. The crickets were quite pleasant too. Much better than the stringy cicadas I tried in Bangkok.

Conceptually it's no worse than eating prawns. My partner Wilma didn't partake. I think she was a bit disturbed by the Psar Thmey vendor who chased her with handfuls of live spiders.

Tarantulas are part of the most feared group of spiders—the primitives. Once I got to know a few up close and personal, my fear turned to fascination yet again!

7

LIVE LONG AND PRIMITIVE—
THE MYGALOMORPHS

A 'mouse-eating' spider, which has recently been added to the zoological society's collection, can only be justified in existing if we consider it to be a supreme effort of nature in the direction of the hideous. It can stretch itself out to several inches, is as black as a bear and as hairy, and is as ugly as a nightmare. Nature constantly makes these efforts to teach us how horrible she can be when she likes; but she slips her horrors at us only one by one, and at long intervals, so that the general impression of her tenderness and grace may not be too roughly shocked.

New York newspaper article, *circa* 1880

I was walking in the footsteps of the expert, but only by luck. Ten years ago, when I was still far from recovered from my arachnophobia, I stayed at a resort in Lamington National Park in southern Queensland. Dr Robert Raven, the leading authority on the deadly funnel-web spiders, had been there only the week before. Raven had located a large number of burrows of different primitive species. Able, by this stage, to be comfortable around my web spinners, I was still mightily afraid of the big black horrible things that rear up and kill people, but I knew that I had to control this fear.

The ranger handed me Raven's list of twelve species of mygalomorphs, some with trapdoors and some with open burrows. 'This includes,' he said with relish, 'the tree funnel-web, *Hadronyche formidabilis*, considered one of the most deadly spiders in the world.' To be fair, he did add that they were very shy, and he didn't think there had been any recorded fatalities.

Off I went, following the ranger and my husband, Damian. I stuck to the middle of the track, expecting huge, ugly black creatures to rear at me from the ground and trees. How could the men be chatting so calmly? The ranger identified a particular section of the track which contained hundreds of burrows and proceeded to point them out. He showed us little trapdoors, open burrows and then, on the tree trunk, the concealed silken tube of a tree funnel-web. Once we knew what to look for, it was easy to see the tube and the radiating silk lines at the twin entrances.

'You'll have to return at night if you want any chance at photographs,' he chirped. The mere thought of walking this track at night with no ranger to protect us started me shaking.

Feeling pretty sick, I started down the track with Damian after night fell. I checked every step ahead with the torch to make sure there were no eight-legged monsters running at me, fangs poised to strike. I checked behind just as regularly, in case they were chasing me. Eventually, unscathed, we returned to the burrows and turned the torch on them. Lids closed and spidery legs disappeared. A solitary spider remained at its burrow entrance, its feet resting on the trip lines. I took a deep breath and one step towards it. It was gone.

From then on, as soon as we managed to sight a spider, it disappeared down its burrow. At the dreaded tree funnel-web site, too, we caught only a fleeting glimpse of spider. That was the night I grew to fully understand just how frightened spiders are of us. By the end of the expedition, I thought I had my fear of them under control, but there was only one way to find out.

It was time for me to confront a large, primitive spider up close. At the time, Alan Henderson and his brother Robbie were running Minibeast Wildlife, a fascinating invertebrate zoo. I had become a regular visitor, using the Hendersons' enthusiasm and knowledge to combat my fear. Alan took Olive, an Australian tarantula (*Selenocosmia sp.*) from her enclosure and placed her on the table in front of me. There was nothing between the massive creature of my nightmares and me. To my surprise, my first instinct was to pat her velvety abdomen, it looked so soft. I was not foolish enough to do so. Alan showed how she would become aggressive, when gently touched by a pencil, but I can honestly say I felt no fear. In fact, I thought Olive was beautiful. At that point I knew that I had my arachnophobia conquered.

*Olive, an Australian tarantula (*Selenocosmia sp.*). (Photo: Alan Henderson)

*An Arizona blond tarantula (*Aphonopelma chalcodes*) emerging from her burrow, displaying her huge chelicerae.* (Photo: Alan Henderson)

As we saw in Chapter 4, the most obvious distinguishing features of the primitives are their downwards-pointing fangs and two pairs of book lungs. The spiders rear up to expose their threatening fangs, although the aggressive stance is often one of self-defence.

Unlike most modern species, female primitives continue to moult for their entire lives. Many species live over twenty years, allowing them to grow very large. Males rarely moult once they are sexually mature, nor live long after mating.

The largest spiders in the world are the primitive spiders of the family Theraphosidae. It is the theraphosids which are now accepted as the true tarantulas. It is often thought that all primitive spiders are large. In fact, some species are less than a millimetre long; they are just not as noticeable as the large and threatening species which star in so many horror movies. It is also often mistakenly believed that a big spider means a lot of venom. The venom glands for the primitive spiders are contained wholly in their chelicerae. The large tarantulas actually have very small venom glands.

The primitives are common across the tropics and subtropics, as well as in the southern and western regions of the United States, but there are only a few primitive species in Europe. Britain, for example, has only two mygalomorph species—both purse-web spiders, genus *Atypus* in the family Atypidae. But what the Brits lack in quantity they gain in quality. Purse-web spiders display some of the most intriguing behaviour of all the spiders. Also found in the United States, Europe, Asia and Africa, *Atypus* lives in a silken tube, sealed at both ends, which she never leaves. So how does she eat and mate?

A clumsy, thick-bodied spider reaching a bit over a centimetre in body length, *Atypus'* tube of silk is mostly underground. The upper five or six centimetres lie on the ground, or are held upright by foliage, much like the inflated finger of a glove. The spider disguises her tube by weaving particles of soil into the mesh and waits for prey to walk on her trap. In *The World of Spiders*, W.S. Bristowe describes what happens next:

> The way in which an insect is seized can be watched by tickling the tube with a grass stem. Quite suddenly two shining curved fangs are violently protruded through the web; and it can be seen from their position that the spider strikes in a shark-like manner with lower side uppermost. If a buzzing fly is held against the tube the fangs pierce its body and hold it like fish-hooks. The fangs are, of course, hinged to the massive basal segment of the chelicerae and a clenching movement now pulls and presses the insect against the tube wall beneath which the basal segment lies. After a certain amount of tugging and jerking, in the course of which one fang at a time may be withdrawn from its victim to assist in the next operation, a slit appears in the tube wall through which the insect is pulled . . .

Once the insect is inside the tube, *Atypus* carries it down to the chamber at the bottom and then usually fastens it to one side whilst a return journey is made to the surface. Here the fangs are employed to pull the gaping edges of the slit together before it is patched by a number of zig-zag lateral sweeps of the spinnerets across it.

Male purse-web spiders have to make sure the female knows they are not prey, which they do by tapping out their status on the female's silk tube, usually late in autumn. Should his overtures be accepted, the male will tear a slit in the silk and join the female. After mating, the two will often cohabit in the tube, sometimes for months. If the male dies a natural death, or the female gets particularly hungry, she will eat him. No need to waste valuable protein. But many males leave at the end of winter. The young will stay with their mother for a year or so.

We don't have any purse-web spiders in Australia, but we do have over 450 primitive species, in ten different families. Years after following Dr Raven's footsteps along the paths of Lamington National Park, I was delighted to discover a small burrow in the narrow passage of rockery next to the Garret. I carefully photographed the owner, whose tiny, close-grouped eyes told me she wasn't a wolf spider. As I had arranged to meet Dr Robert Raven the next week, I took the photos with me, hoping that I had located my first primitive.

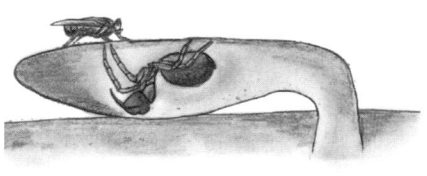

'You've got a young *Stanwellia* there,' he informed me—a Melbourne trapdoor spider (*Stanwellia sp.*, family

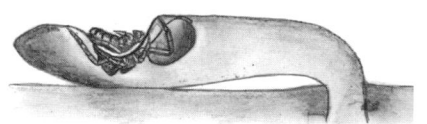

Purse-web spiders, family Atypidae, hunt from within a silk tube which the females never leave. (Adapted from Bristowe, p. 74)

Nemesiidae). I had been visiting the same spot every night for months, checking on Twiggy and her egg sacs, and I was amazed I hadn't noticed the burrow only a hand's width from her log.

Raven, too, was once an arachnophobe. His father was a mine engineer who terrified his small son with stories of lighting newspapers when down in the mine shaft and having red-backs drop down his back. When a zoology student at university Raven took to spiders to confront this fear. He specialised in our largest spiders, the Australian tarantulas, and our most deadly, the Sydney funnel-web and its relatives. Now he calls himself 'a spider man'.

On my return, I proudly went to check out Twiggy and my new primitive friend. There was another burrow, and another. And a good few more. Hunting around with the torch I found more than 50 burrows, all within a few metres of the original, many much larger. As long as I didn't thump around too much, each burrow had a spider sitting at the mouth, red-tinged legs elegantly spread ready to detect the slightest movement of approaching prey. They seemed unconcerned by the torch or the camera flash. Every night, as I visited Twiggy, 50 or more spiders had been sitting at the top of their burrows and I had never noticed them. That's how it is with spiders.

A few weeks later, I had over three hundred trapdoor burrows marked out in our large bush

Dr Robert Raven at his desk at the Queensland Museum.
(Photo: D. and L. Kelly)

garden within 50 metres of the house. Some were very large, many very small. Wherever I found a large burrow, I would usually find more within a few centimetres of it. Between each group of burrows would be stretches of ground which looked very similar to me, but in which there were no burrows. Most primitive species disperse on foot so these groups of burrows are known as matriarchal clusters.

I marked every burrow I found with a numbered plastic white knife, so I could find it easily at night when I did my rounds. By the time I had located three hundred burrows it looked like I was starting up a plastic cutlery plantation. The knives were my cuttings.

Then we had the first heavy rain after years of drought. Many of the small trapdoors in the softer ground next to the Garret were gone. I was briefly saddened by their loss. Very briefly. I turned the torch on part of the bank just above the lost burrow site, and there was a group of new burrows, each with a little trapdoor spider at its entrance. The following

*Annie, a Melbourne trapdoor spider, (*Stanwellia sp.*), adding a grass waterway with her spinnerets to divert the rain around her burrow. With her head down the burrow she is attaching the grass by feel alone.* (Photo: D. and L. Kelly)

Having protected her burrow from the rain, Annie is ready to wait for prey. (Photo: D. and L. Kelly)

summer most covered their burrows, remaining underground through the heat and dry.

All over the world are tracts of ground riddled with burrows. We walk the surface, ignorant of the fact that beneath our feet are hundreds, if not thousands, of spiders who are aware of our presence and will consequently stay well hidden.

Trapdoor spiders are incredible in the variety of their burrows and the brilliance with which they use silk. My particular genus of trapdoors don't build doors, but many are true to their common name. Having read about the ingenious trappings of the trapdoor burrows, I was very keen to learn more.

On a visit to Perth, I nervously prepared for an interview with one of the world's authorities on trapdoor spiders. I knew Professor Barbara York Main was well beyond her allotted three-score years and ten and part of me wondered if she would still be lucid enough for me to talk to. I learned a great deal about trapdoors that day. I also learned an important lesson about age and my own attitudes.

I had asked Dr Mark Harvey, at the Museum of Western Australia, how he would describe Professor Main. He said only two words, 'An inspiration' and his colleagues gathered in the tea room all nodded and said no more. As I waited in reception at the University of Western Australia's School of Animal Biology, the reception staff spoke of Professor Main in awe. I soon discovered why. In strode a fit and lively woman, who started talking enthusiastically about spiders and continued for the next three hours. Not one word was dull. Piling into her new four-wheel drive, essential for her fieldwork in the state's wheatbelt, we went to a nearby shopping centre to grab some dinner so we could keep talking. Walking from the car to the shops, I struggled to keep up with her. Decades younger, and considering myself to be pretty fit, I resolved never again to judge someone on their age.

Professor Barbara York Main in her office at the University of Western Australia. (Photo: D. and L. Kelly)

As the oldest member of staff at the university, Professor Main still lectured and conducted extensive field research in remote areas. We talked for three more hours, and wandered her backyard searching for spiders. There are only two words to describe Professor Barbara York Main—an inspiration.

ARTISTS OF LEAF, TWIG AND STONE

Trapdoor spiders are the architects of the arachnid world. Found over much of the world, they need to protect themselves against dehydration and flooding. Preyed upon by wasps, large centipedes and scorpions, they have evolved a wide range of burrow designs to protect themselves and their young.

Many trapdoor spiders protect themselves just by closing their doors and hanging on to them from beneath. They are surprisingly strong, bracing themselves against the burrow walls. The genus *Cyclocosmia* (family Ctenizidae), found in the United States, China, Thailand, Mexico and Guatemala, has an armour-plated flattened rear end of its abdomen, which it wedges into the sides of the burrow, blocking the entrance and giving a solid defence against attack. Like the other members of the widespread family Ctenizidae, they build a thick, cork-lid to close their burrow. The family Cyrtaucheniidae is widespread over much of the world. Most members of this family, but not all, build wafer-thin doors to their burrows.

Some trapdoors have flaps of silk, often disguised with stones or soil, while others have no door at all. My own Melbourne trapdoors (*Stanwellia sp.*, family Nemesiidae) have no door, but often cover their burrows with a thin layer of silk.

Most trapdoors spend their entire lives in their burrows, which are wallpapered with silk. The level of ingenuity displayed in creating these homes is amazing. Some glue soil and litter fragments into lids to ensure they blend with their surrounding soil. The untrained eye passes over them without ever registering their existence. As the spider grows and enlarges its burrow, it tears down its old wallpaper and redecorates with new silk. Some may enlarge the lids of their burrows, leaving rings which are sometimes visible.

Main lifts the trapdoor on an Anidiops villosus *burrow in a bucket in her office.* (Photo: D. and L. Kelly)

Professor Main showed me real trapdoors in buckets of sand as well as carefully preserved excavated burrows.

One of Main's favourites is *Anidiops villosus* (family Idiopidae). *Anidiops villosus* has a soil- and litter-covered door at the top of its burrow, and a silk sock halfway down. The top of the silk lining of the bottom half of the burrow is loosely attached to the wall, and detached when the spider wishes to dispose of its food scraps. Sewn neatly back into place, the rubbish-bag acts as a defence. When under attack, the spider releases the sock-top completely, which creates a false bottom to the burrow, effectively covered with the food remains predators are used to finding at the bottom of empty burrows. Main has found centipedes and spider-hunting scorpions on top of the sock, unaware of *Anidiops* concealed beneath them.

I thought that was unbeatable until Main started talking about the pellet spider. As she wrote in her book, *Spiders*:

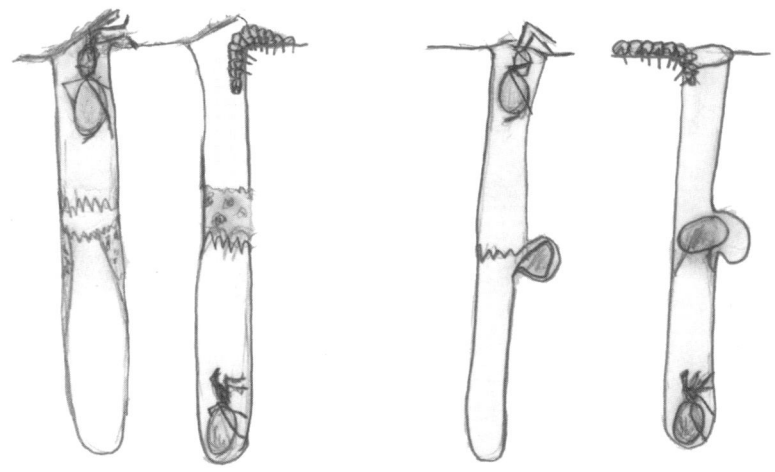

The burrow of Anidiops villosus *showing the false bottom generated with a sock of silk. The pellet spider,* Stanwellia nebulosa, *builds a burrow with a pellet to protect itself from intruders.* (Adapted from *Spiders* by Barbara York Main)

A common South Australian spider, *Stanwellia nebulosa* or the pellet spider builds an elaborate variation of the sock . . . Only the lower part of this spider's burrow is lined with silk. About half way up the lining forms a loose, upstanding collar to one side of which is attached the neck end of a pear-shaped pebble. When the collar is open, the pebble fits into a pocket in the soil wall of the nest. If disturbed from above the spider is able to tug on the collar from below and draw it closed, meanwhile pulling the pebble down on top of it and thus blocking the burrow. The pebble, being pear-shaped, is heavier at one end, thus when the spider chooses to push the collar open again, the counterweighted pebble drops neatly back into its socket. When I first observed these ingenious nests I marvelled at the symmetry of the pebbles. They were all perfect pear shapes but I could never find any similarly shaped pebbles on the ground! Where did the spiders get them? Then I realised that the spiders made the pebbles or pellets by combining silk and saliva into mud, which they then carefully moulded into shape. Also the little pocket in the wall of the burrow was scooped out and the walls packed down until the pebble made a perfect but loose fit.

The lidded trapdoor species peer out from the edge of their capped domains, waiting for the patter of insect feet. The hinged lids restrict the angles at which the spiders can detect prey. A strongly hinged lid offers good protection, but restricts the spider's foraging angle to as little as 180 degrees. If there is no lid, the spider has a 360-degree range, but little protection. The citrine spider (*Teyl luculentus*, family Nemesiidae) pushes its silken lid fully open to lie flat on the ground to use the full 360-degree range.

Many trapdoors use trip lines of leaves and twigs, especially those that feed on ants. Ants tend to follow the line of a twig or blade of grass, and careful positioning takes the insects directly to the waiting spider, which can leap to life with alarming rapidity. I was shocked when

I realised how quickly a *Stanwellia* of the same species as mine could move. Alan Henderson, now Curator of Live Exhibits at the Melbourne Museum, fed the spider a live cricket for a group of students who displayed a great deal of ghoulish glee. It was all over before you could say 'trapdoor'.

The variety of entrances to my hundreds of *Stanwellia* burrows enthrals me. The trapdoors are often in terrain which is so hard it is almost impossible for me to insert my plastic-knife marker. Some spiders burrow through the compacted surface of gravel paths, arranging stones in a neat circle around the entrance; others use leaves or strands of grass, either to deflect water or to make trip lines. I've seen burrows on slopes with little soil turrets above the entrance, to protect them when the rain strikes; others have no adornment at all. Yet they are all made by the same species.

The primitives are much more sensitive to drying out than their modern cousins. Barbara York Main tells how this impacts on both spiders and campers in outback Western Australia:

*A Melbourne trapdoor spider (*Stanwellia sp.*), just inside her burrow entrance, to which she has drawn live blades of grass from a nearby plant to guide insects to her waiting fangs.* (Photo: D. and L. Kelly)

This Melbourne trapdoor spider burrowed through the hard surface of a compacted gravel path, securing a circle of stones with silk. (Photo: D. and L. Kelly)

A Melbourne trapdoor spider has used twigs to direct insects to her burrow. She has temporarily webbed over her burrow, possibly to moult.
(Photo: D. and L. Kelly)

Another Melbourne trapdoor spider using leaves and twigs to direct traffic. A passing ant on one of her leaves is drawing her from the burrow even though it is still daylight.
(Photo: D. and L. Kelly)

It is significant that in much of the interior desert regions some of the spiders are opportunistic: they can moult, mate and disperse any time of the year but only during or after rain, which usually is associated with summer thunderstorms. This often results in a mass irruption of male spiders which can turn a campsite into pandemonium. This is what we experienced one hot (31° C) muggy December evening at Magooninya near Balladonia in Western Australia. With the first drops of rain of an impending thunderstorm, male diplurids seemed to scatter like dry leaves between the campfires of our party of ten. However it was a good haul for me as everyone dashed around putting upturned bottles over scurrying spiders. I collected males of three diplurid species and one barychelid.

When dead black spiders were found in my neighbour's swimming pool, I thought they must be the same species as my trapdoors. Males often end up in swimming pools when they go wandering in search of females. Needing a firm classification for my spiders, I took them to

Alan Henderson, who used a magnifier to check the eye pattern. He drew some pictures of spider heads on his whiteboard. Instead of the close cluster of eight eyes you would expect with a trapdoor, there was a row of eyes right across the carapace.

'Male mouse spiders,' he announced. '*Missulena*.'

I described my reluctance to touch them despite their being clearly dead. Henderson told me how he had once collected one from the bottom of a pond and laid the floppy, limp, inert body on a dry towel. Half-an-hour later it stood up and walked away. Primitive spiders are known to be able to survive under water for days.

Mouse spiders (family Actinopodidae) are so called because of a mistaken belief that their burrows were extremely deep, like those of burrowing mice. They are very deep for spiders—up to 30 centimetres—and have twin entries with silken trapdoors on each. Mouse spiders vary in body length from one to three centimetres. My local species, almost certainly *Missulena bradleyi*, are in the middle of this range. Mouse spiders are found in Australia, with one species in Chile. Their venom is potentially the most deadly in the world, but the spiders rarely release the venom when they bite, although they are particularly aggressive. I clearly have a significant population of them, yet have never found a single burrow. (See Plate 32.)

I was very excited. I now had at least three families of burrowing spider—trapdoors, wolf spiders and, now, mouse spiders. I could distinguish my trapdoor burrows from the wolf spider burrows, often side-by-side, by the trapdoors' thick silken lining which descends deep down into the ground. I wondered how so many different burrowing spiders could occupy the same ecological niche? Given their aggressive carnivorous tendencies, why weren't they consuming each other?

A much better authority than me had asked the same question. The difference was that she went on to answer it. In her book, *Spiders*, Barbara York Main noted that each of the five species of burrowing spider she discovered in a 40-hectare area of bush lived in a slightly different habitat, or had a different type of burrow. For example, a wolf spider and a trapdoor species that were living in the same surface environment had superficially identical, circular open burrow entrances. There the resemblance stopped.

> when we dug the burrows out we found that some stopped at about twenty centimetres while others penetrated the hard-pan. It turned out that the deeper burrows *all* belonged to the mygalomorph species, the citrine spider *Teyl luculentus,* while the burrows terminating at the hard-pan were either those of the lycosids or juvenile specimens of the citrine spider. The significance of this seemed pretty obvious.
>
> Firstly, lycosids are not equipped to dig burrows in very hard compacted soil whereas many mygalomorphs (including the citrine spider) have special tooth-like spines on the front of the chelicerae with which to pick at the soil and break it up into removable fragments. Secondly, mygalomorphs are all long-lived and take at least four or five years to mature whereas the lifespan of a lycosid is at most two years and of many species not more than one year. The burrows penetrating the hard-pan would be insulated against summer drought characteristic of the region, whereas spiders with burrows terminating above the hard-pan would be liable to desiccation and heat stress during an extreme summer. Probably most of the lycosids would live out their lives before being subjected to an unfavourable summer, while the mygalomorphs at greater depth would be protected.

After reading this, I went out and studied my own burrows. All the burrows in the softer soil, such as the vegetable patch and disturbed garden beds, belonged to lycosids. Where the ground was harder but with a soft surface layer of moss, leaf matter and soil, the two families overlapped. In the very hard clay and quartz rock terrain, I nicknamed the lycosids I had found 'BBLW'—Big Burrow Little Wolf—as tiny spiders peered from the humungous entrances of burrows clearly excavated by others.

Very soon I noticed that trapdoor and lycosid burrows were sometimes covered with silk. Most were not, but a few were almost always webbed in. If a group was doing it, then it was possibly a response to the environment, perhaps the heat or humidity of the air temperature. If it was one or two individuals, then perhaps they were moulting. Or young had hatched. I have enough to explore with my population of burrowers to last a lifetime.

One of the greatest pleasures I have gained from my spider observations is the chance to experience my own little patch of bush on an invertebrate scale. Instead of eight hectares of dry open bush, I now see eight hectares as a complex multitude of mini-environments, each with their own resident population—spiders and insects, slugs, millipedes and centipedes, snails and skinks. Each tiny locale has its own dramas being played out as the spiders eat the insects, and the centipedes attack the spiders; as the wasps who don't get caught in the webs parasitise spiders who aren't well enough hidden; and as the birds attack and the echidnas excavate.

How many mini-enviroments will you find in your own backyard? Suburban gardens, apartment balconies, nature strips—each has its particular miniature ecosystem for you to explore, observe and enjoy.

TARANTULAS

An American couple went to Mexico and brought home a rare and precious cactus. They planted it in their living room and cared for it. One hot summer's day they watered their cactus. It started moving. Vibrating and expanding. They rang their state department of agriculture who told them to close all windows and doors, lock the house and get out of there as quickly as they could. They escaped just in time. Hundreds of deadly tarantulas burst from the cactus only moments after they left the house.

Or so the story goes. The spider-spewing prickly plant story has been told and retold in newspapers and on the internet. It has absolutely no basis in fact. No spider burrows into plants to burst forth later in an explosion of hairy legs but, thanks to the excesses of the media, tarantulas have become the much-maligned giants of the arachnid world. In the flesh, they are beautiful creatures, with none of the horrible habits commonly ascribed to them.

One version of the tarantula story starts in a small town called Taranto in southern Italy. In the sixteenth and seventeenth centuries, a strange and mysterious disease broke out every time the days grew long and summer arrived. The bite of a large, hairy wolf spider (*Lycosa tarentula*), was blamed for the townsfolk's woes. Heightened excitability and restlessness gripped the victims who, it was believed, needed to engage in frenzied dancing to prevent certain death. A wild dance involving rapidly swirling couples—the Tarantella—evolved as the cure. (Of course, this unorthodox therapy may have had something to do with getting around religious prohibitions against dancing.)

It is now known that the maligned wolf spiders are harmless. Those who really did become ill from a spider bite had probably been bitten by the European or Mediterranean black widow, sometimes called the malmignatte spider, *Latrodectus tredecimguttatus*. There are many other theories on the real cause of the symptoms, but it is unlikely that spiders were involved at all.

The name 'tarantula' stuck, however, and many Europeans still refer to wolf spiders as 'tarantulas'. Only the large, hairy spiders of the family Theraphosidae are now referred to by arachnologists as 'tarantulas', and it is the theraphosids we will be looking at for the rest of this chapter.

With 908 species, the family Theraphosidae is generally broken up into Old World (Asia, Africa, Europe and Australia) and New World (The Americas). The New World can claim most identified tarantula species. Australia has only half-a-dozen species in a few genera, while mainland Europe has even fewer.

Tarantulas are the largest spiders in the world. Africans call them baboon spiders; to Asians they are tiger or bird spiders. In Australia, they are barking or whistling spiders while in the Americas they are just tarantulas.

The largest of the largest is the goliath birdeater tarantula (*Theraphosa blondi*), which can reach a leg span of nearly 30 centimetres and a weight of over 100 grams. Despite its common name, it poses no threat to the birds. The same cannot be said for the insects, frogs and mice which inhabit the wet rainforests of north-eastern South America. Like the rest of the New World species, the goliath is unlikely to bite, but will defend itself with irritating barbed hairs known as urticating setae. These hairs

A goliath birdeater tarantula, Theraphosa blondi, *the largest spider in the world.* (Photo: Alan Henderson)

are located on the spider's abdomen. Some spiders will deliver their barbs by pressing themselves directly on their enemy, but most will use their rear legs to direct a shower of barbs at an attacker. Some species even line their retreats and protect their egg sacs with their barbed hairs, possibly to discourage predators who prey on the eggs and young.

There are basically three lifestyles among theraphosids. Arboreal tarantulas live in trees and bushes in specially constructed silken tube webs, holes in the trunk, behind loose bark, or among upper-storey plant growth. Those known as bird spiders have been observed going into free-fall to avoid danger, spreading their hairy legs to form an arachnid parachute. The second group of theraphosids are believed to do without a permanent home, taking refuge under foliage when they need to. The third group is the largest—those who live in burrows. One of the most stunning of the New World burrowers is so gentle it is much favoured as a pet. The Mexican red-kneed tarantula (*Brachypelma smithi*) lives both in burrows and under rocks in the dry Pacific coastal region of Mexico. It preys on large insects and can live for more than twenty years. Usually very docile, it will throw off barbed hairs from its abdomen if provoked. These beautiful spiders have been collected for the pet trade to such an extent that they are now considered endangered and have been listed by CITES (the Convention on International Trade in Endangered Species of Wild Fauna and Flora). CITES is an international agreement between governments intended to ensure that international trade in specimens of wild animals and plants does not threaten species' survival. At the time of writing, the only spiders listed by CITES are about twenty tarantulas out of the 40 000 spider species now described.

Theraphosids can deliver a painful bite because of the sheer size of their fangs, but their venom does not seem to be harmful to humans. Mostly, they seem to be pretty gentle creatures, which rely on threatening behaviour rather than actual aggression to deter predators. Many tarantula species produce threatening sounds by means of specially developed hairs. This is known as stridulation. In both males and females, various appendages carry these stiff bristles—chelicerae, coxal segments of legs and maxillae. By rubbing opposing patches of these stridulating bristles together, the spiders can produce hissing and rasping sounds. Although we can hear some of them, other spiders sense them as vibrations. The goliath birdeater can produce a hissing noise loud enough to be heard over distances of more than four metres.

Stridulation is also known among some of the modern spiders. The male wolf spider *Pardosa fulvipes* (family Lycosidae), for example, uses spiny bristles on his legs to rub over the rills on the cover of his book lungs. It is thought that stridulation may play some part in courtship as well as defence, as it is often only the male of the species that stridulates.

The whistling spider (*Selenocosmia crassipes*) lives in tropical north-eastern Australia and Papua New Guinea and feeds on insects and small vertebrates like frogs. All of Australia's tarantulas 'whistle', but Australian tarantulas differ from those in South America in the way they produce the sound. The Australian species have spines and picks on the opposing faces of the mouthparts known as maxillae. When aggravated, the spider rubs its maxillae together to make an audible whistle or hiss. The noise can be heard a few metres away.

As it is illegal to import the more docile tarantulas kept as pets in other countries, the pet trade in Australia revolves around this species, which does occasionally bite. Although its bite is not harmful to humans, it has been known to kill small mammals such as puppies and kittens.

AS PETS

If you want to keep a tarantula as a pet, here are a few basic guidelines.

Some of the arboreal tarantulas can be kept as pets, but the most popular are the New World burrowing species. These can be housed in a small, glass fish-tank. Remember, however, that tarantulas can walk up glass and are strong enough to open lightweight lids and wander off, to be stumbled on by some unsuspecting visitor. As they are cannibals, it is a good idea to have a separate tank for each one. Tarantulas can go without food for over a month, but most owners feed their pets with about four live crickets a week, supplemented with a variety of other arthropods.

It is not cruel to keep a spider in a small tank as long as there is enough soil for it to burrow. In the wild, many species rarely venture more than a few centimetres from their burrow entrance with the exception of mature males, for which instinct tells them to wander in search of females. Try to keep a mature male in captivity without a supply of females, and you will have a large, strong, determined spider constantly trying to escape.

Temperature and humidity are far more important to the spider than living space. The tank needs to be kept between 22 and 30 degrees Celsius. If you heat only part of the tank, your spider will be able to regulate its own body temperature by moving. Do *not* heat the tank with lights. As nocturnal hunters, tarantulas don't like light.

Decorations are more important to you than the spider. Despite appearances, tarantulas are extremely fragile, easily damaged creatures. Too many unfortunates have been caught in fancy little fish-tank bridges, added to satisfy the owner's sense of décor. Given the fragile nature of a spider's abdomen, cacti are not recommended. Placing a spider tank near a sunlit window for effect will more than likely kill its inhabitant. Tarantulas do not bounce and falls can be fatal. It's not a good idea to give your pet to a visitor to hold. A sudden fright and a dropped spider will leave you with one less pet.

Australia's very strict quarantine laws ban the importation of *any* foreign species. As long as there are fools to buy them, however, smugglers will try to bring in New World tarantulas and other 'desirable species'. Museum Victoria is an approved quarantine site where most confiscated spiders can live out their lives. Within the museum's own secure premises, three separately keyed locks stand between the handful of authorised staff and the spiders. All vents are covered with 100-micron mesh, every crack and crevice is sealed and all surfaces are painted white and brightly lit 24 hours a day. As tarantulas dislike the light, dark boxes are placed in each chamber to attract any which might escape. And, finally, only one sex of each species is held, to ensure there is no breeding.

As a recovered arachnophobe, I knew the final stage in my journey would be to hold a tarantula and allow it to walk on me. And so I did.

I was very nervous the night I met with tarantula owner Jennifer Burge in Texas. I had no fear of looking at live spiders or even allowing tiny salticids to wander over my hands. However, I was very afraid that, confronted with the touch of a huge hairy spider, I would revert to my old ways. If I should jump and drop the spider, I could kill it.

Jennifer arrived with Arabella, a pink zebra beauty (*Eupalaestrus campestratus*), Dozer, a young curly hair (*Brachypelma albopilosum*) and the impressive Albus Bumblebee, an Arizona or Mexican blond (*Aphonopelma chalcodes*). I asked why she chose spiders as pets rather than a cute puppy. She explained:

> I learn something new every day. We don't know even half of everything there is to know. They are so different from us biologically. They are very quiet roommates. They are low maintenance. They never complain. There are people who will argue that they don't have person-alities, only temperaments, but they are not the same thing. They definitely have individual personalities.

As it happened, Dozer was too busy eating. The usually docile Arabella made a run for it, relaxing only when Jennifer put her very gently back into her container. But Albus was a gem. With her hand under mine—out of concern for Albus, not me—Jennifer carefully placed Albus on my hands. There was no fear at all. He was gorgeous!

Arachnophobe no more.
(Photo: Peter Turlo)

8

NO-ONE DOES IT
LIKE A SPIDER

Conflict between the sexes occurs because males try to mate with every female they encounter. Females, meanwhile, choose only the strongest male to father their young and are vicious in their rejection of others. The mating game is played right across the animal world, but spiders take it to quirky extremes.

There is a common misconception that all male spiders die at the venom-dripping tips of their cannibalistic mates' fangs—tragic victims of their sexual impulses. The truth is that the males of most species leave the mating arena alive—even if some have to make a fairly hasty retreat.

Spiders' mating behaviour can only be interpreted by taking their unique arachnid biology into account. For most species, two effectively blind carnivores must meet and mate when each is almost indistinguishable from the other's last meal. As it is the male who approaches the female, he must make that distinction very, very clear to her.

Helen and Frank were a match made in huntsman heaven. This pair of Australia's giant huntsmen (*Holconia immanis*, family Sparassidae) each had their own terrarium at the home of Alan Henderson, Curator of Live Exhibits at Museum Victoria.

Frank's pedipalps were swollen like boxing gloves, indicating that he had reached maturity. Helen was significantly larger in body size—the female *Holconia* being much more robust than the male—but Frank was her equal in leg span. When Frank was introduced into Helen's spacious terrarium the initial signs were not promising. They mostly ignored each other, with Helen eventually displaying signs of aggression. Frank was removed to his own terrarium. The timing obviously wasn't right. A previous huntsman pairing Henderson had made had not gone well. The male had moved so quickly that he had killed the female before Henderson could intervene.

A few weeks later the reason for their lack of romance was revealed. Helen moulted. She had not been fully mature.

Frank was introduced again and, sensing Helen's pheromones, immediately began to explore his new environment by touching the ground with his pedipalps. He moved around the terrarium, constantly touching the ground and walls, locked in to Helen's trail. Every so often his whole body would begin to shudder and he would stop moving until the tremors had passed.

After a few minutes, Frank found Helen and made contact with his long front legs. As soon as he touched her, he froze momentarily. Then he started shuddering again. Frank began tapping gently on Helen's legs and body with his long forelegs, an overture to which she obviously responded as there was no sign of aggression. Helen was moving gently around, accepting Frank's constant tapping, then she appeared to go into a trance-like state.

Frank didn't just climb straight on and mate. He kept circling her, touching her all the time, ensuring that he had her total consent. Huntsmen don't have good eyesight so touch is a crucial part of their mating ritual. After a few more minutes Helen was flat on the ground, not moving at all. Frank climbed over her, reached over with his pedipalps and lifted her abdomen. Keeping his own body at right angles to hers, he reached his left pedipalp into her epigynum.

For the next few hours Helen remained in her trance while Frank crouched over her, from time to time changing palps. When they separated, each wandered off to opposite sides of the terrarium and rested on the walls.

Frank was moved back to his own terrarium, and Helen started feeding. She ate and ate, becoming bigger and bigger until she was the largest *Holconia* Henderson had ever seen. A few weeks after mating Helen produced an egg sac in the lid of her terrarium. As Helen stayed

Helen, a female huntsman, Holconia immanis. (Photo: Alan Henderson)

Frank makes his entrance.
(Photo: Alan Henderson)

with her egg sac at all times, this made it pretty difficult for Henderson to open the terrarium without damaging Helen or her sac.

Another few weeks passed and her young emerged. As Henderson remembers, with a wry smile, 'I didn't seal the holes on the lid of her terrarium quickly enough. We ended up with a hundred tiny Franks and Helens all over the house.'

Helen and Frank mating. (Photo: Alan Henderson)

Frank's embolus, the tip of his palp engorged with semen.
(Photo: Alan Henderson)

If you are going to have huntsmen babies by the hundred roaming your home, it is a very good idea to be married to someone who shares your passion for them. Deanna Henderson is a Senior Keeper at Museum Victoria, and shares her husband's passion for mini-beasts. While Helen was producing her young, Deanna was working towards a similar goal. And so was Tiger.

Tiger is a tiger huntsman who doesn't have a scientific name—yet. She is the first of her kind known in captivity, and is

Helen with her egg sac on the lid of her terrarium.
(Photo: Alan Henderson)

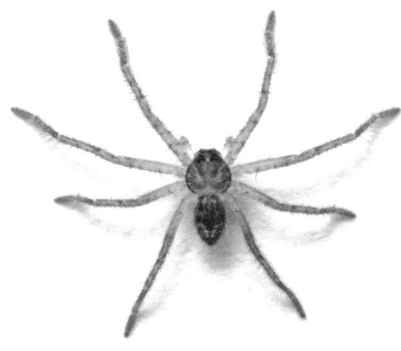

Helen and Frank's offspring, a miniature of its parents.
(Photo: Alan Henderson)

the prize exhibit in the museum's *Bugs Alive!* display. Henderson suspects she is a new species in the genus *Typostola*. The only way to know for sure is for her dead body to be shoved under a microscope, and Henderson isn't ready for that just yet!

Henderson collected Tiger early in December 2006. By May 2007, the museum staff had given up hope of her being fertile, but then she grew and produced her egg sac. Tiger must have mated over five months before and stored the sperm until she was ready to lay her eggs. The young emerged on 2 May, the very same day Deanna and Alan's daughter, Tayen, was born. For all her effort, Deanna had produced one child. Tiger produced hundreds, and months later did so again, still using the sperm she had stored before coming to the museum.

But what about Frank and Helen? Unfortunately, the romance didn't last. When Frank was reintroduced into Helen's terrarium he approached her in exactly the same manner as before but Helen became aggressive. Frank fled to the other side of the terrarium and stayed there, perfectly still. Henderson removed Frank for his own safety. Helen went on to lay another sac of eggs. She simply didn't need Frank any more.

Both Helen and Tiger were able to reproduce second egg sacs because they had stored their mates' sperm. How do female spiders do this? In fact, how do spiders do *it*? It's time to look at the mechanics of mating.

SEXUAL REPRODUCTION—THE SPIDER'S WAY

A mature male spider displays his status in his palps.

As discussed in Chapter 3, the palps are two leg-like structures next to the chelicerae. Unlike the actual legs, which have seven segments, the palps have only six, lacking the metatarsus. Female palps stay like shortened legs and are generally used for carrying and manoeuvring prey. The male emerges from his final moult with palps now specialised for the storage and transfer of sperm. The palps have become copulatory organs, unlike anything found in any other arthropod. For one thing, they are the copulatory organs, but not where the sperm is produced. The two acts—sperm production and copulation—do not happen at the same time or in the same place. Of course, there are exceptions. Some males stop the courting ritual to charge their palps with sperm but most get the job done first. In anthropomorphic terms, it's a case of the male masturbating then going in search of a female with sperm in hand.

To charge his palps with sperm, a male spider transfers some of the sperm fluid from his internal testes through his genital opening, the genopore, onto a sheet of silken web he has prepared—the sperm web. At the tip of his palp is a narrow, coiled tube called the embolus,

*A male social huntsman (*Delena cancerides, *family Sparassidae), has entered the house in search of a female.* (Photo: D. and L. Kelly)

which the spider uses to suck up the sperm. The sperm is then stored in the engorged bulb until needed.

With charged palps, the male seeks a female that is his perfect match. That is not a bit of romantic anthropomorphism, but a physical necessity. The degree of modification of the male palp in any given species is matched to the complexity, or lack of it, of the female. Most female spiders have two genital pores covered by a sclerotised plate known as the epigyne. These are known as entelegyne species. Haplogyne spiders, such as the daddy long-legs, have a single opening and no epigyne. The male needs to insert the sperm-laden palp into the female's genital pore or pores. The semen is then sucked into one of the female's two long, coiled sperm ducts.

The shape of the external sexual organs are so specific to a given spider species, that they are often used as the definitive guide to classification. In most cases, the male palpal 'key' fits only into the

A male garden orb weaver with engorged palps in his diurnal retreat having just done his final moult. He was gone the following day. (Photo: D. and L. Kelly)

female 'lock' of his own species. The simplest form of the male palp is a bit like an eye dropper, with a flexible bulb filled with semen. If the male has a long, convoluted embolus, then the female of his species must have a matching convoluted sperm duct.

In some species, such as the golden orb weaver, *Nephila clavipes*, and the widow spiders, *Latrodectus*, the embolus will stretch out into a long, spiralled tube more than double the length of the male's body! This lengthy embolus can break off during mating and remain in the female's epigyne. It has been hypothesised that this remaining 'plug' will stop further mating. Arachnologists have shown that the females may still mate again, and that damaged males can also mate again. Spider sexual organs are so varied and complex that this is an area in which there is still a lot to learn.

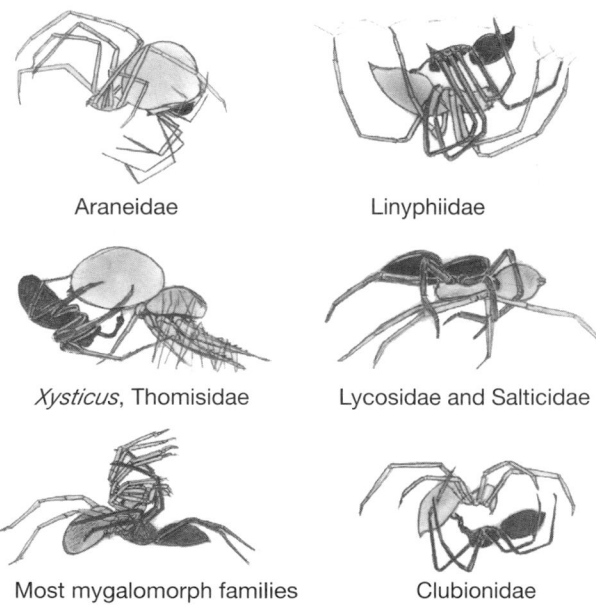

Araneidae   Linyphiidae

Xysticus, Thomisidae   Lycosidae and Salticidae

Most mygalomorph families   Clubionidae

Typical sexual positions for some spider families. (Diagram: L. Kelly)

The male's sperm passes down the female's sperm duct into the spermathecae where it is stored until it is needed to fertilise the eggs. The female may be ready to fertilise the eggs fairly soon, or she may retain the sperm for months—until she is ready to lay. Once the female has mated, she aggressively seeks prey and her ovaries expand visibly.

Although the genetalia of the male and female must match exactly, which tends to ensure same-species sex, behaviour is a key indicator of whether a female will accept a male's sexual advances. Two species of wolf spider (*Schizocosa ocreata* and *Schizocosa rovneri*) have almost identical genital organs. Under normal conditions, the females will mate only with males whose behaviour indicates they are the same species. When females of either species were briefly anaesthetised with carbon dioxide, the males of the other species would mount them and successfully copulate. Fertile eggs resulted in hybrid young.

SIGNALLING HIS STATUS

Male spiders of species with poor sight use touch to alert females to their status as potential mates. For example, they might twang a female's web in a particular way, thump the ground or touch her legs.

Species which have better eyesight, the wolf and the jumping spiders for example, incorporate elaborate visual displays into their mating rituals. Current opinion holds that these displays, which can be spectacular, could fill a dual role. They may not only enable the female to identify a male of her own species, but also enable her to choose the fittest of the available males.

The male jumping spider will approach the female with an elaborate dance. Each species has its own distinctive choreography. Waving his legs and palps in jerky, yet rhythmic, motions, the male displays his colouring to great effect. If his display is successful, he will mate quickly

A jumping spider, family Salticidae, signals his intentions with a display which indicates to the female he is a member of her species.
(Photo: Alan Henderson)

and leave. When two males meet each other, the display is equally impressive, but the dance is different, with a different message. Circling each other, with front legs spread, if one doesn't clearly dominate, they will fight. It is not usually a fight to the

Two male long-jawed jumping spiders sizing each other up for battle.
(Photo: Alan Henderson)

death, though, just a fight to dominate the hunting space or a nearby female. The defeated male usually turns and retreats.

One of the nursery-web spiders, *Pisaura mirabilis*, gives gifts of wrapped-up prey to his potential partner. The female nursery-web spider is prone to cannibalising her partners and the male will put on a remarkable death-feigning display known as thanatosis, as part of the courtship ritual. Many animal species use thanatosis to deter potential predators, but spiders are the only animal to have made it part of the sexual act. As the male offers up his precious gift, the female approaches. She usually shows interest in the gift but can sometimes attack its bearer, at which point the male collapses into a death-like stillness, still holding his gift. As the female starts sucking the juices from his offering, the male will cautiously revive and use her momentary distraction to initiate copulation. Despite his offering, the male may end up eaten as well when the mating is done.

LIVING TO MATE AGAIN

Some spider species have worked out ingenious ways to mate and live to mate again. They use bondage. Some crab spiders of the genus *Xysticus* (family Thomisidae) bind the female's legs and body to a leaf with ties of silk, crawl under her abdomen and mate.

To be honest, the ties are not particularly binding, nor does the female resist the truss. Like many spider species, she appears to go into a form of temporary trance when accepting the male's attention. After the male has left, the female quite easily breaks the bonds. Some of the tiny male orb weavers in the genus *Nephila* (family Nephilidae) also place threads over the legs of the much larger females, but these ties appear to be no more than show.

Another nursery-web species, *Pisaurina mira* (family Pisauridae) wanders randomly until he detects the dragline of a female of his species.

Passing his palps over the silken trail he stops periodically, raising and extending his front legs. As he draws nearer to the female, he increases the duration of the leg-waving ritual. On reaching her, the male touches the female's hind legs with his front pair. If she is not suitably impressed she will move away, and descend instantly on another dragline to a lower branch of her plant. Should she be receptive, however, she will remain in contact briefly, before climbing and attaching another dragline to a leaf or stem of her choice. The male follows, and waits a short distance above her chosen location. The female draws in her front two pairs of legs close to her body and descends freely on a dragline. Descending after her, the male lands on the back of her abdomen and, using his front two pairs of legs, he spins her gently. As she is turning he pulls a veil of silk over her front legs, to bind them, before attaching his own dragline to hers.

With the female's body firmly supported by two draglines, the male folds her back two pairs of legs and takes up a position on her abdomen at right angles to her. He passes his palps through his chelicerae to moisten them, and inserts a palp into one of the female's genital openings. Turning to the other side, he repeats the process. He may have time to turn again, but as the female emerges from her trance and becomes increasingly active, the male adds an additional veil of silk over her front pair of legs, then climbs her dragline and retreats. Freeing herself, the female drops further on her dragline and moves to another part of the plant. Their brief encounter is over.

The nursery-web spider will live to mate another day. Many other males are not as fortunate.

SEXUAL CANNIBALISM

When a male spider is killed by a female of the same species, it may have nothing to do with sex. It may just be that his signals weren't clear enough and instead of being a potential mate he became dinner. Even having got the signals right, many male spiders are killed before, during or after copulation. Laboratory observations indicate that the female orb-web spider, *Argiope bruennichi* (family Araneidae), attack every male during his first copulation. Only 20 per cent survive this attack. The female St Andrew's Cross spider (*Argiope keyserlingi*) is limited to a maximum of two copulations. The male transfers sperm from only one pedipalp per copulation and although almost 50 per cent survive their first attempt, they are guaranteed to become a post-coital meal after their second.

One of my most precious memories is of about twenty huge golden orb weaver (*Nephila sp.*, family Nephilidae) webs overlapping each other in southern Queensland. On every web there were tiny males, just a fraction the size of the host. (See Plate 31.)

The leaf-curling spider *Phonognatha graeffei* (family Tetragnathidae) weaves a curled leaf into its orb web as a retreat. A male *Phonognatha* who comes across an immature female will share her leaf retreat, waiting for her to moult. Immediately after she has moulted, while her fangs are still soft, he will mate safely. The male *Phonognatha* will respond aggressively to the presence of rival males while he waits. Mature female *Phonognatha* have been observed cohabiting with males, and males copulate with previously mated females for significantly longer than with virgin females. But the male *Phonognatha* doesn't get it all his own way. Some do get eaten.

Those best known for killing their mates are the widow spiders. The genus *Latrodectus* (family Theridiidae) earned its common name by the female's tendency to devour her mate before or after mating. Widow spiders are found on every continent, except Antarctica. Black widow is the common name used for a range of widow spiders of which the best known is America's *L. mactans*. The American black widow is identified by her red hourglass marking on the underside of her abdomen.

Australia boasts the red-back spider (*L. hasselti*), with the hourglass as well as a red stripe on the upper side of her abdomen. New Zealand has katipo spiders (*L. atritus and L. katipo*), while in Africa widows are known as button spiders.

Every rule has its exceptions. In some *Latrodectus* species, the male has been observed to live in the female's web for an extended time, in perfect safety. Unlike most other species, the northern black widow (*L. variolus*) male is larger than the female. It's never safe to make assumptions about spiders.

The nature of sexual cannibalism varies even between species of the same genus. It is a very complex area, and is the subject of fascinating ongoing research.

In understanding the intriguing and, to humans, often gruesome mating behaviour, it is essential to look at the interactions from a spider perspective. And then, from a male or a female spider perspective, for

*A female red-back spider (*Latrodectus hasselti, *family Theridiidae), guards her egg sac.* (Photo: D. and L. Kelly)

they are different. Professor Mark Elgar from the Department of Zoology at the University of Melbourne is an evolutionary biologist who likes to explore ideas about why certain bizarre behaviours have evolved in the animal world. He explained to me that female behaviour favours characteristics that take the most advantage of resources to produce offspring. She needs to be well fed and mate with the strongest male. For males, selection favours characteristics that maximise the number of eggs he can fertilise. In understanding the behaviour, it is essential not to generalise for all spiders, but consider each species in turn. For example, the European garden orb weaver will often cannibalise the similarly sized male before copulation. As Elgar wrote:

> Preinsemination sexual cannibalism may provide females with an opportunity to assess aspects of male quality, by challenging them with a radical form of mate choice. Males that succeed in avoiding sexual cannibalism may be of better quality, and males of lesser quality are nonetheless nutritious fodder. Males of the garden spider *Araneus diadematus* court the female on a specially constructed mating thread that is suspended from the edge of the orb-web to either the vegetation or surrounding web support threads. The male drums and plucks the mating thread with his legs and the vibrations attract the female, who must hang from this thread in order to mate. As the female approaches the male, he lightly touches her body with his legs before attempting to copulate. Females may capture and cannibalize males before copulation takes place, but larger males are less likely to be caught than smaller males. Thus, females may benefit from preinsemination sexual cannibalism because it allows them to distinguish between males on the basis of both their size (which might reflect their foraging ability as juveniles) and their competence at avoiding cannibalism. In this context, the cost of sexual cannibalism to females, in terms of risking remaining unmated, is no greater than that experienced

in other species with discriminating females. The only difference is that sexually cannibalistic females do not have the opportunity to mate with males that were previously rejected.

With a second example, Elgar showed how cannibalism after the sexual act is a mechanism for increasing the male's paternity share in a sperm competitive environment for the tiny red-back male (*Latrodectus hasselti*, family Theridiidae):

> All males of *L. hasselti* perform a somersault during copulation that places their abdomen directly onto the female mouthparts. Females excrete digestive fluids onto the male that slowly digest his body . . . After two insertions, the damage to the male's copulatory organs, the pedipalps, renders him functionally sterile. Males that are cannibalized more than double the duration of copulation (from 11 to 25 minutes), which effectively doubles the paternity share of that particular male under sperm competition. Hence self-sacrifice provides a competitive advantage to males by extending the duration of sperm transfer. In addition, sexually cannibalistic females are less receptive to other mating partners, thereby reducing the risk of sperm competition.

But let's get this into perspective. The male red-back will only live eight weeks. Less than 20 per cent will even manage to find a female in the short time between maturity and death. If he doesn't manage to copulate in that time, he will leave no offspring. If he does hit the arachnid jackpot, then he could reproduce a thousand times over. From that one mating, the female can produce eggs in batches of 100 to 300, every month for up to two years.

The spider world displays endless variation on every theme. There is a tiny spider, *Tidarren sp.* (family Theridiidae), which possesses such huge palps that two would be unmanageable. Two moults before the end, all species of *Tidarren* males twist off one of their own palps, which will never regrow. The Yemeni species, *Tidarren argo*, takes this even further. The remaining palp is then torn off by the female immediately after insertion. The palp transfers semen into the female which remains attached to her epigyne for about four hours during which it apparently continues to function without him. Meanwhile, the female feeds on what's left of the male.

FROM EGG TO ADULT

After mating, the female will create her egg sac when she is well fed and ready to lay. Most spiders lay their eggs onto a silken sheet, but the actual structure varies greatly between families and even between species of the same family. For example, daddy long-legs (family Pholcidae) uses only a few loose threads to bind her eggs in a net which she then carries in her chelicerae.

In many species, when the female makes her egg sac, she binds the silk with a sticky substance that includes the contents of her spermathecae—the storage place for the male's sperm—which allows the sperm to then fertilise the still-soft eggs. Fertilisation takes place at the time of laying, not at the time of copulation.

Egg sacs take many forms. Some spiders weave simple silken sacs, while others create multiple ornate chambers. Like everything with the vast number of spider species, the variation is enormous and we still have a great deal to learn. One of the great joys of constant observation of individual spiders is to see the life cycle of the females through to the end and discover just where they lay and what their egg sac is like. But be ready for a challenge—spiders have a vested interest in keeping their future young well hidden!

If you are lucky enough to see the tiny young emerge, you will be seeing them after their first or second moult. They will be tiny, pale versions of the adult. If you examine the egg sacs with a magnifying glass or macro lens of a camera, you can sometimes see the result of those initial moults as debris in the egg sac. After the first moult, the young can feed as their tiny mouthparts are now developed. They will go on feeding from the nutrition stored in the egg yolk until forced to forage for themselves. They are carnivores. If the nearest moving creature of the right size is a brother or sister, then they may well become a sibling-snack. So the tiny spiders leave the area and find domains of their own in which to set up their killing fields. At this stage, they become highly cannibalistic and if it moves, it will be eaten.

Some spiders seem to care for their young. As we saw in Chapter 6, wolf spiders carry their egg sacs on their spinnerets. When the young leave the sac they ride on special nobbly hairs on their mothers' backs. Nursery-web spiders (family Pisauridae), are very like wolf spiders, although the egg sacs are carried in the chelicerae and, rather than offering a piggy-back ride, the mother pisaurid builds a silk tent for her young to hatch into. After a few days of webbed protection, they will emerge to hunt alone. Like bees, ants and termites, a few species of the families Theridiidae and Eresidae will regurgitate a substance which the mother feeds mouth to mouth to her young.

You may be thinking that life is just peachy for female spiders compared to the males. Consider matriphagy however, when the mother sacrifices herself to be eaten by her young. The Australian social spider, *Diaea ergandros* (family Thomisidae), lives in large colonies, with many spiders creating their nests of leaves in the same tree. There the mother will care for her young—the only batch she will ever produce. She will guard them and provide them with prey. If young of another mother are introduced into her nest, she will not feed them. Unlike most spiders, she can recognise her own offspring. In her final gesture of maternal care, she will provide the spiderlings with the nutrients from trophic eggs, unfertilised and unlaid eggs created for the nutrition of her young. When the spiderlings have reached their fourth instar, each instar representing a moult toward maturity, they slowly start to cannibalise their mother. Initially they will take small quantities of haemolymph from her leg joints. She will not resist, even as she loses mobility and her abdomen shrinks as her trophic eggs are transformed into haemolymph. When, weeks later, she is decrepit and unable to move, the offspring will consume her completely. This is thought to be a rare evolutionary behaviour which enables these cannibalistic creatures to live in social groups.

What happens when the young spiders are ready to leave their mothers? As we saw in Chapter 7, most primitive species disperse on foot, which is why groups of burrows can be found in close proximity to the mother's original burrow. The vast majority of spiders venture into the unknown on tiny threads of silk—ballooning. Some can travel on air currents for many kilometres, as Charles Darwin recorded in his journal on the HMS *Beagle*:

> On several occasions, when the *Beagle* has been within the mouth of the Plata, the rigging has been coated with the web of the Gossamer Spider. One day (November 1st, 1832) I paid particular attention to this subject. The weather had been fine and clear, and in the morning the air was full of patches of the flocculent web, as on an autumnal day in England. The ship was sixty miles distant from the land, in the direction of a steady though light breeze. Vast numbers of a small spider, about one-tenth of an inch in length, and of a dusky red colour, were attached to the webs. There must have been, I should suppose, some thousands on the ship. The little spider, when first coming in contact with the rigging, was always seated on a single thread, and not on the flocculent mass. This latter seems merely to be produced by the entanglement of the single threads. The spiders were all of one species, but of both sexes, together with young ones. These latter were distin-

guished by their smaller size and more dusky colour. I will not give the description of this spider, but merely state that it does not appear to me to be included in any of Latreille's genera. The little aeronaut as soon as it arrived on board was very active, running about, sometimes letting itself fall, and then reascending the same thread; sometimes employing itself in making a small and very irregular mesh in the corners between the ropes. It could run with facility on the surface of the water. When disturbed it lifted up its front legs, in the attitude of attention. On its first arrival it appeared very thirsty, and with exserted maxillae drank eagerly of drops of water, this same circumstance has been observed by Strack: may it not be in consequence of the little insect having passed through a dry and rarefied atmosphere? Its stock of web seemed inexhaustible. While watching some that were suspended by a single thread, I several times observed that the slightest breath of air bore them away out of sight, in a horizontal line.

Some spiderlings balloon over tens of kilometres. Some end their journey much sooner. Twice I saw my wolf spider, Theresa, rear young last summer. Just before her untimely death, I watched her spiderlings balloon. Most of the tiny specks of spider faded into the bright blue skies that afternoon but a few floated only a metre or so, caught by the bushes nearby. A small burrow appeared on the other side of Theresa's pelargonium bed. It grew over the months until one day I glimpsed her—a stunning wolf spider at the burrow entrance basking in the winter sun. Later, in the summer, she covered her burrow, just as Theresa had done. Then she emerged with a brood of tiny spiderlings on her back, and the cycle had started again.

9

MURDEROUS OR MISUNDERSTOOD— THE SPIDER BITE

> Spiders are one group of arthropods that are very well known by the common person yet are terribly misunderstood; because of the rare occasion of a deleterious venom incident, almost all spiders are lumped into the category of 'squish first and ask questions later'.

So writes toxicologist Dr Rick Vetter. And he should know. He is one of the world authorities on the effects of spider bites.

What springs to your mind if someone mentions 'deadly' spiders? It's a fair bet your first thought will be of the widow and red-back spiders, the Sydney funnel-web and perhaps some vague notion about the Brazilian wandering spider. Fair enough. And if they move on to necrotic flesh festering agonisingly for months, even years, what spider springs to mind? The brown recluse? The white-tailed spider? The hobo spider, maybe? Your answer will depend where you are, but myth and mystery will be woven between the facts. Although death as a result of spider bites is now almost unknown, paranoia about spider bites is a global phenomenon.

Spider venom works on humans in two different ways. Neurotoxins, such as those found in the venom of the widow, mouse and Australasian funnel-web spiders, attack the nervous system. They can kill. Necrotoxins, such as are found in the venom of the recluse spiders, attack the tissue surrounding the bite. They can cause painful lesions, can sometimes penetrate vital organs and can, very rarely, be fatal. In both cases fear greatly outweighs fact.

Out of the 3681 genera containing 40 024 spider species described at the time of writing, only four have species that have been known to kill—the Brazilian wandering spider (*Phoneutria*), Sydney funnel-web (*Atrax*), a few of the widow spiders (*Latrodectus*) and a few of the recluses (*Loxosceles*). Three other genera include species that toxologists believe have the *potential* to kill: Australian funnel-webs (*Hadronyche*), mouse spiders (*Missulena*) and the six-eyed sand spiders (*Sicarius*). Even then, many species within these genera are not fatal to humans.

Hollywood victims of spider bites die in a rapid, writhing rumpus. It might be effective cinema, but it never happens. Deadly bites take hours, if not days, to kill and in almost all cases, the antivenom is now available.

NEUROTOXIC KILLERS

Spiders bite for two reasons—to feed and to defend themselves. They can control the amount of venom they deliver. At any one time, a spider will have limited reserves so it will inject its precious venom only when absolutely necessary. A small prey will receive much less of the deadly toxin than a larger one. A spider that is defending itself will often dry-bite; that is, without delivering any venom.

Dr Robert Raven is a world authority on the Australian funnel-web. He told me about a new claimant in the 'most deadly of all' stakes—

a spider I had just discovered to be common in my own backyard—the mouse spider, *Missulena sp.* (family Actinopodidae). This gave me an added interest in discovering exactly what is meant by the words 'the most deadly'. Are we talking about the spider that kills the most often or that has the most lethal venom?

Laboratory experiments seem to indicate that the female mouse spider may have the most powerful venom of all. With her squat body alone measuring up to three centimetres, she has huge fangs. However, she rarely delivers any venom when she bites. Raven cited the example of a seven-year-old boy who presented at a Queensland hospital with one of these monsters firmly gripping his finger in her powerful fangs. Painful? Without a doubt. Deadly? No. Despite the trauma of being carried on a child's finger to a hospital and then forcibly removed, the spider didn't deliver any venom. The boy left the hospital only hours later, fully recovered.

Researchers had to 'stimulate' their mouse spiders with electric shocks before they could extract any venom. Interestingly, although a primitive spider, the mouse spider's powerful fangs are not paraxially aligned but work at an angle. (See Plate 32.)

If we take 'the most deadly' to mean the spider who kills most often, which are the contenders? The most often nominated is the Sydney funnel-web (*Atrax robustus*, family Hexathelidae). Three of the eleven genera in this family contain species capable of causing genuine harm to humans—*Atrax*, *Hadronyche* (found in Australia and the South Pacific) and *Macrothele* (found in eastern Asia). All are neurotoxic spiders, their venom attacking the human nervous system.

Atrax is known only in the Sydney region. Despite the funnel-web's fearful reputation, there are only thirteen recorded deaths which can be reliably attributed to it, all of which took place before the 1981 introduction of an antivenom.

The Sydney funnel-web, Atrax robustus, *reputed to be the most deadly spider in the world.* (Photo: Alan Henderson)

Sydney funnel-webs are stocky spiders, with thick, hairy legs, a shiny black head, tiny, closely grouped eyes and long spinnerets extending well beyond the body. As mygalo-morphs, they rear to attack and are one of the most aggressive spiders. Funnel-web fangs can penetrate the nails of fingers and toes, as well as soft shoe leather. Usually black all over, with no discernible pattern, a well-fed female may have a lighter coloured abdomen as her skin is distended.

A large female, with her legs extended, could cover an adult human hand. Most Sydneysiders never sight a funnel-web. If they do, it will be during summer, when the smaller males wander in search of a female. The females rarely leave their burrows unless disturbed. They build silk-lined funnels either in the ground or crevices in trees. The strong, parchment-like silk divides into two, three or four openings, usually with silk trap lines extending from them.

The bite of both the male and female funnel-web is potentially dangerous, even fatal, to humans, but Sydney's pets are safe. The funnel-web's venom has evolved to be incredibly effective on invertebrates and primates, but have minimal impact on other vertebrate species.

Unlike the widow spiders, in which the female is deadlier than the male, a male funnel-web produces venom three to five times more potent than that of the female. The female of the Toowoomba funnel-web (*Hadronyche infensa*) has been found to be more toxic than the male of the Sydney funnel-web. This means that a male *H. infensa* must be many times more dangerous than the well-known 'most deadly' spider.

Can you imagine the feelings of the father, living in range of funnel-web spiders, who found his previously healthy eight-month-old son lethargic and covered in vomit, with a large, black hairy spider beside him in the cot? The puncture marks were clearly visible on the baby's tiny hand. The child was sweating profusely, had a high pulse rate and kept vomiting. The man rushed his son to the local hospital. He also took the spider.

Although deadly, these spiders bite so rarely that the local country hospital at Maleny did not have any antivenom on hand. An emergency physician and nurse were rushed to the hospital via helicopter with funnel-web antivenom. With no time to identify the spider formally, the worst case assumption was made and the antivenom administered. The 1999 report in the *Medical Journal of Australia* went on to say:

> Almost four hours after the bite, the infant's conscious state had deteriorated, with minimal response to painful stimuli during intravenous cannulation. Antivenom premedication of adrenaline 0.1 mg intramuscularly, combined with hydrocortisone 30 mg and promethazine 5 mg, was given intravenously. The on-call toxinologist at the Australian Venom Research Unit advised treatment with two ampoules of antivenom. After the first ampoule (125 units intravenously over 10 minutes), the infant showed rapid and almost complete recovery. Within minutes of treatment he sat up, smiled and began to interact with his parents and hospital staff. The profuse sweating settled and his pupils dilated to 3 mm, with a brisk response to light. His pulse rate dropped to 130 beats/min and all other vital signs were normal.
>
> He was then transferred by helicopter 100 km to the Brisbane Royal Children's Hospital Paediatric Intensive Care Unit, where he was

observed overnight and discharged without further sequelae. The live spider was identified by the Queensland Museum as a male *H. infensa*.

Maleny Hospital now has antivenom in stock.

Australia's spiders are so commonly assumed to be dangerous, if not deadly, that medical professionals always assume the worst, as can be seen from this 2005 report in *Emergency Medicine Australasia*:

> I report the first case of survival from a 'Big Black Spider Bite' from the desert region of Western Australia.
>
> A 27-year-old Maori reported being bitten on his left forearm by a big black spider (BBS), the size of his palm whilst working on a mine site 300 km NE of Kalgoorlie. Soon after the bite he developed localized pain at the bite site, sweating, small (3 cm) lumps on both arms, pleuritic chest pain, shortness of breath and haemoptysis. His pain was not relieved with oral Panadeine Forte and he was transferred from the mine site clinic to the regional hospital. Examination was unremarkable other than multiple subcutaneous lumps over his entire body. The bite site could not be identified.
>
> After a 4-day stay, where extensive blood, radiological (including a CT pulmonary angiogram) and microbiological investigations were all normal, he was transferred to Sir Charles Gairdner Hospital for admission and further investigation by the Clinical Toxicology Service. On arrival the patient was distressed as he felt the body lumps were becoming more prevalent.
>
> Ongoing pain was managed with regular pethidine. He was admitted for observation. Advice from other toxicologists in Perth and Dr Geoff Isbister, a toxicologist with much expertise in spider bites, was uniformly unhelpful. I could find no reports in the medical literature of such a spider bite, and it was apparent to me that I was on the verge of describing a new spider bite syndrome.

My intern then handed me a fax. She had obtained the patient's medical record from New Zealand that reported numerous hospital presentations with chest pain, shortness of breath, haemoptysis and generalized subcutaneous lumps. The patient had always received large doses of pethidine during these admissions.

Biopsy of the lumps had revealed they were angiolipomata. This patient was thought to be narcotic-seeking and his name had been placed on a national register of drug-seeking individuals.

Another deadly neurotoxic spider genus is *Latrodectus*, the widow, red-back, or button spiders, part of the huge family Theridiidae. There are over 2000 theridiid species, found all over the world. Often known as tangle-web spiders, they have tiny cephalothoraxes and pea-shaped bodies. Their long, spindly legs deal efficiently and elegantly with webs and prey. Messy at the top, with long sticky traplines extending well below the web, often to the ground, theridiid webs are incredibly effective.

Commonly found theridiids include the common house spiders (*Achaearanea spp.*) and the false widow spiders (*Steatoda spp.*). These are very shy spiders and will only bite if grabbed or pressed against flesh in cloth.

America's most notorious theridiid is the black widow (*Latrodectus mactans*) which is very like Australia's red-back (*L. hasselti*), the latter having a red stripe on her back as well as the distinguishing red hourglass on the underside of the abdomen.

The United States also boasts the grey or brown widow (*L. geometricus*), the red widow (*L. bishopi*),

A red-back, Latrodectus hasselti, *with prey.* (Photo: Alan Henderson)

the northern widow (*L. variolus*) and the western widow (*L. hesperus*). New Zealand has the black katipo (*L. atritus*) and the red katipo (*L. katipo*). It is unclear where these spiders originated, but they have now been discovered in many warm, cosmopolitan locales. As they can live for months without food, there is always a risk of a deadly passenger arriving with the cargo.

In most widow species, the male is tiny. His bite would probably not even pierce the skin. The female's fangs produce a mild to sharp pain. There may be some redness, mild swelling and itching at the wound, but the really harmful effects are on the nervous system. Within an hour, the victim will experience severe pain radiating from the site of the bite then constant, cramping pain over much of the body. Pain and cramping peaks in a few hours but can last a few days. With profuse perspiration, nausea, fatigue, shock and possibly coma, this is not a fun bite, but healthy individuals usually recover completely without treatment. In some cases severe cramping can lead to respiratory distress, shock and, rarely, death in children or the frail. Death has been reported in fewer than 1 per cent of documented cases. A range of antivenoms has now been developed and there have been no reported deaths resulting from the bites of the various widow species for decades.

The third deadly neurotoxic genus is *Phoneutria*. The 'Brazilian wandering spider' is the name given to a few very similar spiders in the genus *Phoneutria* (family Ctenidae)—aggressive and highly venomous spiders first discovered in Brazil, but now found elsewhere in South and Central America. They can grow to a leg span of over twelve centimetres. They are a wandering spider, not a web-builder or burrower, and are known to hide in household items during the day. Looking much like a wolf spider, the Brazilian wandering spider has been known to travel in bunches of bananas and hence is sometimes known as the banana spider. It is claimed that many bites this spider inflicts may be dry; that is, no venom is released. When it does deliver venom, the effects are reputed to be excruciatingly painful. Although young and infirm have been killed by this spider in the past, since the antivenom was developed in 1996 there have been no further deaths reported. However, the Brazilian wandering spider has been blamed for causing uncomfortable erections, lasting for many hours and possibly leading to impotence. The venom may end up providing valuable information for the development of erectile dysfunction treatments.

NECROTOXIC FLESH DESTROYERS— FACT AND FICTION

The fourth deadly genus, *Loxosceles*, kills in a very different manner. The recluse spiders produce venom that is necrotoxic, attacking the skin and causing blistering and weeping lesions. The brown recluse is a very common spider in parts of America. Australians have told me similar stories of the horrid blisters caused by white-tailed spiders (*Lampona spp.*), which I see almost every night, all summer. Sensational media reports show sickening images of these necrotic wounds in both countries. The experts tell a different story.

I approached two of the world's authorities on spider venom, Dr Geoff Isbister from the Department of Clinical Toxicology and Pharmacology, Newcastle Mater Hospital, and Dr Rick Vetter from the Department of Entomology, University of California, Riverside, California. Their lively emails, papers and websites soon clarified the whole confusing mess.

Brown recluse spider is the name given to one species, *Loxosceles reclusa*, found in the Midwest states of America. A woman in Lenexa, Kansas, collected 2055 brown recluse spiders in six months in the house where her family of four had been living for eight years without sustaining a single bite. An 8th Grade teacher in Oklahoma took his students on an insect-collecting trip. In about seven minutes, eight students collected 60 brown recluses. They picked them up with their fingers without a single child being bitten. 'With the current paranoia, if we had populations like that in California, they would evacuate the state and close it down,' Vetter says. Only about ten specimens have ever been found in California, probably individuals brought in by travellers or in freight, yet apparently Californians live in constant fear of them. Vetter described his own experience:

> Folks are always telling me that they have found brown recluses, are afraid of brown recluses, have been bitten by brown recluses, have had neighbors die or lose limbs to brown recluses. The brown recluse has been elevated to a major urban legend status very much like UFOs, Bigfoot and Elvis . . . The biological evidence that is available resoundingly deflates any of the arachno-propaganda that is constantly being given new life with each newspaper story or word-of-mouth tale of terror. I emphatically state THERE ARE NO BROWN RECLUSE SPIDERS LIVING IN CALIFORNIA.

In contrast, Kathleen Hawkins, whom I quoted in the second chapter, listed the spiders she had identified in Texas: 'wolf spiders, garden orbs, black fishing spiders (maybe), tarantulas, brown recluses, daddy long-legs . . .'—with brown recluses merely listed in passing.

This is not to say that the brown recluse is a harmless little arachnid. The recluse spiders produce venom that is necrotoxic, attacking the skin and causing blistering and weeping lesions. With approximately 100 *Loxosceles* species (family Sicariidae) worldwide, the most famous is the brown recluse spider, *L. reclusa*. Recluses are also known as fiddle-back and violin spiders, due to the dark-coloured violin-shaped marking on the back of the cephalothorax. However, this marking is not always visible.

Recluse spiders are shy spiders—hence their common name. They stay well hidden during the day, becoming active at night. They wander with a languid gait, interspersed with occasional sudden dashes. It is hard to get bitten by this reclusive creature. When hiding in clothing or towels, for example, the spider may, if pressed against the body, react with its fangs. All have potent venoms, containing the dermonecrotic agent *sphingomyelinase D*, which is otherwise found only in a few pathogenic bacteria, although different members of the genus have different levels of toxicity. It's very hard to positively identify a bite from the lesions due to the similar symptoms of various fungal and bacterial infections, Lyme disease, and the first sore of syphilis. As the spiders themselves are seldom caught in the act or properly identified, they get the blame far more than is deserved.

Although most recluse bites are minor, very occasionally a rare dermonecrotic reaction can destroy tissue, producing open wounds which take months, or even years, to heal. Some such wounds have been measured at 25 centimetres in length. As the lesion becomes gangrenous, the dead skin will drop away leaving weeping raw flesh. Very occasionally, a severe systemic reaction occurs which can cause renal failure and even death. Deaths have been recorded not only for the brown recluse, but also for the South American species *L. laeta* and *L. intermedia*. Common in Chile and occurring throughout South America, the Chilean recluse (*L. laeta*) is considered to be the most dangerous of the recluse spiders. The bite frequently results in severe systemic reactions. Most of the recorded fatalities are children.

Yet recluses do cause necrotic lesions—if only occasionally. Other species are also feared for the same reason, with no evidence of ever having commited the crime. Americans blame their hobo spider (*Tegenaria agrestis*, family Agelenidae) while Australians are terrified of their white-tailed spiders (*Lampona spp.*, family Lamponidae).

Tegenaria agrestis is in the same genus as the common house spider (*T. domestica*) found all over Europe and the United States. Despite its reputation, the hobo spider has never been known to cause any serious reactions, let alone deaths, in Europe where it is very common. The hobo spider first appeared in the United States early last century. By attaching its egg sacs to crates which were shipped from Europe, it was then transported across America by train. The common name reflects this stowaway heritage. In North America, hobo spiders have been blamed for serious symptoms and even deaths. Yet according to experts there is serious doubt as to whether the hobo spider poses any danger at all.

The vast majority of Australians today will tell you that the long purplish spider with the prominent white dot on its rear is a very dangerous creature indeed. Yet the poor white-tailed spiders (*Lampona spp.*, family Lamponidae) were never mentioned by my grandparents or parents when I was young, although they made very sure I could recognise a red-back. *Lampona* species are extremely common in houses all over Australia. I see quite a few daily. Yet the fear has only been prevalent in the last few decades. This is a fine example of the power of the media. It is also a fine example of the irresponsibility of the media.

It started with a woman and a bite. In 1981, while gardening, the woman suffered a nasty wound and went to the local doctor. About ten hours later, a search was made in the garden where she had been working and they found a spider. It wasn't a white-tailed spider, despite what the newspaper later reported. Rather the spider was identified as a wolf spider, with no evidence that it was the one that bit the woman. The media nevertheless published a photo of a white-tailed spider, reported the necrotic sores and linked it to deathly infections in the United Kingdom. The picture of the white-tailed spider was subsequently pushed into every home in newspapers, magazines and on television, accompanied by horrifying images of decaying flesh.

Toxicologists have done extensive studies of patients who they know were definitely bitten by white-tailed spiders. These are very common

*The white-tailed spider (*Lampona cylindrata*, family Lamponidae), showing the white spot on the end of the abdomen.* (Photo: Alan Henderson)

spiders who bite often. None of the many bites recorded resulted in more than minor temporary reactions. There have been no cases of necrotic lesions in which a firm identification of the white-tailed spider has been made. Not one.

Debate continues about the actual cause of the severe reaction, one theory being that it is due to the bacterium *Mycobacterium ulcerans*, which may exist on the fangs of a spider or other invertebrates, picked up from the soil or water.

As we saw in the mysterious case of the Big Black Spider Bite, the spider-bite diagnosis is often given or accepted by doctors. They trust their journals, and it seems many of the journals print material that is not up to par. This is why arachnid toxicologists such as Isbister and Vetter are forced to rebut articles printed in reputable journals promulgating these myths. One such article gave a table of the spiders which have been linked to 'necrotic arachnidism'—which included Legless (*Badumna insignis*) and Theresa (*Lycosa godeffroyi*) along with the white-taileds! To be fair, the same article also listed the very many conditions which have been misdiagnosed as necrotic arachnidism. The recommendation from every expert in the field is the same: do not to treat any necrotic reaction as a spider bite unless the spider is presented or has been identified by someone qualified to do so.

Of course, there is a very good reason to beat up the dangers of spiders—if you happen to be a pest-control agency. Although most professionals in this field are fairly accurate in their assessment of spiders and the possibility of their eradicating them, some are quite ludicrous. One American site had Australia's mouse, black house and white-tailed spiders listed as 'toxic (poisonous)' in the United States. Given that in scientific terms 'poisonous' generally means dangerous when eaten, I am left wondering how many Americans feed on Australia's indigenous spiders.

Kill off all the spiders in a small area and they will soon be back. The problem with spiders is really not an entomological one. It is psychological. It is irrational. It is arachnophobic.

It's time to change the image.

10

CHANGING THE IMAGE

'Do you understand how there could be any writing in a spider's web?'

'Oh, no,' said Dr Dorian. 'I don't understand it. But for that matter I don't understand how a spider learned to weave a web in the first place. When the words appeared, everyone said they were a miracle. But nobody pointed out that the web itself is a miracle.'

'What's miraculous about a spider's web?' said Mrs Arable. 'I don't see why you say a web is a miracle—it's just a web.'

'Ever tried to spin one?' asked Dr Dorian.

Mrs Arable shifted uneasily in her chair. 'No.' she replied. 'But I can crochet a doily and I can knit a sock.'

'Sure,' said the doctor. 'But someone taught you, didn't they?'

'My mother taught me.'

'Well, who taught a spider? A young spider knows how to spin a web without any instructions from anybody. Don't you regard that as a miracle?'

Charlotte's Web, E.B. White

American writer Elwyn Brooks White wrote three children's books, *Charlotte's Web*, *Stuart Little* and *The Trumpet of the Swan*. All are now regarded as classics. First published in 1952, *Charlotte's Web* extolled the wonders of the little creature in the corner of a barn, so often ignored although each night she performs a miracle.

White based his creation on the common barn spider (*Araneus cavaticus*) found in North America and Canada. The title character's full name is Charlotte A. Cavatica, reflecting the barn spider's scientific name. One of Charlotte's daughters, after being told her mother's middle initial was 'A', named herself Aranea.

The barn spider is very similar to the other garden orb weavers found all over the world. Like many species of garden orb weaver, it takes down its web each morning and builds a new web every night. For the sake of the story, Charlotte had to vary from this behaviour when her words needed to be read. Like most orb weavers, Charlotte would spend many hours very still, head down, waiting for prey and, in her case, waiting for ideas on how to save the loveable pig, Wilbur, from becoming bacon.

For years, I've talked to students of all ages in many schools about my passion for spiders. Once the 2006 film of *Charlotte's Web* had hit the cinemas, I found a significant change in attitude. When I showed an image of my wolf spiders ballooning, the room would suddenly be filled, unprompted, by a chorus of 'Wheeeeee' in exactly the tone of Charlotte's babies in the film. I shared my observations with John Dietz, the visual effects supervisor at Rising Sun Pictures and head of the team responsible for the animation of Charlotte. He replied:

> What you're saying about changing attitudes of children has really made a lot of people in the office very proud. Anytime we can transcend bounds of film-making into an impact on society, it makes all the effort seem way more worthwhile.

I asked Dietz how he and his team went about creating a realistic spider who also had the emotional impact of Charlotte. He wrote:

There were basically two tracks of immersion that took place. First because she is a spider, and she was going to have naturalistic tendencies, we buried ourselves in arachnid photos, movies, books, anatomy and webs. We even had a spider specialist come to our office and let us film and photograph spiders ourselves. I'd say we'd probably have one of the largest collections of spider material. While gathering that material you have a tendency to take it in at the same time, so we were really learning about spider anatomy, look, behavior, tendencies. The second thing the team was doing was breaking down the screenplay, the original book, and ultimately the shots that go into the film. This includes many conversations with the director, and people in-charge of making the movie. What you're doing there is trying to find out the requirements to tell the story with her character.

In this case, we knew she's a very complex character in a story. In the barn all the animals are always bickering and fighting and just plain-old don't get along. Charlotte comes along and she's a bit of the woman scorned, she is immediately looked down upon, and feared by the other animals because she is a spider, and that's the stereotype of an arachnid. She's outcast by everyone except for this innocent, naive little pig. So because she sees something different in this pig, she makes the leap to come down and befriend him. Ultimately she becomes an endearing motherly teacher to the pig and eventually gives her own life to save his. Not only that, but this unlikely friendship between spider and pig actually changes the attitudes of the characters around them (the barn animals), who can now live together and enjoy their lives together more thoroughly. This little spider changes the world around her. So in trying to find that character you look to the past for ideas. Because Charlotte was voiced by Julia Roberts we studied her behavior in previous films and life. So we figured out how we want her to act.

Next you begin to put the two together to actually make her character. Because the other animals in the barn were going to be real animals, and have their mouths adjusted to make them talk, we knew she was going to have to be based on a real looking, behaving spider. In the story she writes words in her webs so from our research we knew she was gonna be an orb spider. We began there by doing a lot of drawing and artwork to change an orb weaver into something that can act. What we're basically doing at that time is defining the amount of anthropomorphism she'd have in her design. Because she's endearing, and has to 'act' in close up we needed to design her face so an audience could understand what she was emoting. So things like giving her more almond-shaped main eyes, using the secondary eyes as a brown line, using the line between the head and the chelicerae as a sort of line that acts as a mouth, subtleties that become human landmarks. Another issue in the motherly aspects of the design was femininity. So things like 'grooming' her hair not all spikey like a real arachnid, and making her face more of a heart shape all started to make her more feminine. These are all things that took her away from a real spider in subtlety, but all are intentional for story telling.

All that work was basically the design of Charlotte. Now we sculpted a model of Charlotte in clay that was then scanned into the computer and turned into a digital model. It's what we call a 'wireframe' model, which is what you see in making of movies, and hi-tech displays. That model is then 'rigged' which is defining controllers to make her move. It's basically the muscles and bones that define motor-skills that animators will move around to make her behave. Then her surface properties are defined, every little detail like the translucency of her exoskeleton, the look of her eyes, the sheen of her hair, her colour, her slightest little surface textures, everything.

Then there is behavior design where we build a language for Charlotte to emote to an audience. This has to do with facial expressions, and in her posture.

For a spider, this was quite difficult. At this time we also defined how Charlotte would talk, what we call lip sync. We didn't want her to have a mouth because it just went too far away from keeping her anatomically a spider. We came up with this technique that her mouth was behind the chelicerae, and they were like a veil that moved secondarily while she talks.

I then asked Dietz how the team went about getting the right balance between the reality of a barn spider's behaviour and the demands of the narrative. He replied:

One main way was by framing Charlotte in a shot, and by editing. Typically, if it's a wider shot, then she behaves more like a spider, a little twitchy in her legs, and more of a real spider feel. When the story calls for her to emote to the audience the camera will move in and get close. She then becomes more calm and acts with her face, and subtleties in her posture, and only feels (hopefully) subconsciously like a spider, and fully like Charlotte the character. This makes an audience feel endeared to her, then you cut wide again and the audience remembers 'Oh yeah, she's a spider'.

You want the audience to go on the same arc as the barn animals. At first she comes down and the audience is really feeling the naturalistic spider Charlotte. At the end she dies, and hopefully she's not a spider to anyone, but this character that gave her life to save another.

Because of the contradiction in mentality of the audience in endearing character and spider, it was the hardest thing I've ever dealt with by far. There are just so many perceptions out there about a spider not being a 'nice' thing, that to make a character emote like Charlotte was nearly impossible. Also we were dealing with an iconic story, and doing the title character in it, which in itself hasn't been done very many times in CGI. All we could do really is prepare as well as possible.

I commented that details of Charlotte's movement, web-making and egg sac were very realistic.

For story-telling there are a few licenses we took anatomically in her physicality. Orb weavers really drag their back legs when they're on a surface. The joints are more horizontal. Because she's completely synthetic we took the liberty to keep them orb-spider like when she's in her web, and more of a ground-based spider when she's on the ground. Using license like this basically is appealing to the perception of a generic 'spider' and lets us tell a story and keep it moving. Spinning was the same type of story. In the sequence where she spins her first word she is at her best, she is just really, really good at what she does. She's dynamic, and almost balletic. We used the natural world to set up techniques of how she uses her abdomen, or how she would lay down one type of web strand before another as a starting point, but then enhanced the dynamism to tell the story that she's just really special at this! Later when she's at the end of her life, she's making her 'humble' web. She is listless and slow, still good, still using the base of the naturalistic techniques, but her elegance is gone, she slips even as she struggles.

As she's getting older she ages, she gets grayer, her abdomen grown with pregnancy, her posture changes, she has to carry around the extra weight. So always the balance between performance and naturalistic.

Her egg sac was based on nature, but again it was sized properly for Templeton to carry away, and lit and coloured almost gold to show its magic.

Charlotte's webs were actually treated like a character in the story. Before she writes any words the webs are completely real, always subtly in the background, but there! Then when she writes 'some pig' it's magical, she's at the top of her game. It sparkles and glitters like the miracle that it is, a little more over the top like you'd see in a real web. By the time she does 'humble' its design is not as clean, and a little disorganized. It's harder for her then! Then she passes away and her last web is dusty and dead, like her. Wilbur goes back to the barn with his medal and doesn't say a word to the animals. He walks to Charlotte's door and bows his head in memory while the 'radiant' web, tattered and almost gone, waves in the wind like a memorial flag. The other animals join and bow together, changed.

I have watched my garden orb weavers' webs change from the glorious, perfect creations of early summer, to the tattered efforts of their last few days. I stand in awe of John Dietz and his team in their creation of Charlotte, and in the incredible impact they have had in changing the attitude of an entire generation of children to spiders.

Although many people react with disgust at the mere mention of a spider, there is a rich tradition of admiration of the spider's skills. The very name 'arachnid' is taken from the ancient Greek story of Arachne.

Athena, daughter of Zeus, was the goddess of wisdom who presided over the arts of men, such as agriculture and navigation, and those of women—spinning, weaving and needle-work. Arachne was a mortal maiden, famed for her stunning weaving. Many would come just to watch her weave. Proud of her skill, Arachne dared compare herself to Athena and challenged her to a competition. The goddess was, of course, displeased when she heard of the girl's audacity. Disguising herself as an old woman, Athena advised Arachne not to compete with a goddess but to ask her forgiveness. Arachne not only refused the advice but agreed to compete with Athena, so confident of winning that she would accept any punishment should she lose. The contest began and the two weavers wove with speed and skill unrivalled anywhere. Athena wrought on her web the scene of her contest with Poseidon. In the four corners she showed punishments the gods had dealt to mortals who had dared to challenge them. Arachne ignored the magnificently woven warning.

On her tapestry, Arachne showed the failings and errors of the gods. She did so with brilliance, the cloth astounding all who watched. Even Athena was forced to admire her skill, but despised her presumption. Athena struck Arachne's web with her shuttle and destroyed it. She touched Arachne's forehead, making the maiden feel such guilt and shame that she hanged herself. Athena took pity on her and sprinkled her with the juices of aconite. Arachne shrank and her nimble fingers became legs on the body which serves only to make silk. Athena had transformed her into a spider.

The Pueblo and Navajo Native American tradition tells how Spider Woman was the originator of all the living creatures, which she created from the very clay of the earth. All people are forever connected to her by a thread of silk. Long ago a Navajo woman descended deep into the earth to watch Spider Woman as she wove her stunning and delicate webs. The woman watched and learned every step of the warp and waft, every part of the weaving and designing of wonderful fabric. Spider Woman taught the Navajo to build a loom from sunshine, rain, lightning, sky and earth. Spider Woman taught them how to weave.

Robert Bruce, King of Scotland, it is said, was inspired to try just one more time, when watching a spider. Six times he had fought his English enemies in battle and six times he had been beaten. Bruce was in despair, hiding in a cave, ready to give up. Then, he noticed a spider trying to spin a thread across the cave entrance. Once, twice, three times she failed. Eventually, like Bruce, she had failed six times. He decided he would do as the spider did. Should she succeed in her next attempt, then he, too, would try one more time. On her seventh attempt she crossed the gap. Bruce called together his soldiers for one last effort. He led them in a great battle and won.

The spider as trickster—Anansi—is an all-time favourite in West African folk tales. He uses his wits to make up for his lack of size. There are many Anansi stories, each containing a lesson to be learned. The story of how Anansi came to own all the tales of Africa tells of Nyame the Sky God, who owned every tale told in the world. Anansi went to Nyame asking if he could buy the stories. Many had tried before, but Nyame always asked a price that not even the rich and powerful could pay. He asked for Mmoboro, the hornets, Onini, the python, and Osebo, the leopard.

Anansi found a gourd and made a hole in it. Splashing himself with water at the river so that he was dripping, he filled his gourd and carried it to the tree. He splashed the hornets, calling to them to move out of the rain to some place dry. They asked where they should go. Anansi generously offered them his gourd! Locking them inside, he carried the hornets to Nyame.

Anansi then cut a bamboo pole and carried it to Onini's house, muttering to himself. He told Onini that he was arguing with his wife about which was longer and stronger, the pole or Onini. When Onini stretched himself beside the pole, Anansi tied him to it to stop him slipping, and took his captive to Nyame.

Anansi went to the forest where Osebo prowled. He dug a pit, and covered it with leaves and branches. The mighty Osebo fell into the trap. Osebo begged Anansi to help him escape but Anansi first made him promise that he would not be eaten. Anansi then bent a tree over the pit and tied it down. He attached a rope to the top of the tree and threw it down to Osebo, who attached it to his tail as instructed. Anansi cut the rope which held the tree, releasing the tree. Osebo was left hanging upside down, struggling to be free. Anansi killed him and took his body to Nyame, who was duly impressed. The Sky God gave Anansi all the stories, stating that the tellers of tales must acknowledge him as the owner. The lesson is that through cleverness, not strength and riches, Anansi the spider became the owner of all tales that are told.

Film and legend alone, however, cannot change the image of spiders. It is the spiders themselves, their surprising beauty and their crucial role in the environment, which tell the most important story of all.

Some museums and zoos are now drawing large crowds to live spiders exhibited for their beauty, not their shock factor. Museum Victoria's *Bugs Alive!* display at the Melbourne Museum has gained a worldwide reputation for putting live invertebrates on display.

At the museum, I watched Alan Henderson talking to a group of students, showing them his live spiders and stunning photographs. He answered their questions with the same enthusiasm which had converted me. Another group of children left his presence enthralled by spiders. A huge dark space, with no glass and no barriers, is filled with St Andrew's Cross spiders weaving their webs with the lighting set so all can marvel at their skill. Preserved leftovers from the essential role of quarantine for illegally imported tarantulas are mounted in a glass wall so all can see what gloriously furred creatures they are.

And then there is Tiger sitting in her luxury glass-walled apartment with her egg sac and food delivered whenever she wants. Her sign tells everyone that she is, as yet, unclassified. We have so much to learn.

Alan Henderson in the Bugs Alive! *display at the Melbourne Museum, with Tiger.* (Photo: D. and L. Kelly)

Mary Ann Hamilton works as Curatorial Manager at the Butterfly Pavilion in Westminster, Colorado. There are far more creatures in this wonderful educational centre than just butterflies. According to Hamilton, 'The children start screaming as soon as they walk in the door: "I want to hold Rosie!" You hear that maybe 400 times a day.' Rosie is one of a collection of Chilean rosehair tarantulas (*Grammostola rosea*, family Theraphosidae) which are gently placed on the hands of the visitors to show them just what gentle creatures they are. Mary Ann allowed me behind the scenes where I met Scary Spice. A salmon pink birdeater (*Lasiodora parahybana*), she was much larger than any tarantula I had seen before. She was anything but scary!

Sir David Attenborough has said that: 'If we and the rest of the back-boned animals were to disappear overnight, the rest of the world would get on pretty well. But if the invertebrates were to disappear, the world's ecosystems would collapse.' So we need to change spiders' image for the sake of the planet! Sound like an extravagant claim? Not at all! I am

Scary Spice on the author's hands. (Photo: Peter King-Smith)

deadly serious. Spiders are the best indicator we have to the health of the local environment.

When I see a home with immaculate brickwork and concrete, or perfectly maintained, bug-free garden or, worse still, no garden, I am greatly saddened. If you spray the insects and kill the spiders and their food, you starve the reptiles, birds and all the higher animals who depend on those lower down the food chain.

The presence of spiders isn't a sign of shoddy housekeeping but of a healthy environment. The presence of lots of spiders means that their local environment is making a real contribution to the health of the planet.

In a 2006 article for *BBC Wildlife* magazine, Mark Stratton wrote:

> A series of UK studies is now providing hard evidence that invertebrates are experiencing alarming declines in abundance and diversity. The figures make grim reading: 70 per cent of British butterfly species are reportedly losing numbers . . . riverflies down 66 per cent in three decades (the rare caddisfly *Glossosoma intermedium* is now restricted to just one river); nine of our 22 bumblebee species have declined in range by 70 per cent post-war; and 250 of our 4000 beetles have not been seen since 1970, confirms Buglife, the Invertebrate Conservation Trust.
>
> 'Invertebrates are disappearing faster than any other organisms,' explains Buglife's Matt Shardlow. 'Bumblebees, mayflies and beetles are in serious trouble. Halting their extinction is currently the biggest challenge for UK biodiversity conservation.'
>
> English Nature lists 200 invertebrate species lost to the UK in the past 50 years. But does it matter? After all, our world has survived megafauna extinctions—surely we can cope without Essex emerald moths and Sussex diving beetles?
>
> 'It's like a game of Jenga,' disagrees Shardlow. 'Take the bricks out one by one and the tower stays up, but take out one too many and the whole countryside may come crushing down.'

> The house sparrow's tumble towards *Red Data Book* status is linked to chick starvation, as aphids, spiders and craneflies have become scarcer.

Stratton goes on to describe how Britain's farmlands have become unfit for invertebrates. Seventy-five per cent of Britain's countryside is used for agricultural purposes. The continuous cropping made possible by artificial fertilisation, together with overgrazing and the removal of hedgerows, leaves little behind to sustain invertebrate populations. But worst of all is the spraying of pesticides. The farmer might be targeting species detrimental to the crop but many other invertebrates will also die. Residues of sprays and worming chemicals persist in the environment, kill the dung feeders—and so it goes on. If the spiders themselves are not killed, their food supply is.

The entire food chain is affected. In the short term, we get more food for humans. In the long term, we have done irreparable damage to our environment.

The more I observe spiders in their tiny worlds, the more I learn about caring for the environment. The microfauna don't waste a thing. I was intrigued by one little orb weaver who I called Spinnelein. Deciding one night that I was a massive risk, she suddenly took down her web. She didn't just abandon it, but pulled it in systematically, balled it up and scuttled with it to her retreat under the pelargonium leaves. There she ate it. Without that protein, she may have struggled to build a web again, so she risked a few extra seconds in the face of a predatory monster to gather it up. We can learn from the spiders. (See Plates 36–38.)

The greatest joy I have gained from my obsession with spiders is the insight they have given me to their little worlds and all the invertebrates, birds, reptiles and mammals who populate their perilous lives. I have hundreds of tiny worlds in my own garden. Constant observation alerts me to every sign of activity and offers free entertainment of the highest order which will last a lifetime. I just have to walk out the back door.

From the viewpoint of my protagonists, my spiders, and their many antagonists, I start in the very middle of the food chain and live the intricate balance between animals therein. Each night I venture forth with torch in hand, to turn my spotlight on their stages and witness some new intrigue. I have never been disappointed.

This excitement is on offer to anyone who has at least one spider in their backyard—which is everyone. Leave a few of the common house spiders (*Achaearanea spp.*), found all over the world, on your outside walls and you can watch a whole soap opera. There will be the killing of prey, mating and dying, young and new webs—all going on every night all year round. Their cobwebs are full of the evidence of their active lives. I have half-a-dozen on the back porch and there is always something happening. And they tend to do things slowly, which gives you plenty of time to watch. Small and harmless—what more can you ask? And the price is just a few messy webs.

Many spiders are stationary, living either in burrows or webs. Once you know how to find them, you can monitor their numbers. Every new spider you find is an indicator of the good health of your environment. By adding garden which is not

*Femme-fatale, one of my many common house spiders (*Achaearanea sp.*) had two males living and mating with her over a week.* (Photo: D. and L. Kelly)

constantly manicured to within an inch of its life, and by reducing your use of pesticides, your spider numbers will increase and you can know that you are helping to feed the birds and save the planet.

You don't need university qualifications or complicated equipment to make your own observation on the biodiversity and health of your backyard environment. Spiders are easy to monitor and, above all, they are just so cute.

To convince everyone in the world that spiders are the good guys, we need to change their image. Each of us can do our bit by ensuring our own small territory is spider friendly. That way we can save the planet—eight legs at a time.

GLOSSARY

Abdomen: the rear of the two major parts of the body of a spider. Despite many amateurish drawings and pieces of jewellery implying otherwise, there are no legs attached to the abdomen. Also known as the opisthosoma.

Aciniform silk: the rapidly produced shroud of silk with which the spider binds a struggling insect, now considered to be the strongest silk of all in terms of both flexibility and breaking stress. Male spiders use aciniform silk to make their sperm web while females may use it for the outer wall of the egg sac.

Aggregate glands: glands which produce the gluey substance added to silk as it is laid down in the web.

Ampullate silk: dragline silk, which is known technically as major ampullate silk, used for the radials of an orb web among other things. Temporary scaffold silk in the orb web is known as minor ampullate silk.

Araneomorph: the spiders, often called modern spiders, who have their fangs directed inwards in a pincer-like movement. The spider does not rear to attack prey.

Autotomy: the ability to amputate one of their own legs. They autotomise them.

Book lungs: book-like organs, with a single lung slit opening, on the underside of the abdomen. Most araneomorphs have one pair of book lungs, while mygalomorphs have two pairs.

Calamistrum: a row of toothed bristles on the metatarsal segment of the last leg, used to comb out cribellate silk.

Carapace: the hard upper shell covering the cephalothorax, the front body part of the spider.

Cephalothorax: the foremost of the two major body parts of the body of a spider, consisting of the head and thorax in a single part. The cephalothorax has the chelicerae with fangs attached to it, as well as the pair of palps and the four pairs of legs. Also known as the prosoma.

Chelicerae: the pair of short appendages at the front of a spider holding the fangs.

Claw tuft: a thick brush-like set of hairs located just behind the tarsal claws on the foot, used to help with gripping smooth surfaces.

Cloaca: the internal organs used to store the waste products from digestion.

Coxa: the first of the seven segments of a spider's leg, counting from the body.

Coronate silk: see *flagelliform.*

Cribellate silk: the woolly, non-sticky silk produced from the cribellum of some spiders.

Cribellum: a sieve-like spinning plate situated in front of the spinnerets.

Diaxial fangs: a pair of fangs that operate in a pincer-like action as found on araneomorph (or modern) spiders.

Embolus: the narrow portion of the tip of the male papal organ, through which the sperm is expelled into the female.

Entelegyne: species in which the female has two genital pores covered by a sclerotised plate.

Envenomation: poisoning following the injection of a spider's venom from the fangs into the skin.

Epigastric furrow: a groove on the underside of the abdomen.

Epigynum/epigyne: the hardened, external genital structure found on the underside of the abdomen of a female spider just in front of the epigastric furrow.

Eye patterns: the arrangement of the eight (or sometimes less) eyes found on the raised front upper end of the cephalothorax. Two rows of four eyes are common. The anterior eyes form the front row and the posterior eyes are in the second row, starting from the fangs. The middle pair of eyes in each row is known as the median eyes, with the outer pair known as the lateral eyes.

Fangs: tapering curved needles used by a spider to inject venom into prey and to perform physical tasks such as burrowing and holding objects. Fangs move parallel to the ground in the moderns, such as the orb weavers, and vertically to the ground in the primitives, such as the trapdoor spiders.

Femur: the third of the seven segments of a spider's leg, counting from the body.

Flagelliform or coronate silk: the extremely stretchy sticky capture silk which can be stretched to more than three times its length before snapping.

Fovea: a hollow visible in the centre of the upper surface of the carapace, to which muscles supporting the sucking stomach are attached.

Haemolymph: a fluid which transports oxygen and nutrients around the spider's open circulatory system, taking the place of mammalian's haemoglobin.

Haplogyne: species of spiders in which the female has a single genital opening.

Instar: an immature form of a spider; spiders pass through at least five instar sizes before reaching adulthood.

Malpighian tubule: an organ which removes nitrogenous waste during digestion.

Maxillae: a pair of flexible plates on either side of the mouth. A thick border of hairs on the maxillae acts as a filter to ensure only liquid food enters the mouth.

Metatarsus: the sixth of the seven segments of a spider's leg, counting from the body.

Modern spiders: a common language description applied to the araneomorph spiders, those whose fangs move together in a pincer-like movement.

Moult: the process by which immature spiders break out of the hard body shell to grow larger. Moulting occurs at least five times before the spider reaches maturity.

Mygalomorph: the spiders, often called primitive spiders, who have their fangs directed vertically. The spider rears to attack prey.

Necrotising arachnidism: the mostly mythical progressive ulceration and loss of skin around the site of a bite, attributed to spiders. Research has shown that most of the accused spiders do not cause necrotising arachnidism.

Neurotoxin: a toxin which is present in the venom of most spiders to enable them to immobilise prey. As we are not the target prey, very few arachnid neurotoxins have a severe impact on humans.

Opisthosoma: see *abdomen.*

Palps: short, leg-like structures on the front of the cephalothorax between the fangs and the first pair of legs. In females and in immature males they resemble small legs, with one less segment. In some spiders they are very small, in others quite prominent. In mature males the endmost segments are modified into a boxing glove-like sexual organ.

Paraxial fangs: a pair of fangs that strikes downwards in parallel, as is usual for a mygalomorph, or primitive, spider.

Patella: the fourth of the seven segments of a spider's leg, counting from the body.

Pedicel: the narrow waist which joins the two major body parts, the cephalothorax and the abdomen.

Pedipalps: see *palps.*

Piriform silk: used to attach webs and draglines to their anchor points.

Primitive spiders: a common language term used for the mygalomorph spiders, those whose fangs strike vertically down on prey. They live a burrowing lifestyle, like the ancestor species.

Prosoma: see *cephalothorax.*

Scapus: part of the epigyne, the female genital organs, visible on some orb weavers.

Scopula: a dense brush of hairs on the underside of the endmost segments of the legs of some spiders.

Sexual dimorphism: male and female spiders of the same species can look very different. A common difference is in size. Mature males of some species are very much smaller than their female counterpart.

Spermathecae: a receptacle in the female spider in which semen is stored until fertilisation of the eggs.

Spigot: the tiny tubes on the tip of the spinnerets, releasing the silk.

Spinnerets: the silk-spinning organs found on the rear underside of the abdomen.

Spiracle, or tracheal spiracle: an opening on the ventral side of the abdomen, enabling air to reach the tracheal system.

Stabilimentum: a band of dense silk woven into a web, often in the form of a cross.

Tarsal bulb: the bulbous endmost segment of the palps of a mature male spider.

Tarsus: the last of the seven segments of a spider's leg, counting from the body.

Tarsal claws: a pair of small claws at the end of each leg, used by the spider to hold onto its own web as well as other structures. Some species have a smaller median claw behind the main pair.

Tibia: the fifth segment of a spider's leg, counting from the body.

Trachea: thin internal tubes which form part of the respiratory system for some of the araneomorph spiders.

Trichobothria: (singular *trichobothrium*) are long bristle-like hairs which detect vibrations and currents in the air.

Trochanter: the second of the seven segments of a spider's leg, counting from the body.

Tubuliform silk: used by female spiders in the construction of the egg sac.

APPENDIX 1:
SPIDER FAMILIES

At the time of writing, 40 462 spider species in 3694 genera in 109 families are listed.

This listing has been taken from *The World Spider Catalog*, version 9.0 found at <http://research.amnh.org/entomology/spiders/catalog/>, dated 23 June 2008. It is maintained by Dr Norman Platnick and is recognised globally as the authorative source on spider taxonomy.

The families are ordered alphabetically within the three suborders. Common names for spiders representative of the family have been added. Because of the confusion caused by the use of common names, arachnologists refer to groups of spiders by their scientific family names. For ease of reading, however, the common names given in R. Jocqué and A.S. Dippenaar-Schoeman (2006), have been included.

The taxonomy in every family has changed since version 8.5 of *The World Spider Catalog*, December 2007, which indicates the state of flux of the field. The number in the second column gives the cladistic order of the families.

		Family	Genera	Species	
		Suborder Mesothelae			
1	1.	Liphistiidae	5	87	Segmented spiders

		Family	Genera	Species	
		Suborder Mygalomorphae			Also known as Orthognatha
2	10.	Actinopodidae	3	41	Mouse spiders
3	3.	Antrodiaetidae	2	32	Folding-trapdoor spiders
4	2.	Atypidae	3	43	Purse-web spiders
5	14.	Barychelidae	44	300	Brush-footed trapdoor spiders
6	8.	Ctenizidae	9	121	Cork-lid trapdoor spiders
7	7.	Cyrtaucheniidae	18	132	Wafer-lid trapdoor spiders
8	6.	Dipluridae	24	175	Sheet-web mygalomorphs
9	5.	Hexathelidae	11	86	Funnel-web mygalomorphs
10	9.	Idiopidae	22	281	Spurred trapdoor spiders
11	4.	Mecicobothriidae	4	9	Midget funnel-web tarantulas
12	13.	Microstigmatidae	7	14	Micro-mygalomorphs
13	11.	Migidae	10	91	Ridgefanged trapdoors
14	12.	Nemesiidae	41	341	Tube trapdoors, wishbone trapdoors
15	16.	Paratropididae	4	8	Hunting micro-tarantulas
16	15.	Theraphosidae	113	908	Baboon spiders/tarantulas
		Suborder Araneomorphae			Also known as Labidognatha
17	78.	Agelenidae	42	511	Funnel-web spiders
18	85.	Amaurobiidae	72	717	Mesh-web weavers
19	98.	Ammoxenidae	4	18	Termite hunters
20	81.	Amphinectidae	36	187	Forest hunters
21	58.	Anapidae	36	146	Ground orb-web weavers
22	91.	Anyphaenidae	56	508	Tube spiders, phantom spiders
23	66.	Araneidae	166	2979	Orb-web spiders
24	37.	Archaeidae	3	37	Long-necked spiders
25	18.	Austrochilidae	3	9	Junction-web weavers
26	31.	Caponiidae	12	71	Bright lungless spiders
27	96.	Chummidae	1	2	Spiny-backed spiders
28	99.	Cithaeronidae	2	6	Swift ground spiders/curly-legged spiders
29	93.	Clubionidae	14	552	Sac spiders
30	94.	Corinnidae	77	944	Dark sac spiders/ant-like sac spiders
31	77.	Ctenidae	39	477	Tropical wolf spiders
32	52.	Cyatholipidae	23	58	Tree sheet-web spiders
33	79.	Cybaeidae	12	161	Water spider/soft spider
34	82.	Cycloctenidae	5	36	Scuttling spiders
35	50.	Deinopidae	4	57	Net-casting spiders/ogre-faced spiders
36	80.	Desidae	38	182	Long-jawed intertidal black house spiders
37	84.	Dictynidae	48	562	Mesh-web spiders
38	30.	Diguetidae	2	15	Cone-web spiders
39	24.	Drymusidae	1	15	False violin spiders

		Family	Genera	Species	
40	34.	Dysderidae	24	497	Long-fanged six-eyed spiders
41	47.	Eresidae	10	101	Velvet spiders
42	20.	Filistatidae	16	109	Crevice spiders
43	100.	Gallieniellidae	10	48	Long-jawed ground spiders
44	104.	Gnaphosidae	110	2032	Flat-bellied ground spiders
45	19.	Gradungulidae	7	16	Long claw spiders
46	83.	Hahniidae	26	238	Comb-tailed spiders
47	49.	Hersiliidae	11	157	Long-spinnered spiders/ two-tailed spiders
48	40.	Holarchaeidae	1	2	Minute long-jawed spiders
49	97.	Homalonychidae	1	3	Desert sand spiders
50	42.	Huttoniidae	1	1	New Zealand palp-footed spiders
51	17.	Hypochilidae	2	11	Lampshade web spiders
52	102.	Lamponidae	23	191	Australian ground spiders/white-tailed spiders
53	25.	Leptonetidae	15	203	Midget cave spiders
54	63.	Linyphiidae	576	4345	Hammock-web spiders/dwarf spiders/ money spiders
55	92.	Liocranidae	29	163	Spiny-legged sac spiders
56	67.	Lycosidae	110	2336	Wolf spiders
57	45.	Malkaridae	4	10	Pitted spiders
58	38.	Mecysmaucheniidae	7	25	Striped long-jawed spiders
59	41.	Micropholcommatidae	8	33	Micro-gondwana spiders
60	46.	Mimetidae	13	153	Pirate spiders
61	90.	Miturgidae	25	325	Prowling spiders
62	59.	Mysmenidae	21	96	Minute clasping weavers
63	65.	Nephilidae	4	57	Giant golden orb-web/ coin spiders
64	54.	Nesticidae	9	206	Cave cobweb spiders
65	88.	Nicodamidae	9	29	Red-and-black spiders
66	27.	Ochyroceratidae	14	155	Midget ground weavers
67	48.	Oecobiidae	6	105	Dwarf round-headed spiders/star-legged spiders
68	35.	Oonopidae	74	505	Dwarf hunting/dwarf armoured/goblin spiders
69	36.	Orsolobidae	28	178	Six-eyed ground spiders
70	70.	Oxyopidae	9	426	Lynx spiders
71	44.	Palpimanidae	15	130	Palp-footed spiders
72	39.	Pararchaeidae	7	34	Tiny thick-necked spiders
73	23.	Periegopidae	1	2	Wide-clawed spiders
74	107.	Philodromidae	29	530	Small huntsmen spiders
75	28.	Pholcidae	85	999	Daddy long-legs
76	86.	Phyxelididae	12	54	Hackled mesh weavers/ lace-web weavers
77	61.	Pimoidae	4	31	Large hammock web spiders
78	69.	Pisauridae	53	336	Nursery-web/fish-eating spiders

	Family	Genera	Species	
79	29. Plectreuridae	2	30	Spur-lipped spiders
80	103. Prodidomidae	30	302	Long-spinnered ground/prodidomid spiders
81	74. Psechridae	2	26	Cribellate sheet-web spiders
82	109. Salticidae	560	5188	Jumping spiders
83	22. Scytodidae	5	193	Spitting spiders
84	33. Segestriidae	3	106	Tube-web spiders
85	105. Selenopidae	4	190	Flatties/wall spiders
86	71. Senoculidae	1	31	Bark spiders
87	21. Sicariidae	2	122	Six-eyed sand/violin/ recluse spiders
88	62. Sinopimoidae	1	1	New family from China
89	106. Sparassidae	83	1038	Huntsmen/giant crab/ rain spiders
90	43. Stenochilidae	2	12	Diamond-shaped spiders
91	72. Stiphidiidae	13	94	Cone-web spiders
92	57. Symphytognathidae	6	45	Dwarf orb weavers
93	60. Synaphridae	3	12	Midget spiders
94	53. Synotaxidae	13	68	Chicken-wire-web spiders
95	26. Telemidae	7	26	Long-legged cave spiders
96	89. Tengellidae	8	50	Post spiders
97	32. Tetrablemmidae	30	131	Armoured spiders
98	64. Tetragnathidae	48	938	Water orb weavers
99	55. Theridiidae	96	2288	Cobweb/gum-foot web/button spiders
100	56. Theridiosomatidae	12	75	Ray spiders
101	108. Thomisidae	173	2085	Crab/flower spiders
102	87. Titanoecidae	5	46	Rock spiders
103	68. Trechaleidae	18	96	Leaf hunters
104	101. Trochanteriidae	19	152	Scorpion spiders
105	51. Uloboridae	18	265	Hackled orb-web spiders, triangle-web spiders
106	95. Zodariidae	74	868	Burrowing spiders, ant-eating spiders
107	76. Zoridae	13	74	Spiny leg spiders
108	73. Zorocratidae	5	42	Ground spiders
109	75. Zoropsidae	12	77	Ground spiders

APPENDIX 2:
A GUIDE TO THE SILKEN CLUES

1. The ladder orb web is an example of the distinctive shapes that can help to identify the spider.

2. The golden orb weavers, or *Nephila*, build huge permanent orb webs with the lower half larger than the top. *Nephila* will often be in their webs during the day when the web reflects golden in the sun. The pirate spiders and *Argyrodes* can be found around the edges.

3. *Argiope*, or the St Andrew's Cross spider or black and yellow garden spider or writing spider or wasp spider (among many other names all over the world), rest in their large orbs during the day and night. The vivid striped abdomens and white decorations in the web, the stabilimenta, are indicative of this spectacular genus.

4. If you are very lucky, you may discover a really strange web such as the triangle web held in place by its owner, *Hyptiotes*, whose body forms part of the actual web structure.

5. Your best chance of seeing an orb web spun is by locating a garden orb weaver. Each night a new web is created. This awe-inspiring sight is available in gardens the world over.

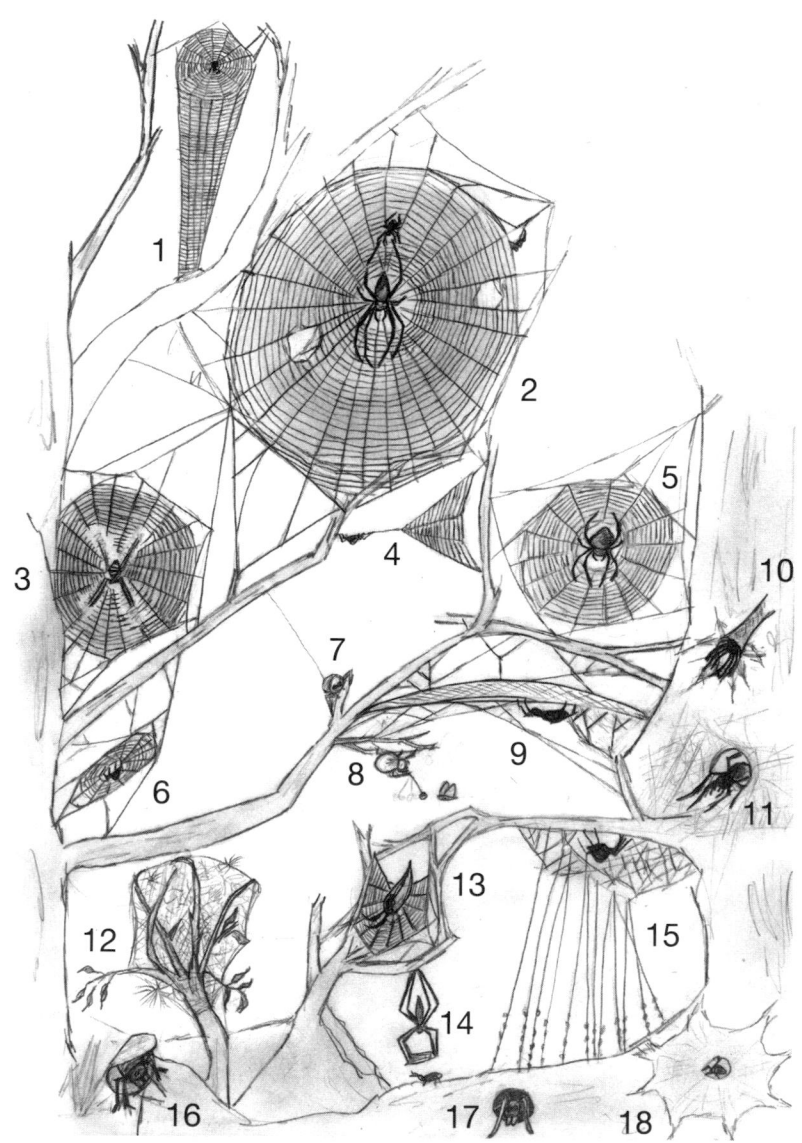

(Diagram: L. Kelly)

6. Uloborids are small humped spiders that build their tiny cribellate orbs at all angles, often in large groups.

7. Dragline silk is the very strong thread left by spiders as a safety line. Following a dragline will sometimes lead you to the owner, such as a curious and cute jumping spider.

8. If you are very lucky you may discover a bolas spider, an orb weaver whose web is now a single line with a glob of glue on the end ready to ensnare a male moth attracted to the spider's mimic of the female moth pheromones.

9. The tent spider (*Cyrtophora spp.*, family Araneidae) builds a horizontal orb web attached with a mass of messy support strands above and below. The spider hunts from the under surface of the web.

10. Tube-web spiders build silken tubes in gaps on bark or buildings. They can be identified, when at the mouth of their tube, by the three pairs of legs they hold in the forward position.

11. Funnel-weaver spiders are extremely widespread, often building their woolly cribellate webs around buildings. Shiny silk indicates a very recent addition and an active web. The spider will emerge from the funnel retreat to wait for vibrations on the web. Try very lightly tickling the web with grass and you may lure it out.

12. The mesh-web spider (family Dictynidae) often build webs over twigs and small branches encasing the foliage. With dead leaves and other debris within the web as a retreat, it is often very difficult to find the owner during the day.

13. Debris in a web may well hide the spider. Many spiders, such as the leaf curler, stitch leaves together to create a retreat.

14. Close observation in the right countries may just reveal a net-casting spider in wait for passing prey.

15. The messy cobwebs of the huge family Theridiidae can be found everywhere. The lower strands are often glue-lines. The inconspicuous owner may be a small pale spider hidden in debris. Get to know a common house spider and you will see lots of action—from hunting to sex to lots of young—all year round.

16. Search by day with a strong torch and you may locate burrows. Just a hint of silk around them indicates a spider lives within. Sneak up at night and you will meet the owner, maybe a trapdoor spider or . . .

17. . . . maybe a burrowing wolf spider. The wolf spider is easily identified by the pair of large eyes above a row of smaller eyes.

18. Sheet-webs become visible on the ground on dewy mornings. Locate the funnel and return at night and you may meet the owner.

If you mark the places where silk gives you clues then you will certainly be rewarded by meeting spiders. The more often you venture out, torch in hand, the more you will discover just how many spiders are there. Scraps of silk will become obvious where none was noticed before. Soon you will learn to find them almost everywhere. If there is silk, then there will be spiders.

APPENDIX 3:
A GUIDE TO
SPIDER-SPOTTING EQUIPMENT

If you want to watch spiders, then you need some basic equipment to improve the quality of your observations. This is my kit:

1. Torch. Day and night, you will see much better with the spider highlighted in the beam of a high-intensity torch. Most spiders do not seem to react to the light. They react to my movement far more. Some arachnologists recommend using red cellophane over the torch so the spiders are less aware of your attention. Silk that you cannot see in normal light will become visible in a strong torch beam.

2. White plastic knives. When you locate a burrow or web, you will often think it will be easy to locate again. It won't. A white knife with the blade pointing towards the spider's location will show up easily at night. Using a permanent marker, you can write names or codes to help when you record the individual's progress.

3. Observation sheets (see Appendix 4: Observation Sheet). If you write it down, then you have the information ready for reflection later. Behaviour may not seem significant until a pattern starts to emerge. Without the notes, you will not know if it is a week or two or more from, say, the covered burrow to the babies emerging. Over time, these observation sheets will contain invaluable data.

4. Camera. A good digital camera with a macro lens will allow you to explore a spider's world in the most extraordinary way. I use a Canon 350D with 100 mm fixed macro and ring flash. By zooming in on the images, I have noticed details I could never see without the lens and computer. We are so lucky to have this technology at our disposal. Not only can you see details of the spider itself, but of its prey, web, burrow and all that is around. By looking back over a series of images you can see what the spider has done to change its own small environment. You will start to get a really strong impression of just what their lives involve as you see prey scraps come and go, webs grow and burrows decorated.

5. The coffins. I have a wooden box full of spiders' leftovers. This is slowly giving me a record of what my black house spiders are eating. I place white card under their webs, held down with rocks. I race the ants to the remains in the morning. I tip them into the sealed coffin. It sounds gruesome, but it is a fascinating insight into my local invertebrate fauna.

I also collect from around the wolf spiders' burrows and under the daddy long-legs' webs into separate coffins. There is no end of information in the detritus on and under spiders' webs and around their burrows. You will occasionally get the remains of a male!

6. The internet. A web search (how appropriate) with the word 'spiders' and your state will almost certainly lead you to sites with images of your local spiders. That's a great place to start identifying your home residents.

APPENDIX 4: OBSERVATION SHEET

SAMPLE OBSERVATION SHEET

Spiders — Observation Sheet

Date: 30 November 2007 **Time:** 10:00 p.m.
Location: Back porch, garden, at home
Weather: Warm, muggy night — lots of bugs!

Type: blackhouse (Badumna insignis) **Individual:** Doora **Location:** above back door	**Notes:** Male, with Doora for fourth night. Doora in and out of funnel entrance. Mostly resting. Male moving around. White-tailed stalking them! (Morning! male still there alive!) — New: Y (N) Ph: (Y) N
Type: blackhouse **Individual:** Cupboardia **Location:** back porch cupboard	**Notes:** Sitting at entrance as usual. Abdomen looking large, well fed? gravid? No reaction to my presence up close. — New: Y (N) Ph: Y (N)
Type: common house (Achaeranea) **Individual:** Femme fatale **Location:** back door, left side	**Notes:** No sign of males. Were in web over a week. Femme tailed up huge beetle. Wrapped its back legs first. Had to keep retreating. Eventually hurled it up into top of web. — New: Y (N) Ph: (Y) N (lots!)
Type: common house **Individual:** Grot-webbia **Location:** back door, right side	**Notes:** Lots of babies around egg sac. They caught fly-thing as group. Six of them and then took it up into web. Had no idea they hunted collectively. Grot-webbia not involved. — New: (Y) N Ph: (Y) N
Type: wolf (Lycosa) **Individual:** Carrotta **Location:** Carrot patch	**Notes:** Out hunting. Saw her grab a woodlice. Subdued it, then slowly back to her burrow. About 10 cm from entrance. Still much smaller than Cabbapia. — New: Y (N) Ph: Y (N)
Type: wolf **Individual:** Cabbapia **Location:** Cabbage patch	**Notes:** Burrow still covered with leaves. Silk weaving them clearly visible. No sign of Cabbapia! Breeding? — New: Y (N) Ph: Y (N)
Type: flat rock (Morebilus) **Individual:** Little Rebel **Location:** Rebel's place, verandah	**Notes:** Thought it was Rebel back after 5 weeks missing. Definitely much smaller, but in same place. — New: (Y) N Ph: (Y) N
Type: Blackhouse **Individual:** Uppity **Location:** Right kitchen window	**Notes:** Still in her old place. Still upside down. Abdomen thin. Old age? Breed second season? — New: Y (N) Ph: Y (N)
Type: garden orb (Eriophora) **Individual:** ERIO-5 **Location:** hakea on driveway	**Notes:** WOW!! In Erio-three's hakea nuts! About half her final size, with prominent white stripe like male from last year. Couldn't see any enlargement of palps. Immature male or female? Hope it survives! — New: (Y) N Ph: (Y) N
Type: garden orb **Individual:** Erio-6 **Location:** gum, 2 from hakea	**Notes:** Haven't been out for a while and they've appeared! She/he's very like Erio-three but about ½ her size. Full orb web, about 30 cm across. — New: (Y) N Ph: (Y) N

Missing Regulars: Angel (blackhouse) — saw 5 white-taileds — think I've lost Angel! Annie, Babs — almost all trapdoors covered. Only few smaller ones visible.
Notes: Rain?

Saw 5 White-tailed, 1 huntsman (right of kitchen windows), 1 wandering wolf. New! Erio-7 (on ridge track) and Erio-8 (fork of ridge and main track). Wolf: Monster, burrow open, no sign of young left. Mid-Iracbia, Bladerunner, Crystal all sitting out ready. Pholcy-1 and Pholcy-2 both in webs in kitchen as usual. Blackhouse: Boardia, mid-boardia both fine.

237

Spiders – Observation Sheet

Date: **Time:**
Location:
Weather:

Type: / Individual: / Location:	Notes:	New: Y / N Ph: Y / N
Type: **Individual:** **Location:**	Notes:	New: Y / N Ph: Y / N
Type: **Individual:** **Location:**	Notes:	New: Y / N Ph: Y / N
Type: **Individual:** **Location:**	Notes:	New: Y / N Ph: Y / N
Type: **Individual:** **Location:**	Notes:	New: Y / N Ph: Y / N
Type: **Individual:** **Location:**	Notes:	New: Y / N Ph: Y / N
Type: **Individual:** **Location:**	Notes:	New: Y / N Ph: Y / N
Type: **Individual:** **Location:**	Notes:	New: Y / N Ph: Y / N
Type: **Individual:** **Location:**	Notes:	New: Y / N Ph: Y / N
Type: **Individual:** **Location:**	Notes:	New: Y / N Ph: Y / N
Type: **Individual:** **Location:**	Notes:	New: Y / N Ph: Y / N

Missing Regulars:

Notes:

NOTES AND SOURCES

1 Arachnophobia

Your suggested cure of learning about them (p. 6) Russell (2007, personal correspondence).

I think that spiders come and find me (p. 7) *Panic Room* (2007).

It's often called genetic memory (p. 12) Honan (2007, personal conversation).

None of the theories that I have read (p. 13) Honan (2007, personal conversation).

I explained that white-tailed spiders (p. 14) Honan (2007, personal conversation).

As for learning to be phobic (p. 14) Jones (2007, personal correspondence).

We ought to be afraid of guns (p. 15) Pinker (1999, pp. 384–6).

And in general you have to work hard (p. 16) Platnick: <www.nydailynews.com/lifestyle/2007/04/22/2007-04-22_working_with_ webs-2.html>.

The only thing [Bond] is in any peril of (p. 16) Platnick: <www.nydailynews.com/lifestyle/2007/04/22/2007-04-22_working_with_webs-2.html>.

Go? I think not (p. 19) *Harry Potter and the Chamber of Secrets* (2002, film).

There's something about the configuration (p. 19) *Phobia: Arachnophobia* (2002).

2 Spiders, spiders everywhere

These are the spiders I've identified (p. 31) Hawkins (2007, personal correspondence).

I think spiders are absolutely extraordinary (p. 37) David Attenborough in interview with David Parkinson: <http://parkinson.tangozebra.com/guest_transcript.phtml>.

3 Garnishing the garden

The spider's touch, how exquisitely fine! (p. 47) Alexander Pope, *Essay on Man*, Epistle 1, section VII, lines 11–12.

Araneus diadematus is without doubt the commonest (p. 52) Roberts (1995, p. 316).

The actual sequence of placing frame-threads (p. 53) Main (1976, p. 190).

A few rules, with built-in contingency planning (p. 56) Stewart (1998, pp. 197, 202).

The message here is mathematically exciting (p. 57) Stewart (1998, p. 204).

4 Let's get physical

The spider sits inconspicuously (p. 87) Bristowe (1971, pp. 84–5).

5 Classification challenges

What I do for a living (p. 89) Harvey (2007, personal conversation).

Diagram (p. 95) The eye patterns are adapted from the drawings distributed throughout Bristowe, 1971.

There are about 1.75 million species (p. 97) Kumar (2005, p. F3).

What keeps it interesting is that so little is known (p. 98) Pesce (2007).

My experience with adult female (p. 104) Atkinson (2007, personal correspondence).

Many thanks for your email regarding Morebilus (p. 105) Harvey (2007, personal correspondence).

In contrast to other mega-diverse (p. 108) Jocqué & Dippenaar-Schoeman (2006, pp. 12–13).

6 The hunters and the hunted

Have you lost your belief in fairies? (p. 111) Clyne (1979, p. 11).

For several days the burrow occupied by 'Sibyl' (p. 115) McKeown (1963, pp. 81–2).

Unless the spider was marked (p. 117) Humphries (2007, personal correspondence).

Two months pass; and the result (p. 121) Fabre (pp. 78–9).

Worn out with fatigue (p. 122) Fabre (pp. 62–7).

The youngsters may be brushed off (p. 124) Fabre (pp. 69–71).

Wolf spiders are intellectually destitute; At least you're not into; Tuna allowed me to work; They move differently (p. 126) Richardson (2007, personal conversation).

She can visually identify complete (p. 128) Richardson (2007, personal conversation).

What makes salticids special (p. 128) Harland & Jackson (2000, p. 231).

From many years of studying Portia (p. 131) Harland & Jackson (2000, p. 238).

Callilepis runs in short bursts (p. 133) Foelix (1996, pp. 172–3).

I'd been at the Central Market (p. 142) Guest (2007, personal correspondence).

7 Live long and primitive—the mygalomorphs

A 'mouse-eating' spider, which has recently (p. 145) *Harper's* magazine (1994). From 'Concerning Spiders: What Would Happen if These Detested Insects Were as Large as Sheep', in the sixth issue of *Past Deadline: The Magazine of 19th Century News*, a quarterly published by Robert Hudson in Troy, New York, that consists entirely of reprints of news articles from the 1800s. 'Concerning Spiders' appeared in *Past Deadline's* 'Horrible' issue, which also included 'A Child Carried Off by an Eagle and Killed', 'A Preacher Murders a Ranch Proprietor—The Body Cooked and Served to Travellers', and 'Extraordinary Self-Mutilation'. 'Concerning Spiders' originally appeared in the London *Telegraph*; it was reprinted 15 July 1880 Troy *Daily Times*.

The way in which an insect is seized (p. 149) Bristowe (1971, pp. 73–4, 75).

The purse-web diagram (p. 150) is adapted from Bristowe, 1971, by the author.

A common South Australian spider (p. 157) Main (1976, pp. 61–2).

It is significant that in much of the interior (p. 159) Main (1976, p. 53).

. . . when we dug the burrows out (p. 161) Main (1976, pp. 48–9).

I learn something new every day (p. 168) Burge (2007, personal conversation).

8 No-one does it like a spider

Preinsemination sexual cannibalism may (p. 186) Elgar & Schneider (2004, p. 147).

All males of L. hasselti *perform a somersault* (p. 187) Elgar & Schneider (2004, pp. 148–9).

On several occasions, when the Beagle (p. 190) Darwin (1989, p. 148).

9 Murderous or misunderstood—the spider bite

Spiders are one group of arthropods (p. 193) Vetter (2007).

Almost four hours after the bite (p. 197) Harrington, (1999, p. 652).

I report the first case of survival from (p. 198) Little (2005, pp. 181–2).

Folks are always telling me (p. 202) Vetter (2007).

10 Changing the image

Do you understand how there could (p. 207) White (1963, pp. 106–7).

What you're saying about changing (p. 208) Dietz (2007, personal correspondence).

There were basically two tracks (p. 209) Dietz (2007, personal correspondence).

One main way (p. 211) Dietz (2007, personal correspondence).

For story-telling there are (p. 212) Dietz (2007, personal correspondence).

A series of UK studies is now providing (p. 218) Stratton (2006, pp. 45–8).

BIBLIOGRAPHY

Allan, R.A., Capon, R.J., Brown, W.V. and Elgar, M.A. (2002), 'Mimicry of host cuticular hydrocarbons by salticid spider *Cosmophasis bitaeniata* that prey on larvae of tree ants (*Oecophylla smaragina*)', *Journal of Chemical Ecology*, vol. 28, no. 4, pp. 835–48.

American Arachnological Society (2007), at <www.americanarachnology. org> [date accessed 31 July 2007].

American Museum of Natural History (2007), *The Goblin Spider Planetary Biodiversity Inventory* at <http://research.amnh.org/oonopidae/index. php> [date accessed 31 July 2007].

Arachnophobia [DVD] (1990), Burbank: Hollywood Pictures.

Atkinson, Ron (2007), 'The find-a-spider guide' at <www.usq.edu.au/ spider/> [date accessed 31 July 2007].

Australian Museum Online (2007), 'Spiders' at <www.amonline.net.au/ spiders/> [date accessed 8 June 2007].

Avil, Leticia, Maddison, Wayne P. and Agnarsson, Ingi (2006), 'A new independently derived social spider with explosive colony proliferation and a female size dimorphism', *Biotropica*, vol. 38, no. 6, pp. 743–53.

Banks, J., Sirvid, P. and Vink, C.J. (2004), 'White-tailed spider bites— arachnophobic fall-out', *The New Zealand Medical Journal*, vol. 117, no. 1188, pp. 1–7.

Benjamin, S.P. and Zschokke, S. (2003), 'Webs of theridiid spiders: Construction, structure and evolution', *Biological Journal of the Linnean Society*, vol. 78, pp. 293–305.

Bilde, T., Tuni, C., Elsayed, R., Pekar, S. and Toft, S. (2006), 'Death feigning in the face of sexual cannibalism', *Biology Letters*, vol. 2, no. 1, pp. 23–5.

Bristowe, W.S. (1971), *The World of Spiders*, London: Collins.

Bruce, J.A. and Carico, J.E. (1988), 'Silk use during mating in *Pisaurina mira* (Walckenaer) (Araneae, Pisauridae)', *Journal of Arachnology*, vol. 16, pp. 1–4.

Brunet, Bert (1996), *Spiderwatch: A guide to Australian spiders*, Melbourne: Reed Books.

Bucaretchi, Fábio et al. (2000), 'A clinico-epidemiological study of bites by spiders of the genus *Phoneutria*', *Revista do Instituto de Medicina Tropical de São Paulo*, vol. 42, no. 1, pp. 17–21.

Clyne, Densey (1969), *A Guide to Australian Spiders: Their collection and identification*, Melbourne: Thomas Nelson.

——(1979), *The Garden Jungle*, Sydney: Collins.

Dapin, Mark (2007), 'Along came a spider', *The Age Good Weekend*, 24 February, pp. 24–7.

Darwin, Charles (1989), *The Voyage of the Beagle: Charles Darwin's journal of researches*, London: Penguin Classics.

Dawkins, Richard (1997), *Climbing Mount Improbable*, London: Penguin Books.

Dippenaar-Schoeman, A.S. (2002), 'The baboon spiders of South Africa' at <www.scienceinafrica.co.za/2002/november/baboon.htm> [date accessed 25 May 2007].

Dorfman, Andrea (2002), 'Spider silk, goat's milk and fibers strong as steel', *Time South Pacific*, (Australia/New Zealand edn), vol. 3, p. 38.

Edgar, Walter D. (1971), 'Aspects of the ecology and energetics of egg sac parasites of the wolf spider *Pardosa lugubris* (Walckenaer)', *Oecologia*, vol. 7, no. 2, p. 155.

Eight Legged Freaks [DVD] (2002), Burbank: Warner Bros Pictures.

Elgar, Mark A. (1998), 'Sperm competition and sexual selection in spiders and other arachnids' in *Sperm Competition and Sexual Selection*, London: Academic Press.

Elgar, Mark A. and Allan, Rachel (2004), 'Predatory spider mimics acquire colony-specific cuticular hydrocarbons from their ant models', *Natürwissenschaften*, vol. 91, no. 3, pp. 143–7.

Elgar, Mark A. and Schneider, Jutta M. (2004), 'Evolutionary significance of sexual cannibalism', *Advances in the Study of Behavior*, vol. 34, pp. 135–63.

Evans, Theodore A. (1998), 'Offspring recognition by mother crab spiders with extreme maternal care', *Proceedings: Biological Sciences*, vol. 265, no. 1391, pp. 129–34.

Evans, Theodore A., Wallis, Elycia J. and Elgar, Mark A. (1995), 'Making a meal of mother', *Nature*, vol. 376, p. 299.

Fabre, J. Henri (1912), *The Life of A Spider*, Alexander Teixeira de Mattos (trans.), London: Hodder & Stoughton.

Fahey, Babette F. and Elgar, Mark A. (1997), 'Sexual cohabitation as mate-guarding in the leaf-curling spider *Phonognatha graeffei* (Keyserling) (Araneoidea, Araneae)', *Behavioral Ecology and Sociobiology*, vol. 40, no. 2, pp. 127–33.

Foelix, Rainer F. (1996), *Biology of Spiders*, (2nd edn), Oxford: Oxford University Press.

Forster, Ray and Forster, Lyn (1999), *Spiders of New Zealand and Their Worldwide Kin*, Dunedin: University of Otago Press.

Framenau, Volker (2007), 'The wolf spiders of Australia (Araneae, Lycosidae): Checklist, taxonomy and identification' at <www.lycosidae. info/identification/australia/index.html> [date accessed 8 June 2007].

Gallon, Richard C. (2007), 'Keeping tarantulas—the basics' at <www.thebts.co.uk/keeping_tarantulas.html> [date accessed 20 July 2007].

——'The natural history of tarantula spiders' (2007), at <www.thebts.co. uk/old_articles/natural.htm> [date accessed 31 July 2007].

Gaskett, A.C., Herberstein, M.E., Downes, B.J., Elgar, M.A. (2004), 'Changes in male mate choice in a sexually cannibalistic orb-web spider (Araneae: Araneidae)' *Behaviour*, vol. 141, no. 10, pp. 1197–210.

Harland, D.P. and Jackson, R.R. (2000), ' "Eight-legged cats" and how they see—a review of recent research on jumping spiders (Araneae: Salticidae)', *Cimbebasia*, vol. 16, pp. 231–40.

Harper's magazine (1994), 'Arachnophobia circa 1880', vol. 288, no. 1724.

Harrington, Anthony P., Raven, Robert J., Bowe, Paul C., Hawdon, Gabrielle M., and Winkel, Kenneth D. (1999), 'Funnel-web spider (*Hadronyche infensa*) envenomations in coastal south-east Queensland', *Medical Journal of Australia*, vol. 171, pp. 651–3.

Harry Potter and the Chamber of Secrets [DVD] (2002), Burbank: Warner Bros Pictures.

Harry Potter and the Prisoner of Azkaban [DVD] (2004), Burbank: Warner Bros Pictures.

Heller, G. (1974), 'Zur Biologie der ameisenfressenden Spinne *Callilepis nocturna* L. 1758 (Araneae: Drassodidae)', PhD thesis, Johannes Gutenberg–Universitat, Mainz.

——(1976), 'Zum Beutefangverhalten der ameisenfressenden Spinne *Callilepis nocturna* (Arachnida: Araneae: Drassodidae)' *Entomol. Germanica* vol. 3, pp. 100–3.

Henderson, Robbie J. and Elgar, Mark A. (1999), 'Foraging behaviour and the risk of predation in the black house spider, *Badumna insignis* (Desidae)', *Australian Journal of Zoology*, vol. 47, pp. 29–35.

Herberstein, M.E., Craig, C.L., Coddington, J.A. and Elgar, M.A. (2000), 'The functional significance of silk decorations of orb-web spiders: A critical review of the empirical evidence', *Biological Reviews*, vol. 75, pp. 649–69.

Herberstein, M.E. et al. (2005), 'Limits to male copulation frequency: Sexual cannibalism and sterility in St Andrew's Cross spiders (Araneae, Araneidae)', *Ethology*, vol. 111, no. 11, pp. 1050–61.

Hillyard, Paul (1994), *The Book of the Spider*, London: Hutchinson.

Hogan, Christopher J., Barbaro, Katia Cristina and Winkel, Ken (2004), 'Loxoscelism: Old obstacles, new directions', *Annals of Emergency Medicine*, vol. 44, no. 6, pp. 608–24.

Holst, Lisa Birgit (1993), 'Reading is Believing' *PC Professional*, 7 January, p. 71.

Hunt, Helen (1988), *The Puffin Book of Spiders*, Ringwood: Puffin Books.

Isbister, G.K. (2004), 'Mouse spider bites (*Missulena spp.*) and their medical importance', *Medical Journal of Australia*, vol. 180, pp. 225–7.

——(2004), 'Black house spiders are unlikely culprits in necrotic arachnidism: A prospective study', *Internal Medicine Journal*, vol. 34, pp. 287–9.

——(2004), 'Necrotic arachnidism: The mythology of a modern plague', *The Lancet*, vol. 364, pp. 549–53.

Isbister, G.K. and Framenau, V.W. (2004), 'Australian wolf spider bites (Lycosidae): Clinical effects and influence of species on bite circumstances', *Clinical Toxicology*, vol. 42, pp. 153–61.

Isbister, G.K. and Gray, M.R. (2003), 'White-tail spider bite: A prospective study of 130 definite bites by *Lampona* species', *Medical Journal of Australia*, vol. 179, pp. 199–202.

Isbister, G.K. and Gray, M.R. et al. (2005), 'Funnel-web spider bite: A systematic review of recorded clinical cases', *Medical Journal of Australia*, vol. 182, no. 8, pp. 407–11.

Isbister, G.K. and Vetter R.S. (2005), 'Loxoscelism and necrotic arachnidism: More myths and minor corrections (letter)', *Annals of Emergency Medicine*, vol. 46, pp. 205–6.

Isbister, G.K., White, J., Currie, B.J., Bush, S.P., Vetter, R.S. and Warrell, D.A. (2005), 'Spider bites: Addressing mythology and poor evidence (letter)', *American Journal of Tropical Medicine and Hygiene*, vol. 72, pp. 361–4.

Isbister, G.K. and Whyte, I.M. (2004), 'Suspected whitetail spider bite and necrotic ulcers', *Internal Medicine Journal*, vol. 34, pp. 38–44.

Jackson, Robert R. (1992), 'Eight-Legged Tricksters', *Bioscience*, vol. 42, no. 8, pp. 590–8.

——(1995), 'Cues for web invasion and aggressive mimicry signalling in *Portia* (Araneae, Salticidae)', *Journal of Zoology*, vol. 236, pp. 131–49.

——(2002), 'Trial-and-error derivation of aggressive-mimicry signals by *Brettus* and *Cyrba*, spartaeine jumping spiders (Araneae: Salticidae) from Israel, Kenya, and Sri Lanka', *New Zealand Journal of Zoology*, vol. 29, pp. 95–117.

Jackson, R.R. and Wilcox, R.S. (1993), 'Observations in nature of detouring behaviour by *Portia fimbriata*, a web-invading aggressive mimic jumping spider from Queensland', *Journal of Zoology*, vol. 230, pp. 135–9.

Jocqué, R. and Dippenaar-Schoeman, A.S. (2006), *Spider Families of the World*, Tervuren: Royal Museum for Central Africa.

Jones, Susan C. (2000), 'Extension fact sheet: Spiders in and around the house' at <http://ohioline.osu.edu/hyg-fact/2000/ 2060.html> [date accessed 31 July 2007].

Klaas, Peter (2001), *Tarantulas in the Vivarium*, Florida: Krieger Publishing Company.

Krink, T. and Vollrath, F. (1997), 'Analysing spider web-building behaviour with rule-based simulations and genetic algorithms', *Journal of Theoretical Biology*, vol. 185, pp. 321–31.

Kumar, Mohi (2005), 'The Exciting Adventures of Spider Man: From the vial to the tree of life', *The New York Times*, Scientists at Work: Norman Platnick, 25 October, p. F3.

Leroy, Astri and Leroy, John (2003), *Spiders of Southern Africa*, Cape Town: Struik Publishers.

Little, Mark (2005), 'Big black spider bite from the desert region of Western Australia', *Emergency Medicine Australasia*, vol. 17, pp. 181–2.

London Zoo (2007), 'Do you have a spider phobia?' at <www. zsl.org/zsl-london-zoo/news/scared-of-spiders,20,NS.html> [date accessed 31 July 2007].

McKeown, Keith C. (1963), *Australian Spiders*, Sydney: Sirius Books.

Main, Barbara York (1976), *Spiders*, Sydney: Collins.

——(1986), 'Trapdoors of Australian Mygalomorph Spiders: Protection or Predation?', *Actas X Congr. Int. Arachnol. Jaca/Espana*, vol. 1, pp. 95–102.

Museum of Victoria (2002), 'The Spider's Parlour' at <http://museum victoria.com.au/spidersparlour/> [date accessed 31 July 2007].

MythBusters [television programme] (2004), Discovery Channel, season 1, episode 13.

Nelson, Ximena J., Jackson, Robert R., Pollard, Simon D. and Edwards, G.B. (2004), 'Predation by ants on jumping spiders (Araneae: Salticidae) in the Philippines', *New Zealand Journal of Zoology*, vol. 31, pp. 45–56.

Panic Room [television programme] (2007), <www.bbc.co.uk/pressoffice/pressreleases/stories/2007/03_march/20/panic.shtml>.

Pesce, Nicole Lyn (2007), 'Working with webs: 7 questions for a real life spider man' at <www.nydailynews.com/lifestyle/2007/ 04/22/2007-04-22_working_with_webs-2.html> [date accessed 31 July 2007].

Phobia: Arachnophobia [television programme] (2002), Washington: Pangolin Pictures for National Geographic Channel.

Pinker, Steven (1999), *How the Mind Works*, New York: W.W. Norton & Co.

Platnick, N.I. (2008), *The World Spider Catalog*, version 9.0. American Museum of National History at <http://research.amnh.org/entomology/spiders/catalog/index.html> [date accessed 31 July 2007].

Preston-Mafham, Rod and Preston-Mafham, Ken (1984), *Spiders of the World*, Poole: Blandford Press.

Raven, Robert (2007), 'Spiders of Australia' at <www.uq.edu.au/~xxr raven/spiders.html> [date accessed 20 June 2007].

Raven, R.J., Baehr, B.C. and Harvey, M.S. (2002), *Spiders of Australia: Interactive identification to subfamily* [CD-ROM], ABRS Identification Series, Melbourne: CSIRO Publishing.

Reilly, Michael (2006), 'Silky-footed tarantulas don't come unstuck', *New Scientist*, vol. 2571, p. 12.

Roach, John (2006), 'Sexual prime peaks when males "smell" mates, spider study shows', *National Geographic News* at <http://news.nationalgeographic.com/news/2006/06/060616-spiders-sex.html> [date accessed 31 July 2007].

Roberts, Michael J. (1995), *Spiders of Britain and Northern Europe*, London: HarperCollins.

Schneider, J.M., Fromhage, L. and Uhl, G. (2005), 'Extremely short copulations do not affect hatching success in *Argiope bruennichi* (Araneae, Araneidae)', *Journal of Arachnology*, vol. 33, no. 3, pp. 663–9.

Schneider, Jutta M. and Lubin, Yael (1998), 'Intersexual conflict in spiders', *Oikos*, vol. 83, pp. 496–506.

Schneider, Jutta et al. (2006), 'Sexual conflict over copulation duration in a cannibalistic spider', *Animal Behaviour*, vol. 71, pp. 781–8.

Selden, Paul A., Corronca, José A. and Hünicken, Mario A. (2005), 'The true identity of the supposed giant fossil spider Megarachne', *Biology Letters*, The Royal Society, vol. 1, no. 1.

Sezerino, U.M. et al. (1998), 'A clinical and epidemiological study of *Loxosceles* spider envenoming in Santa Catarina, Brazil', *Transactions of the Royal Society of Tropical Medicine and Hygiene*, vol. 92, no. 5, pp. 546–8.

Shao, Z. and Vollrath, F. (2002), 'Materials: Surprising strength of silkworm silk', *Nature*, vol. 418, p. 741.

Shear, William A., Palmer, Jacqueline M., Coddington, Jonathan A. and Bonamo, Patricia M. (1989), 'A Devonian spinneret: Early evidence of spiders and silk use', *Science*, vol. 246, no. 4929, pp. 479–81.

Simon-Brunet, Bert (1994), *The Silken Web: A natural history of Australian spiders*, Sydney: Reed Books.

Snetsinger, Phoebe (2003), *Birding on Borrowed Time*, Colorado Springs: American Birding Association.

Stewart, Ian (1998), *Life's Other Secret: The new mathematics of the living world*, London: Penguin.

Stratton, Mark (2006), 'Where have all our insects gone?', *BBC Wildlife*, vol. 24, no. 12, pp. 45–8.

Sutherland, S. (1987), 'Watch out, Miss Muffet!', *Medical Journal of Australia*, vol. 147, p. 531.

Tarsitano, Micahel S. and Jackson, Robert R. (1997), 'Araneophagic jumping spiders discriminate between detour routes that do and do not lead to prey', *Animal Behaviour*, vol. 53, pp. 257–66.

Thirunavukarasu, P., Nicolson, M. and Elgar, M.A. (1996), 'Leaf selection by the leaf-curling spider *Phonognatha graeffei* (Keyserling) (Araneoidea: Araneae)', *The Bulletin of the British Arachnological Society*, vol. 10, no. 5, pp. 187–9.

Thompson, Lachlan and Mathers, Naomi (2006), 'Spiders in Space: A collaboration between education and research', *Science in School*, vol. 1, pp. 44–8.

Ubick, D., Paquin, P.E. and Roth,V. (eds) (2005), *Spiders of North America: An identification manual*, American Arachnological Society, <www.americanarachnology.com>.

The Ultimate Guide: Spiders [video] (1999), Discovery Communications, Maryland: Silver Spring.

Vetter, Rick (2007), 'Myth of the brown recluse: Fact, fear, and loathing' at <http://spiders.ucr.edu/myth.html> [date accessed 20 April 2007].

Vollrath, Fritz and Knight, David P. (2001), 'Liquid crystalline spinning of spider silk', *Nature*, vol. 410. pp. 541–8.

Waldock, J.M. (1992), 'Recent discoveries of *Tegenaria* (Araneae: Agelenidae) in Australia', *Australasian Arachnolgy*, vol. 44, pp. 4–5.

Walker, Ken L. and Milledge, Graham A. (1992), *Spiders Commonly Found in Melbourne and Surrounding Regions*, Melbourne: Royal Society of Victoria.

White, E.B. (1963), *Charlotte's Web*, London: Puffin Books.

Wilder, Shawn M. and Rypstra, Ann L. (2007), 'Male control of copulation duration in a wolf spider (Araneae, Lycosidae)', *Behaviour*, vol. 144, no. 4, pp. 471–84.

Yeargan, K.V. and Quate, L.W. (1997), 'Adult male bolas spiders retain juvenile hunting tactics', *Oecologia*, vol. 112, no. 4, pp. 572–6.

INDEX